PRAISE FO
THE AMUR RIVER

"Elegant, elegiac, and poignant. . . . Thubron is an intrepid traveler, a shrewd observer, and a lyrical guide . . . to the river, much of it along the border between these two powers at a time of rapid and tense reconfiguration of global geopolitics."

—*Washington Post*

"A mesmerizing trip down Far East Asia's most consequential river reveals the twists and turns of history and politics. . . . It is the troubling tension between Russia and China that lies at the heart of Thubron's book. . . . A poignant contribution to Thubron's acclaimed career, with his trademark lyricism elevating nature to a central breathing character that often reflects the ambivalence of its human counterparts."

—BookBrowse.com

"When a river runs through a good book, a current of expectations irresistibly carries readers along. . . . On this subarctic odyssey, each bend of the Amur brings new sights, new characters, and new revelations. . . . For over a thousand miles, the Amur marks the boundary between two nations, and it is there, crisscrossing the border, that Thubron sees the contrast between an empire in decline and one on the rise."

—*Natural History* magazine

"A journey from a sacred Mongolian source down a river that is also a fault line of history, where empires divide and rivalries begin. . . . The most eloquent travel writer in Britain . . . found a psychic salve in the Amur, whose rugged beauty enchants him even as its history fills him with dread." —*Wall Street Journal*

"Unlike such peers as the Mississippi and the Nile, the Amur is a source of division, with anxiety and distrust seething on both banks. . . . Veteran travel writer Colin Thubron weaves in historical anecdotes, such as the freedom Chekhov felt while sailing down the river to interview convicts in Sakhalin, and his stopover with a Japanese prostitute in Blagoveshchensk."
—*The New Yorker*

"A breathtaking account of the beauty and harshness of the 1,100-mile-long Amur River that forms the border between Russia and China. . . . Thubron documents the interplay of politics and history, contrasting the 'subdued fatalism' of Russians living in the river basin with the bustling optimism of the Chinese, whose glitzy restaurants and markets mask signs of discontent. . . . A top-notch travelogue."
—*Publishers Weekly* (starred review)

"*The Amur River* shows Thubron to be at the peak of his powers . . . as one of our greatest prose writers in any genre. But *The Amur River* is not just beautifully written: it is also a work of great importance. . . . Thubron uses the Amur River as a metaphor to deal with the relationship of two countries now regarded by many as the greatest threat to the West in these dying days of the U.S. Imperium." —*Daily Telegraph*

"A gripping read with fascinating political insight."

—*Sunday Times* (London)

"Enthralling. . . . A captivating portrait of a remote region of the world . . . evoking with beautiful detail and compassion its rich history and culture." —*Kirkus Reviews* (starred review)

"An extraordinary journey. . . . People are characterized with great sympathy. . . . Thubron writes brilliantly about the region's wildlife and folklore. . . . Moments of humor leaven the atmosphere. . . . One can only marvel that Thubron completed his journey and be thankful that this marvelous book came out of it." —*Times Literary Supplement* (London)

THE
AMUR RIVER

BETWEEN RUSSIA
AND CHINA

COLIN THUBRON

HARPER ⚫ PERENNIAL

NEW YORK • LONDON • TORONTO • SYDNEY • NEW DELHI • AUCKLAND

HARPER ● PERENNIAL

FIRST HARPER PERENNIAL EDITION PUBLISHED 2022.

Library of Congress Cataloging-in-Publication Data has been
applied for.

ISBN 978-0-06-309969-2 (pbk.)

22 23 24 25 26 LSC 10 9 8 7 6 5 4 3 2 1

For Austin, Paula and Eliseo

Contents

Map		viii
Chapter 1	The Source	1
Chapter 2	Steppelands	22
Chapter 3	The Treaty	47
Chapter 4	The Shilka	72
Chapter 5	The Lost Fortress	88
Chapter 6	The City of Annunciation	113
Chapter 7	Black Dragon River	146
Chapter 8	Khabarovsk	186
Chapter 9	City of the Dawn	211
Chapter 10	The Promise	240
Acknowledgements		277
Index		279

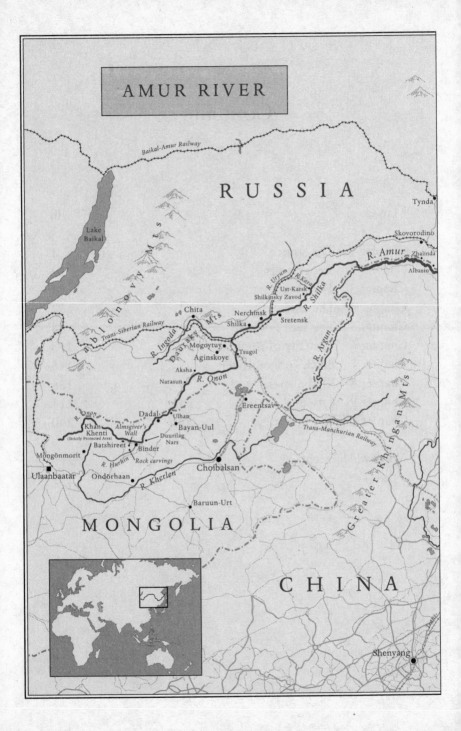

AMUR RIVER

Baikal-Amur Railway

RUSSIA

Tynda

Lake
Baikal

Skovorodino

R. Amur

Zhalinda

Albazin

Yablonovy Mts

R. Uryum

R. Karul

Ust-Karsk

Shilkinsky Zavod

R. Shilka

Chita

Nerchinsk

Trans-Siberian Railway

Shilka

Sretensk

R. Ingoda

Daursky Mts

Mogoytuy

Tsugol

Aginskoye

R. Argun

Aksha

R. Onon

Narasun

Dadal

Ereentsav

Khan
Khenti
(Strictly Protected Area)

Almsgiver's
Wall

Ulhan

Bayan-Uul

Duurilag
Nars

Trans-Manchurian Railway

Batshireet

Binder

Mongönmorit

R. Onon

R. Hurhin

Rock carvings

Choibalsan

Greater Khingan Mts

Ulaanbaatar

Ondörhaan

R. Kherlen

Baruun-Urt

MONGOLIA

CHINA

Shenyang

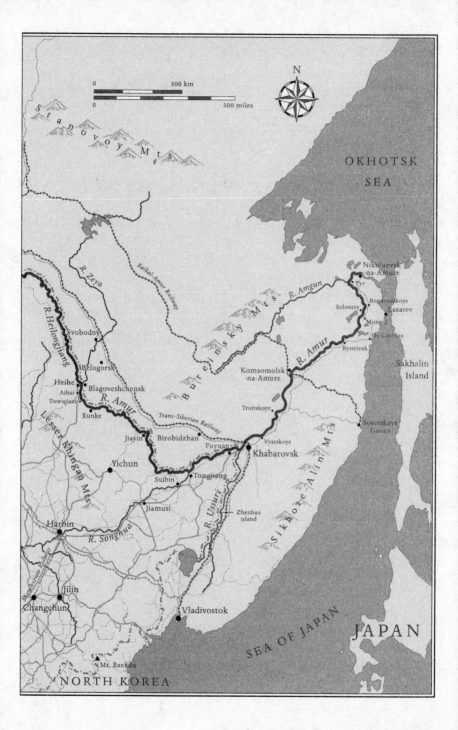

I

The Source

Across the heart of Asia, at the ancient convergence of steppe and forest, the grasslands of Mongolia move towards Siberia in a grey-green sea.

The land's silence is almost unbroken. It is barely inhabited. At its farthest reach, near the Russian frontier, almost five thousand square miles are forbidden to travellers. These mountains, once the homeland of Genghis Khan, are today a near-sacred wilderness. The solitary track that reaches them ends at a barrier and a rangers' lodge. And here we wait – a guide, two horsemen and I – to enter a region that none of us truly knows.

Somewhere deep in this hinterland rises one of the most formidable rivers on earth. It drains a basin twice the size of Pakistan, and more than two hundred tributaries, some of them immense, pour into its flood in spring. For over a thousand miles it forms the border between Russia and China: a fault-line shrouded in old mistrust.

The Amur is elusive. Even the name's origin is obscure. To the West the river seems unreachably remote, and few people have even heard of it. There are wildly different estimates of its length, naming it the tenth or even eighth longest river in the world. Its Chinese shore is almost untravelled, while razor wire and watchtowers shadow its Russian bank from end to end in the most densely fortified frontier on earth.

A day goes by, and then a night, while we wait to cross into these proscribed mountains. The rangers in this country, named the Khenti Strictly Protected Area, are reluctant to release us, although I have permits secured by the trusted agent who found my guide and horsemen. I feel a first twinge of unease. Our three tents, pitched in the meadow grasses, are beginning to look forlorn, and the elation of starting out – the visceral excitement, the tingle of apprehension – is ebbing into the fear that we may never start at all. At night I am woken by our horses cropping the grass outside my tent. It is that hour when the mind darkens; and suddenly the notion of following a river of 2,826 miles (the favoured estimate), as it flows through south-east Siberia then meets China, then breaks for the Pacific, seems little more than a fantasy.

I open my tent-flap on the cold dark, and catch my breath. My shadow falls black over the grass. The night above me blazes with stars, and across that immense Mongolian sky the Milky Way moves in an icy torrent of light.

Dawn spreads the thin radiance of another planet. The world seems still unstained. In the distances around us the sun is lifting a glistening mist above grasslands heavy with dew. It is as if a great fire were burning over the plains. For a while it obscures the hills that fringe the skyline, then its haze dissolves as though we had imagined it. The air grows warmer. Tiny diurnal moths are rising from the grasses, where invisible warblers sing, and the air fills with the click and whirr of grasshoppers. To walk here is to wade through a tide of wildflowers: multicoloured asters, gentians, butter-coloured potentilla, peacock-blue columbines. Over farther slopes, swathes of blown edelweiss make a frosty pallor for miles.

Then the horsemen emerge, heavy in their native *deel* over-coats, their daggers at their belts, to check our tethered mounts. It is well into morning before the rangers appear. They come to our tents on motorbikes, in their outsize boots and piratical headbands. They carry little briefcases. Batmonkh, my guide, a native of Mongolia's capital, says they are feeling important because the prime minister has arrived here on pilgrimage to Burkhan Khaldun, the mountain sacred to Genghis Khan. But they remain with us a long time, eating our biscuits and scrutinizing our papers. The country ahead of us is dangerous, they say, and almost impassable. The most distant tributary of the Amur, the Onon river, rises in remote marshlands, and the monsoons had been heavy that summer. Now, in late August, the ground is flooded and treacherous. And there are bears. Once inside the reserve, we will be beyond help.

Batmonkh listens to them without interest. He says they resent outside intruders in their land. I cannot understand a word they say, only silently hope they will not forbid us. Sometimes Batmonkh wanders away dismissively, while the rangers come and go, and our horsemen laugh at them with the despisal of free men for bureaucracy. Eventually the rangers present us with a document to sign, absolving them of any responsibility, and at last they leave, bouncing over the steppelands on their Chinese motorbikes, after washing their hands of us.

We should have listened to them, of course.

For the last time before we depart the sky looms vaster and more restless than the plains. From end to end the horizon seems sunk beyond the curvature of the earth, and above us spreads a panorama of discordant clouds. On one side they are merely smears of mist, on the other an armada of cumulus rolls into infinity.

For a moment we halt at the edge of the reserve; the next we are in underbush, following the Kherlen river where it descends from its watershed in the east. Already the slopes are steepening and darkening into forest. A late cuckoo calls. Half unconsciously, we are crossing the divide from Eurasian grassland to Siberian taiga, the scent of crushed wildflowers fading under our hooves, and all of us elated by our release.

But soon the terrain grows sodden. Sometimes the horses flounder in bog-water that is still flowing. Once, ominously, the ground beneath the leading horseman gives way, and his stallion – a handsome roan – collapses into a mud hole, and struggles up as he remounts.

By early afternoon we are riding along hills above the river. Buzzards are dropping low over its swamp. For miles we brush through stunted birch thickets, while larches troop down the mountainsides like an invading army, and infiltrate the valleys. The only sounds are our own. As the air sharpens, I sense the deepening remoteness of our path, and feel an old excitement at entering another country.

My horse is a twelve-year-old stallion who has no name. To the horsemen he is simply 'the White Horse'; any other label would be sentimental. He is tough and scarred. We ride in a straggling cavalcade of nine, our tents and food trussed on five packhorses. These beasts are strong and glossy after summer pasturing – not the sickly creatures of late winter. Short-legged and large-headed, they descend from the tireless horses of Mongol conquest, able to gallop ten kilometres without pause, and we ride them in the Mongol way, with legs bent back from the knees on short stirrups. The horsemen are in their early forties, herders and huntsmen, their faces wind-battered raw, their bodies pared lean. They too look tireless.

Yet their ancestors' ancient habitat was not steppeland but forest, from which they first emerged millennia ago, and for a long time our own transition is uneven, where grassy slopes still mingle with woodland as we travel back in time, and the early nomad hoof beats fade into forest silence.

Towards evening comes the first hint of trouble. One of our packhorses is still unbroken, and its wild energy unsettles the others. Ahead of us, in low woodland, they are suddenly thrusting and barging together, then they tear loose from their leading-ropes, three of them bolting back the way they came, their eyes dilated in fear, with the horsemen following.

Batmonkh and I tether the last pair to saplings, and wait. We wait for seeming hours. When the horsemen return with their charges, we find that the recalcitrant palomino has thrown off its baggage, which now lies somewhere – anywhere – in the forest around us. They return to search for it, while Batmonkh and I wonder disconsolately which of the giant saddlebags is missing. If it holds my rucksack, I realize, my passport and visas will be gone, and our journey ended. I tramp back along the way the horses disappeared, but the forest spreads around me in a glaze of concealing birch scrub. I hunt for panicky hoof-prints, smashed branches, and go down tracks that dissipate to the trail of some long-passed animal. The whinnying of the herders' horses sounds farther and farther away as their search widens. Sometimes in the undergrowth a fallen silver birch shines with a moment's hope – they are bright and smooth as china – but soon I cannot imagine finding anything at all in this wilderness.

Batmonkh, when I return, is surveying the leftover luggage still strapped on our tethered horses, alarmed that our food is gone and that we will have to start back at once. Tentatively, with our different hopes, we fumble open one of the mounted packs, but its stallion charges loose – they are all unnerved now – dragging its wooden saddle along the trail behind it. We can only round it up, and wait.

After an hour we hear a far-off shout. Batmonkh says: 'I think they've found it.' And soon afterwards the two men return, still inscrutable, with the lost saddlebags, as if their recovery were expected. And when we unpack that evening, on a tree-sown slope above the marshes, we find that the recovered baggage had contained our food.

We set up our tents at dusk on the rain-softened earth, the horsemen hacking down branches to frame a shelter of their own. Our possessions – food-boxes, water bottles, harness, hatchets, even a canvas chair – lie strewn about the grass, while the horses graze disburdened under the trees. It is strange, in this unpeopled solitude, to realize that our campfire is the sole human light, seen only by wolves or woken bears.

In the chill of nightfall the fire draws us closer, and its smoke repels the mosquitoes that are rising round us. Batmonkh cooks up noodles and scraps of beef on the portable stove, while the horsemen drink salted tea, and smoke. They seemed like twins at first, but now they start to diverge. Mongo looks older than he is, sashed like a brigand, hard-faced and talkative; Ganpurev keeps the appearance of a boy: but of a sharp-eyed boy who has given trouble. He is the youngest son of a family that became poor. They both wear peaked caps and high boots, and anoraks with pirated labels. Around the fire they talk about practicalities: horse-herding and money. In this terrain, eight hours' riding will cover only twenty miles, they say. Their cigarettes flare and die in the dark. Batmonkh, whose English is fluent, sometimes translates. But his world is not theirs, and he may seem as alien to them as I do. The silence, when we at last sleep, is the silence of exhaustion. Even the horses do not stir, asleep on their feet in the starlight.

*

The source of great rivers is often obscure. They descend in a confusion of tributaries, or seep from inaccessible swamps and glaciers. The Indus is born from six contested streams. The Danube, it is claimed, issues from a gutter in the Black Forest. As for the origins of the Amur, when a conclave of geographers from Russia and China met to debate it, they found to their chagrin that its farthest source lay in neither country, but in these remote Mongolian mountains. My horsemen know the river only as the Onon, the 'Holy Mother'; but if the mother herself is born somewhere, few but Ganpurev know quite where this is, and he has been there only once, ten years ago.

It is the profiles of surrounding mountains that guide us, but to me, as the sun rises, they are only snowless shadows. The morning air is cold and pure. The dew on our tent roofs has glazed to ice, and the coats of the tethered horses gleam with frost, their breath pluming over them. All morning we keep to the uplands, riding through larch forests along the tank tracks left by Soviet military exercises decades ago. The Russian border is forty miles to our north. But now the tracks have blurred to rivulets of floodwater, and shrubs and grasses closing over them. Something has happened to the larch forests too. They bank around us in folds of sombre green, but sometimes we find ourselves moving along hillsides ravaged by wildfire. The trees remain upright in death, their charred bark falling away, until our path threads between blackened gibbets. Twice, along these faded trails, we come upon tall sheafs of stacked branches, hung with votive scarves, now turned to rags, left by rangers or poachers. These *ovoo*s mark the summit of mountain ridges that fall within the purlieus of a local spirit. Such spirits are mercurial, and sometimes angry, and here they are unknown to us. Mongo and Ganpurev dismount to circle their *ovoo*s, and sprinkle vodka in propitiation. They ask me to copy them, for our journey's safety.

7

But by noon we are mired in another terrain. Our track thins to a horse's width, and is almost lost among birch scrub, and we are brushing blindly through it. For hours we hear only the sloshing plod of our horses. Then we are plunging into steep-banked streams, tributaries to rivers we do not know, with the packhorses following. Sometimes we dismount and lead them. We sink in shin-deep. My waterproof trainers are useless, and the boots of the others filling with water.

The horses are not used to this. They are the heirs of nomad cavalry, bred for the steppes. Riding them, you forget anything you've been taught. I no longer rein in the White Horse when he nuzzles the buttocks of the packhorse in front. And you spur them forward not with your heels but with a hissing *Chu-chuh*. You never fondle their heads. As we reach higher ground we start to go faster, with relief. But the preferred gait of the White Horse is not a leisurely canter but a fast trot. For mile after mile he insists on this jarring bustle for which the Western rider's inured rise-and-fall in the saddle is hopeless – the tempo is too fast – and instead you stand in your stirrups as the Mongol raiders did.

It is after one of these furious trots that we stop and throw ourselves down in the grass. I remember its softness and the weight of my breathing. A few minutes later, standing up and suddenly dizzy, I recover consciousness at the foot of the White Horse, with my ankle twisted under me. With misgiving I feel its creeping pain. Then Batmonkh helps me into the saddle. For a moment I wonder if I've fallen because of altitude – but we are only at 6,700 feet. Wilfully I decide the ankle can't be broken, and that in the morning I'll be walking. Then I feel the ease of being on horse again, my foot weightless in the stirrup, and the valleys opening before us in a shining sea of green. And with this a chill descends: the cold wonder of travelling a land empty of the memory or scars of human history. Sometimes russet crags break through the forested mountain tops with the semblance of man-made walls and forts, but this is illusion. Human tracks peter out, and the only flight path across the sky is the passage of vultures.

Yet even here this void is not complete. The poaching that broke out in the chaotic years after the Soviet Union's collapse has abated, but not gone, and Russian hunters still occasionally cross the border to feed the Chinese market in traditional medicines by slaughtering musk deer and bears. Yet my companions vouch that wildlife is returning, and for days the only trespasser we meet is an old man in rags gathering pine nuts.

Here the shadows of the past are older, deeper. For this is the Mongol heartland. Eight hundred years ago Genghis Khan decreed the upper valleys of the Onon and Kherlen rivers an inviolable sanctuary, permitted only to Mongol royalty, sealed off for their private rites and burial. It became the spiritual powerhouse of his vast empire. Even now, Batmonkh says, travellers to these mountains are resented. This is holy land. Somewhere to our east, a forested massif lifts to the rocky pate of Khan Khenti, revered as Burkhan Khaldun, on whose slopes the young Genghis Khan, destitute and alone, found a haven from his tribal enemies. On these protective heights, runs the Mongol epic, he sheltered as poor as a grasshopper, and later faced the mountain in grateful worship – a mountain already sacred to his people, close to the Eternal Blue Sky of their ancestral veneration. To this mountain, too, he dedicated the worship of his descendants for ever, and himself returned in times of crisis to breathe again its primal power.

The true site of Burkhan Khaldun is unsure, but beyond us, in the watershed of the Onon, its valley fills with the adversities of the future conqueror. Here, in about 1162, he was born into the clan of a minor chief. On its banks, after his people had abandoned her, his mother dug for roots to keep her children alive, while the boys fished its streams; and here, after escaping from imprisonment by enemy raiders, Genghis submerged himself in the Onon waters, keeping his head afloat in the wooden halter by which they had confined him, then slipped away.

We camp on a shoulder of firm ground. Beyond our firelight the air is cool and still, the forest utterly silent. We eat our mutton stew, and talk, while the sky fills up with stars. Sometimes the horsemen's faces lighten into wry smiles and laughter. They share some old affinity. In the dark their features and ages seem to converge, both born in the Year of the Horse (although they say this means nothing). Batmonkh interprets from the desultory gutturals and aspirants of their exchange. They tell stories of national victimhood: of a Russian robber-baron long ago, who stole Mongolia's gold along a road laid by Chinese slaves. 'Our ancestors told us this.'

Batmonkh gives a ghostly smile. From the vantage of our camp, under that glittering sky, he suddenly starts to talk of natural wonders, as if to replace the horsemen's legend with something stranger and real. Somewhere up there, he says, Titan, the moon of Saturn, has yielded the first signs of life in the solar system.

The horsemen nod silently. It is impossible to tell how this strikes them, or if it seems no more than a distant tale, like many others. It does not, after all, help feed their families, or the horses shifting round us in the night.

But Batmonkh is different. He has a wife and child back in Ulaanbaatar, yet his mind is filled with reflection and dreams. He looks like no Mongolian I've seen. He is dark-skinned and handsome, with large, swimming eyes. Slighter built than the horsemen, he seems at once lither and more vulnerable.

'People think that I'm Indian.' He speaks softly, although the horsemen cannot understand. 'My father is Angolan, you see, from southern Africa. My mother met him in Moscow during Soviet times, as Third World students.' He smiles at the term. 'And I am the result.'

Those had been the years, I remember, when Moscow's Lumumba University took in select students from less developed nations, many from Africa, and gave them a free education, steeped in Soviet ideals. I wonder: 'Where are your parents now?'

'My mother came back to Mongolia, but my father could not follow her. Our government would not allow it, an impoverished African country . . .'

His mother had married again, he says, and had more children, while he gained a place at Harbin University and a degree in geography. 'But when I came back, good jobs were impossible to find. You needed a hook, and I had none . . .'

I guess: 'A contact?'

'Yes.' His voice holds a spark of rebellion. 'It's a kind of corruption.'

I wonder aloud what prejudice festered back in Ulaanbaatar, and if his parentage had hampered him. For a long time he does not answer, then he says: 'No, I don't think so. It's not my colour. It's my family's obscurity. We don't know people. We don't have power.'

Sometimes in that first intimacy, he looks obscurely troubled and goes silent; then his smile returns with a kind of gentle apology. 'It was my grandfather who took my father's place, and brought me up,' he says, and I feel I already knew this. The old man had died a few days before our departure; Batmonkh had shared with me his funeral meats. Now he loads more branches onto our fire, stares at the flames. He says: 'I loved him.'

It happens suddenly. We come down in forest shadow, splashing over streamlets of recent rain. Pink rocks, swept down by meltwater in another age, press up from the alluvial earth. It is almost noon. To our south-east we see a blur of irregular mountains: the two-peaked mass of Mount Khenti, where Genghis Khan may lie. I cannot tell how far away it is. Then the terrain levels out and we go through lashing thickets, our heads bowed, advancing blind. Twice my riding helmet deflects the blows of low-hanging larch branches.

Then the scrub clears before a margin of feathery grass. And here, without warning, we come upon a trickle of water, a yard wide. The horses ahead have already crossed it, and are out of sight. I shout to Batmonkh: 'What is this?'

He calls back: 'The Onon.'

I rein in. Here is the infant Amur. It is, of course, scarcely different from any other runnels we have crossed: only narrower, purer. It has a faint peaty tinge. Upstream it does not bubble whole from the ground, but emerges in a glinting coalescence of marshland waters, edged by fescue grass and willows. I want to drink from it, but as I start to dismount my ankle winces and I cannot stoop. In this river's infancy I feel suddenly old. I imagine a foolish tenderness for it, as if for a child who does not know what will happen. In time it will cease to be the Onon and become the Siberian Shilka, changing gender to the Russians' 'Little Father', before it transforms at last, on the border of China, into the giant Amur.

For the rest of the day, in and out of sight, we follow its gleaming passage eastward.

How still it is. No jungle cries start up at night, or cicada raspings. We are nearing the forest quiet of Russia. In my tent's pitch dark, I'm grateful for my body's weariness that disregards where it sleeps (on a thin foam mat), and I savour our fleeting triumph. The Onon meanders through the night outside, while this dreamy felicity descends, and I lie oblivious in the mosquito-whining air, and sink into sleep.

At dawn a light rain falls, like someone throwing grit on the tent roof, and carries a chill of foreboding. All morning the ground grows slushier under us, as if the whole terrestrial world were turning to water. The Onon is sunk invisibly in its wetlands beside us, where yellowing grasses trace its slow descent. Hour by hour my delight at our finding it dissipates with the splosh of the White Horse's hooves in the deepening morass. Where we are riding no rain falls, but on every side the sky is bruised amber and grey with half-lit clouds. Once only they part to shed down a beam of yellow-gold, which spotlights the river like a benediction.

Towards evening we come upon the only habitation we see in six days: a ranger's cottage and a crude log canopy above thermal springs by the river. The ranger is taciturn, as if we have disturbed him, and assigns us a rough-built hut beyond his own. Mongo and Ganpurev had heard rumours of these springs. Their habitual quiet turns to muttered anticipation, then to boyish glee as they clamber down to bathe. The foliage along the riverbanks has receded before flat grasslands by the springs, where the river flows faster and darker. The springs are four or five pits, edged with planks and sheltered by log ceilings. They look abandoned. Mongo and Ganpurev are already emerging from them in the dusk when I descend. Naked, they do not show the taut bodies I'd expected, but are smooth-muscled, hairless. Ganpurev is growing a belly. Soon they start back to our hut, leaving me alone.

I strip and lower myself into the warmth, hoping to ease my ankle, which has turned amber and black, like the sky. For a few minutes, half floating here, I feel the aching release of my body, and marvel at the strangeness of this thermal eruption into the cold river. Its waters seem already used and cloudy.

Above me, in the gaps of the log roof, a few stars are shining. Then I heave myself out. For an instant I am standing upright in the darkening shelter, above the enigmatic pool. Then the ankle's pain stabs upwards, and I'm falling. I've underestimated the labour of our riding, the insidious weakness, and my ribcage smashes on the solid log bench behind me. For a minute I lie wondering what will happen if I move. What is fractured or punctured? Gingerly I stir and begin to dress, hopelessly trying to avoid pain, and at last climb back towards the hut, clutching at handholds of fescue grass.

Our hut is hacked from raw wood, with twin platforms for sleeping. A rusted stove pushes its chimney into the roof. The place is littered with the detritus of whoever last passed through: discarded cigarette packets, ash, empty bottles. That night, from the upper platform where I try to sleep, with Batmonkh and the horsemen below, I look out at my bitter compensation – the Onon pale in the moonlight, curved below a solitary larch tree. Framed in the rough-hewn window, it has frozen to an engraving, its banks shorn bare, its waters halted in mid-flow: a lost river, winding out of nowhere.

I've borrowed Batmonkh's satellite phone, our only contact with the outside world that cannot help us, and I call my wife in London to say that all is well except for the heavy swamps. There comes the searchlight of her voice. Why do I sound strange? Something has happened. Yes, I've had a couple of falls, but luckily I didn't break my glasses. She laughs. Is this a bad phone connection? You seem far away. Something to do with the satellite orbit . . . I must be sounding sad, because she insists: 'Don't think of me until you come home.' Her voice carries a low, delayed echo. 'Think of your journey.' The roses are blooming in our garden, she says, and will last into winter.

* * *

We were entering a region that even the horsemen did not know. For four days they guided our way by the mountains that now surrounded us. To our south stood the massifs of Mount Khenti and Asralt – not Alpine peaks but ashen silhouettes eight thousand feet high. Ahead of us the Onon flowed invisibly – its course low and flat – through valleys of knee-high grass. Sometimes fir and pine trees descended to the marshlands, or retreated before lawn-smooth hills. From a distance the ground looked innocent, almost landscaped. But to either side of the river its tributaries seeped through a widening waterland where peat-moss and ground-smothering grasses – fescues, needlegrass – had rotted over the millennia into fathomless bog. We crossed to the river's south bank, then back again. It was higher now, faster-flowing, its banks clotted with willows. Our horses plunged in reluctantly. The riverbed was soft under their hooves. Soon I lost count of the tributaries we forded. Often they seemed as full and deep-sunk as the Onon itself. Batmonkh waved me away from the more precarious crossing places, but Mongo and Ganpurev charged in like centaurs, the current streaming over their knees, their cigarettes still dangling from their lips. Once, dropping down the Onon's banks, the packhorses panicked and refused, and had to be rounded up again, the horsemen clouting their flanks in retribution. The White Horse was old, and I felt a clutch of fear each time he descended, but his tread never slowed in midstream, and did not stumble.

We had no track to follow. Beneath grass the subsoil was a squelching morass that seemed only to deepen as we went. Each day, in eight hours' riding, we covered barely twenty miles, as the horsemen had predicted. Often the ground disappeared under a sheen of low-lying scrub, so that neither horse nor rider could see where it was treading. Sometimes this uncertain earth, mined with hidden quagmires, opened like a trapdoor under us. Suddenly the horses would be dropping to their withers and the peat-laden water brimming over their backs. Then they began to struggle out, their eyeballs white and bulging, their forelegs scrabbling for a hold, their hind legs kicking in panic, while we were thrown back and forth in the saddle.

It was in terrain like this that the White Horse sank into a hole and lost his footing. Tilted sideways in that rotting earth, he rolled and threw me. For an instant I found myself trapped beneath his heaving flank, my feet still in the stirrups, my ribcage screaming. Then he started up in fear, and began to bolt. I wrenched one foot free, but the other stayed wedged in its stirrup while he dragged me forward. But my trainer was loose-fitting, and I wrenched my foot out of it as he gathered speed. For a moment I lay in the marsh, oddly at peace, while the trainer went off on its own. But it wasn't funny: I had only one pair.

Batmonkh, on the far side of the swamp, saw the riderless White Horse emerge with only a mud-clogged plimsole in the stirrup. While the horsemen went to round it up, he called into the emptiness: 'Where are you? Can you stand up?'

I heard his voice plaintive and small across the wetland. I got up and walked towards it. There was something a little comical, I thought (but only later). My cut-price trainers, too loose to trap my feet, had saved me. While the other men wore knee-high boots which filled with swamp water, my plimsoles became squelching pouches of warmth. We had long ago ceased to care about the mud and bog water that sprayed up round us. Only at night our discarded footwear steamed by the camp fire alongside the horse blankets.

These hours became a time of drowsy companionship. On a tree-sheltered ridge or knoll, under the waxing moon, Mongo and Ganpurev would talk of their hunting expeditions, guiding oligarch Russian sportsmen in search of game. There was always a tang of danger, they said. In early spring, when bears came out of hibernation, they could be hungry and a little mad. After pillaging ants' nests, the formic acid went to their heads and they ran amok. You had to watch for wild boars too, which turned savage and cunning when injured. Mongo had a deep gash down his thigh to show for it. 'You think you're hunting them, but after they're wounded they will be hunting you.'

No, they didn't mind the Russians. The Russians weren't like the Chinese. Mongo admired Putin, even Trump. He revered rulers with a semblance of strength. Ganpurev stayed silent and Batmonkh shook his head. The horsemen wondered who governed Britain. Wasn't it the royal family? Strange that in this Mongolian fastness they had heard of a British royal prince marrying a mixed-race American. And she from a split family . . .

Batmonkh suddenly said: 'That was my mother's situation too, and mine. Her father was angry with her. "You know what people will say," he told her. "Everyone will say it. Marrying a mixed-race man. Third World Africa. And your children" – that's me – "will show it too. But if you want to do it, all right, you do it." And she did, although they had to separate, and my grandfather supported her to the end.' He shared this with the horsemen in terse phrases.

Hesitantly Ganpurev said: 'I think intermarriage is good. In Mongolia we are too enclosed.'

Suddenly, beyond the thickening darkness, came the cry of a wolf. At first it was only a thread of sound, like a distant scream. Mongo got to his feet, circled his hands round his mouth, and answered it. And the cry came back, closer, from the thickets a hundred yards away: a disembodied howl, pitched high and fluting, then falling away in an inconsolable lament.

When Mongo responded again, his cry sounded identical, and the replies were now echoing back to us – or perhaps to one another – from still-invisible wolves. Our horses stirred uneasily. They would come closer to our tents tonight, Mongo said. The wolves were circling around us, unsure. Something was not right. We never saw them, but they could see us, Mongo said, and now our fire would have disturbed them.

For a time we went on sitting in the dark, while the howling faded away. We were all weary. In more than twenty years' trekking, the horsemen said, this was the worst terrain they had ever known. When the moon sank and our campfire died, the flare of their cigarettes lit their faces with a delusive softness; then they left for their tent.

Batmonkh stayed on, as he often did, staring into the campfire embers while I sat beside him. Usually he liked to talk about his reading. He'd long ago left behind the old Soviet favourites like *White Fang* and *The Last of the Mohicans*, and was devouring books on world history and astronomy, or the origins of humankind, modern warfare, the history of the Huns. But tonight he said: 'I have much to be sad over.' He was remembering his grandfather, the powerful old man, his surrogate father, whose funeral he had left to accompany me. 'He was the one who encouraged me. When I guided historians and palaeontologists in the Gobi Desert, he said that was a fine thing to do, that was my contribution to the world.' Then Batmonkh voiced the old lament of the bereaved. 'I never told him how much I loved him.'

'He must have known,' I said.

'He knew he was near the end. He had blood entering his brain. He went to a river to die. They found him after four days, with a bottle of vodka, barely touched. They identified him only by his watch.'

*

Dawn brings a soft illumination to the land, as if the night had cleaned it. Below our camp the still-weak sun lifts a long sheet of mist above the valley, where the river meanders in and out of sight through scrub burnishing into autumn. I emerge from a sleepless night with aching body. But the land's human emptiness and its deep silence stir a pang of wonder, as if the world were young again. The keen eyes of the horsemen descry Siberian red deer grazing more than a mile away. Batmonkh puts his binoculars to my eyes. The animals have moved out from protective trees, and are standing in open meadowland. The distance, and the pale pink light, turn them a little spectral. They seem to be grazing in another ether than ours, in the peace of a different sunlight.

The day breaks in. The horses glisten and champ at their tethering trees. Mongo and Ganpurev sing low, tuneless songs to themselves as they heave our baggage over the wooden saddles and brace their feet against the horses' flanks to pull the cords tighter. We set off without knowing where this will end. Almost at once we are in swamp again. Clouds of black flies and mosquitoes follow us. We make for higher ground, but the unbroken packhorse runs wild, spreading its fear to the others, who scatter along the hillside. We lose more hours retrieving our thrown-off baggage, and come to rest in a copse where Mongo tries to subdue the maverick horse. When it rears against him, the two men take up heavy branches and bring them crashing down on its neck and shoulders. Their shouts and blows only incense it, and it breaks free again. These tough, patient animals, it seems, are broken by violence – a sheer test of wills – and I now understand the dents and scars on my White Horse's neck. Batmonkh remonstrates with the men, but they only reply that this is how they've always done it. And when the horses become old, they say, 'they're quite good to eat.'

*

This may be the nadir of our journey, I thought. I no longer recognized myself. I knew I was weakening. Sometimes one of the horsemen steadied me into the saddle, and I dismounted by swinging one leg over the horse's neck, to save my ribs. Small things – shaving, brushing teeth – became an ordeal. I gave up searching my body for ticks or snatching at the mosquitoes that whined in my tent's dark. My appetite had gone. Batmonkh, one evening, said sadly: 'Don't you like my cooking?' But I had only a raging thirst. Sometimes I caught the horsemen looking at me and I thought I could read their minds: *How long can he last?* By now even they were reduced. The rioting of the packhorses over the marshes had grown unremitting. At night it was Batmonkh, not I, who set up my tent, and the horsemen no longer talked around our fire but retreated to sleep, exhausted, with their boots still on. As for me, I lay fully clothed on my tent's thin mattress, glad of the tiredness that overcame all hurt.

Batmonkh would sit on alone beside the fire, thinking. He seemed, in the end, the hardiest of us. It was too late to go back, he agreed, even if we'd wanted to. A better rider than me, he'd been thrown from his horse that morning while the horsemen laughed at him – but recovered unscathed. He kept a boyish pride in our endeavour. 'This is the hardest journey I've ever done,' he said. 'In ten years' time I'll still be telling people about it.' Yet we would be on horseback for barely more than a week, covering only two hundred miles. It was the peat bogs that reduced us, the sopping underworld which forced our detours and submerged and panicked our horses.

But then came a morning when we realized that something was changing. The hills grew balder, stonier. The bleached swamplands thinned away. Suddenly we were trotting along tracks of pulverized sandstone, and around us the grasslands of the steppe were returning. Soon the hills subsided to slopes where orange and grey bluffs burst up in isolation, and buzzards were circling the sky on frayed wings. And now the steppeland flora lapped round us in its remembered glory. Asters, sweet vetch, gentians, and purple and red clover were whirring with wasps and flies, and tiny marbled butterflies careering above. Soon red admirals and painted ladies appeared, and fast-flying tortoiseshells with many others I did not know, and wagtails were shrilling by the river. A weathered noticeboard told us that we were leaving the Strictly Protected Area. Signs of habitation emerged: broken-down corrals, abandoned paddocks, some stray cattle. A solitary farmer, reaping hay, barely turned to look at us. And at the day's end the jeep that had carried us to the edge of this region – a Ukrainian UAZ with its imperturbable driver – had circled round three hundred miles to meet us on the track.

2

Steppelands

The land looks empty. The rivers that enter it out of the mountains are stilled to slow motion across the undulating grass. Human life is a scatter of semi-nomad herders whose felt yurts, their *gers*, blur into a sky-filled distance. In these bright-lit plains the memory of desolate marshlands returns only in the peaty outflow of the Onon waters, in the mountain profiles dropping behind us, and perhaps in the body's pain.

But to the eyes of its inhabitants, whose shamanism has accommodated Buddhism and outlived Communism, the whole country is animate. They must use it delicately, because it is not precisely theirs. Invisible spirit-masters hold sway from its hilltops, each crowned by an *ovoo* or rising bare but alive in native memory. In them the land breathes. Mountains harbour unpredictable power, second only to the overarching aegis of the Eternal Sky, and flowing waters are the corporeal lifeblood of the earth. The Onon especially is 'Holy Mother' or 'Mother Queen', come down from the Mongol heartland. Even the souls of ancestors remain in the mortal world, lingering unrealized beyond a hill or river bend or behind an unseen door in a mountainside.

The country grows wider and brighter as our UAZ shudders eastward along tracks of hardened mud at dawn. Mongo and

Ganpurev have left, driving their horses ahead of them, jubilant with their bonus money. The Onon has swerved north in a tall, momentary loop, grazing the Russian border, while we follow its tributary Egiyn towards the village of Batshireet. Our driver, Tochtor, is a barrel-chested townsman whose genial eyes are embedded in a face of massive calm. He steers by no landmark I can see.

Even the steppeland villages, when we find them, seem the lightest human presence on an ancient land. Their stockaded huts are bright with metal roofs in carnival colours – scarlet, orange, enamel blue – as if they were toys dropped all of a piece onto the grass. Sometimes the mushroom cupola of a *ger* rises from someone's courtyard, as though its family were still dreaming of their old unconstraint and might one day depart. More often their compounds contain nothing but the shacks of their toilets, a Chinese motor-scooter, or a broken-down truck. The flimsy paling that encloses every dwelling, wavering along the wide, muddy streets, heightens the feel of a settlement that the next storm might sweep away.

Batshireet, which we reach at noon, is the first of these transient-looking places. Almost nobody is about. There are faded advertisements for G-Mobile and karaoke, but most shops are locked or wrecked. A group of women in flowery skirts and dresses is bargaining at the main-street store for household goods. Their cheeks are burnt raw by winter wind, and their hair in horsetails. They laugh blithely together.

The valleys flatten and open eastward into pure steppe. The hills have shrunk to rock-littered folds, and huge, multi-coloured cattle herds, sometimes two hundred strong, drift over the pastures. To our north the horizon pales beyond plains dreamy with seasonal lakes. The tracks meander and converge, and Tochtor seems to choose our way at random. The rutted surfaces tremble and jolt the chassis, and I sit with my ribs cushioned in baggage, imagining them only bruised and my ankle merely sprained (but months later X-rays show two fractured ribs and an ankle fibula broken).

Over this north-east wilderness we make for a far-off Russian border. The Onon flows in an arc of light to our north, and we are crossing a land unfamiliar even to Batmonkh. Overnight we find simple hikers' camps, but there are no hikers. In the guest *ger*s the walls are of beaten felt, thick and warm, and breakfast, if we are lucky, includes fried dumplings and home-made yoghurt. One night some weathered herdsmen vacate a family *ger* for us, its walls weighted with logs against the wind. Inside, the nomad furnishings are still in place. Its willow framework radiates down from a circular smoke-hole, and a stove on the floor sends a rusted pipe skyward. The household altar no longer harbours photographs of Party leaders, but has returned to older sanctities. Crude paintings of Tibetan Buddhist deities and protectors – the benign White Tara and the fearsome Black Mahakala – are propped on a tin of Imperial Best Quality Biscuits. Beneath them, beside a miniature prayer wheel, some juniper seeds are burning, while behind hangs a bundle of dried curds for sacrifice to the local mountain spirit. The family gives us a dish of cold mutton bones, then leaves us to sleep: I on the only bed, while Batmonkh and Tochtor lie among blankets on the floor.

These mobile dwellings, and the fragile villages that absorb them, seem natural to the Buryat Mongols who inhabit this region. Their recent past is dark with flight and persecution. Early in the last century, with revolution and civil war engulfing their Russian homeland, they fled south into a more tranquil Mongolia. But already the country was sliding under Russia's shadow, and soon Stalin's flail fell on them at the hands of Khorloogiin Choibalsan, a Mongolian despot as ruthless as his Soviet mentor. Through the 1930s night-time arrests took away thousands of Buryats for execution or the labour camps. They were charged with pan-Mongol conspiracies or with spying for a newly aggressive Japan. In an age of fear, they were judged fatally different. Between 1937 and '38, at the height of the bloodbath, half Mongolia's intelligentsia was purged, along with 17,000 monks.

Yet the Buryats remain settled in a deep band south of the Russian border. At 42,000 people, they number less than 2 per cent of Mongolia's population; but their talents have won them unequal influence and resentment, and it is they who occupy the watershed of the sacred Onon river from its source in the Khenti mountains to its departure over the Siberian frontier to our east.

Those dark years have receded almost beyond living memory, but their shadow may fall even on people too young to recall: the orphaned woman, shorn of her history, living in the town still named Choibalsan, or the man I meet one afternoon in Ulaanbaatar, who sips his tea in a hotel foyer. He must be in late middle age, but his hair is jet black and his face scarcely lined. He trusts me, I think, because we meet through a mutual friend, and his English is fluent: a Buryat civil servant working in a young and vulnerable democracy. A century ago, he says, his grandparents fled the Bolshevik Revolution, travelling south from Buryatia, the Russian territory that is still his people's homeland, and settled in Mongolia where the Onon river flows into Siberia.

He says: 'I still return to my birthplace there. I can't explain this, but sometimes I lie on the ground at that spot, and knead its earth in my hands. Then I feel the land, its mountains, entering my body.' He opens his arms to express this, admitting some deep, inherited insight or delusion, I think he is not sure. He is talking of his 'placenta homeland', I realize, of his people's immemorial practice of burying a baby's afterbirth in the place of its delivery. I want to ask him this, but hesitate, and he only says: 'There is this compulsion to return,' and I've heard that such a birth site can bind a person always, and even pull him back in death.

Into Soviet times this ritual of homecoming quietly continued, a lifeline more profound than simple nationhood. Then the 1930s Terror brought a bewildering dislocation in which the Buryat identity became itself a crime, and people burned or hid their genealogies, erasing their own past in a severance that is even now unhealed.

'We lost our inheritance.' He is talking in a sombre monotone. For him, his people's authenticity springs from the steppelands. 'But our nomad children go to boarding schools now, where they learn Russian or Chinese curricula. Soon they no longer remember how they enjoyed riding a horse or milking a cow. They probably don't even know what a cow is.'

I stare at him, at his formal suit and tie, and wonder how many urban dwellers feel their true homeland to be a remote campsite where the earth throbs under them. Yet his grandfather was not a herdsman, he says, but a talented journalist. He was the wrong class from the start.

'One evening, in 1941, he thought he was among friends and said he hoped Hitler would win the war so that the Reds would stop oppressing Mongolia. That night the KGB took him away. He vanished into the Gulag. In those days Germany was closing in on one side, Japan on the other. No one felt safe. My grandfather returned only with the death of Stalin in 1953. He died three months later, peacefully, at home, as if this was what he'd been waiting for.'

'Does your father remember him?'

'My father never spoke of it. I grew up in ignorance. Then came the fall of the Berlin Wall, and Gorbachev's *perestroika*, but that all seemed far away to us, not like with you. But we had our own revolution and in 1991 our archives were opened. Then I was able to read my grandfather's interrogation. And suddenly all that had happened struck home. We were very Sovietized, you know, very brainwashed. And when I read, I broke down and wept.'

In this time of resurgent nationalism people's anger found its target not in Choibalsan – long promoted as a patriot hero – but in the distant abstraction of Stalin.

'Yes, some of us hate Stalin. But we don't mind the Russians, you know. We quite like them.' He suddenly frowns. 'I don't quite understand this either, after everything they did. Perhaps it's because they brought us culture, European culture. They gave us medicine and education. We started from very low down, you see, started from almost nowhere. A century ago we were at the mercy of the Chinese, and they robbed us . . .'

This still astonishes me. The Russians crushed the Mongolians' native culture, devastated their monasteries and almost liquidated their elite. Yet it is the Chinese, dominant in the country for three centuries until 1921, who are regarded with visceral loathing and distrust. Their instruments of torture are lavishly displayed in the state museum, beside the account books of their avaricious traders. And it is the merciless usury of Chinese merchants that has endured in people's imagination. Half the country was said to be in their debt. There are Mongolians even now who believe themselves haunted by long-dead Chinese, warning them away from buried treasure. Neither lamas nor shamans had been able to exorcize them.

Soviet propaganda may have prolonged this old antipathy; but it was the avalanche of Chinese immigration early in the last century that turned the country to violence and at last into the arms of Russia.

'The Chinese would have massacred us all,' the man says. In illustration, he pushes a Chinese teacup and a Russian bottle across the table, to either side of a piece of crinkled paper that he calls Mongolia. 'The Chinese only took from us, whereas the Russians gave things back. When we shop for anything, we'll always buy Russian, even though it's ten times more expensive and there's so little of it.' Ruefully he advances the teacup against the paper Mongolia, while the vodka bottle retreats. 'We hate the Chinese, but we have to do business with them. They're everywhere. In the end I fear they'll take us over.' His voice drops to an involuntary whisper. 'It's said that they are even herding our flocks.'

By now the teacup has edged forward under his hands, and I hear the paper crumpling beneath.

As we drive south from Batshireet, the steppelands surge to the horizon in waves of grass and stone, and a few kites speckle the sky. Here and there a herd of cattle moves, or a *ger* lifts a white dome above the grasses. Somewhere here, in 1206, a great conclave of the Mongol peoples, the *khural*, united by the warring genius of Genghis Khan, proclaimed him their supreme leader. We approach the site over a mass of whitened rocks, and come to a hexagonal corral enclosing a heap of grey stones, and a platform festooned with votive scarves. The notice that identifies this as the place of that momentous congress has gone; but people have left offerings of sweets, lamps and crushed tea, and now a cyclist appears out of the emptiness, rides three times round the mound, tosses on a pebble and disappears into the blue.

The veneration of Genghis Khan, with other signs of Mongolian nationalism, was smothered in Soviet times, and with independence a great craving has arisen for any vestige of him in the landscape. A swathe of dedicatory pillars and *ovoo*s has appeared, and a monstrous steel statue, the largest equestrian figure in the world, shatters the landscape east of Ulaanbaatar. But almost every location is spurious or ill-grounded. The site of the first *khural* is unknown, and rival sites for Genghis's birth and burial abound. In the village of Binder, whose web of stockades and harlequin rooftops echo those of Batshireet, a competing *khural* venue has been set up by an ex-premier (he was born in Binder, that's why, says Batmonkh): an unsightly pillar inset with portraits of the khan, where little piles of devotees' money lie undisturbed.

At evening we come to where the steppeland darkens into a wooded valley. A precipitous hillside, crowded with boulders and larches, breaks open at its summit into blades of orange rock. They bulge from the undergrowth, and litter the skyline like broken teeth. At the hill's foot runs a long drystone wall whose uncut stones leave no clue to the era of its building. In this bare land, where scarcely a solid structure exists, its rampart leaves a baffling question mark. On either side it travels up the hill slope to the skyline, running for two miles in ruined bursts. It is as if a whole battlemented city had once covered this hill, then returned, weather-worn, to earth and rock.

In 2002 this enigmatic place, locally named the Almsgiver's Wall, became the site of a passionately driven archaeological search. It was financed through a Chicago commodities broker named Maury Kravitz, whose obsession persuaded him that here lay the tomb of Genghis Khan, heaped with the treasure of his conquests. The excavations went forward in a gale of optimism. Batmonkh, who worked here as a youth, still remembered their pace and intensity. A detritus of smooth, post-glacial rocks covers the hill with the illusion of human activity. More than forty supposed graves were identified. A corpse in lamellar armour was labelled a Mongol warrior, and returned to the grave without DNA testing. Ironically it was the publicity surrounding the project that led to its downfall. Genghis Khan, by now, was all but a national god, and the prospect of his grave being desecrated – above all, by a foreigner – brought mounting official outrage. The search was forcibly closed down.

Yet we enter the breached wall with a tinge of expectation. Its outer course is canted back to rest on grass-sown rubble, and often sinks wholesale under the earth. Batmonkh climbs high up to where he thinks he remembers graves. I go lower, wading through faded flowers and blown thistles, to rock formations that lose their man-made shape as I approach them. These outcrops are said to be infested by vipers, but I see only marmots running to invisible burrows, and a vulture cruising overhead. I rest in a stone-rimmed hollow that I had thought might be a grave, and hear the drowsing of grasshoppers. Nothing here bears any likeness to the imperial burial place that emerges from the confusion of written history: a plateau on a mountainside, perhaps, where Genghis's sepulchre was returned to secrecy by horses driven over its earth until nothing could be seen. At this Almsgiver's Wall the few artefacts that came to light – broken ceramics, some charcoal fragments – yielded a different story. The archaeologists remained obdurate, and longed to return; but the great enclosure, it seems, had nothing to do with Genghis Khan at all. It was a necropolis of the once-formidable Khitans, whose centuries-long rule of northern China and Mongolia, as the Liao dynasty, came to an end almost forty years before the Mongol emperor was born.

The nearest source for Genghis Khan's life, *The Secret History of the Mongols*, says nothing of his grave. Its omission from this extraordinary document suggests a prohibition against disclosing it; but it is *The Secret History* that fills the Onon valley with Genghis's youth and early conflicts. The anonymous epic, written in a lost Mongolian original a few years after Genghis's death, was discovered in the nineteenth century on the shelves of a Peking library. The work is redolent of oral tradition, where history merges with legend, and vivid detail with archaic epithet. It was written, it seems, as an instructive history for the Mongol royal family, and follows their great progenitor's ascent from youthful fears and crimes – he murdered his own half-brother – to the fulfilment of his divine calling from the Eternal Sky. A complex character – both politic and visionary – emerges alongside the tempest of shocking cruelty familiar to the West. It was on the Onon's banks that the Mongols at last united under him, and it was in its valleys, in collective hunting and early battles, that the way was paved for an empire founded on horseback. *The Secret History* relegates the two decades of his later campaigns to a few cursory sentences, but by his death in 1227 his empire stretched from the Pacific to the Caspian Sea, and his descendants extended it to form the largest contiguous empire ever known, conquering China in the east and harassing Vienna to the west. By 1290 the whole breadth of Asia was bruised into one vast confederacy whose Pax Mongolica endured for another century, while commerce flourished and an exhausted peace reigned. A virgin with a dish of gold, it was said, could walk unmolested from China to Turkey.

Perhaps Genghis Khan, leaving no material trace on the Onon watershed, permeates it the more powerfully in imagination. This evening, when we regain it, the river seems no longer an incident in the landscape, but its surging heart. It is stronger now, fed by mountain tributaries, and deeper. Its surface glimmers in steely troughs and ridges that reach its banks gently, while eating them away. Yet it is still small – a moving sliver in the darkness – and no theory quite dispels the wonder that it engendered this cataclysmic transformation of Asia, and that today's Mongolia, with a population of barely three million, once poured out such a flood of concentrated power.

The Russian frontier runs barely fifty miles away, but at Genghis's death it lay more than three thousand miles to the west in a mosaic of refractory princedoms that constituted early Russia. Between 1237 and 1239 the north-west Mongol power, the Golden Horde, overswept this vulnerable region, crushing Kiev, the most powerful and refined of its states, and settled to impose fearsome levies on the surviving Slavic peoples. For over two centuries Russia's subjugation under the Mongols drastically realigned it, impairing its future convergence with western Europe. The so-called 'Tartar yoke', some historians suggest, gave birth to Russia's stoic fatalism, freezing it in serfdom and autocracy. Thus, by an outrageous sleight of mind, Ivan the Terrible, Stalin and Putin become the offspring of Genghis Khan, and the country's perennial split between Western civilization and an 'Asiatic' destiny originated in the moonlit river beneath us.

Next morning, no cloud disturbs the sky. To our south, across a watery horizon, we see cranes flying. It is impossible to tell to which species they belong – the stately white-naped or the silvery demoiselle – and their sad voices are almost inaudibly far away; but we glimpse the strong trajectory of their flight – their extended necks and tattered wing-tips – as they make for the Himalayas and beyond for India. Their beauty and their dancing, even their rumoured monogamy, clothed them in myth all over Asia – the Chinese imagined they carried the dead to immortality – and I watch them vanish with obscure regret, as if they will never return.

Tochtor spies a quartet of swans floating on the prairie. They have alighted on the seasonal marsh, and are swimming among its waterlogged grasses. Beyond them, on a slight rise, three deer-stones appear. Such monoliths are scattered over the whole steppeland. Whether they were sites of ceremony or burial is unsure, but they seem to be the figures of standing men, and are carved with flying deer, whose significance remains unknown. The ones we find are so worn that only ghostly incisions remain. Two of them are taller than I am, and stand in solid granite: the figures of warriors three thousand years old, perhaps, still bolt upright on the empty plain.

An hour later we reach a place where the ground falls away and a scarp of granite bursts from its grassland cover. Perhaps the water that sometimes trickles among its rocks invited the settlement of Mesolithic hunters, who left their trace some 15,000 years ago. The flakes from their stone workings are still scattered downhill. Months ago, I had seen photographs of a rock face here, covered in petroglyphs of ibex with elegantly backswept horns, stocky horses like the wild Mongol breed, a wonderfully antlered reindeer and a pair of prowling big cats (I thought). In this constellation of minutely carved beasts stood a man with bow and arrows, and a swastika, a benign symbol in ancient Eurasia, was engraved above.

I scramble over the rocks with Batmonkh in the hope of finding these, but the rock walls show blank and the clefts between them bare. Batmonkh is as baffled as I am. He aches to fill in the gaps of his Soviet-style schooling. We sit in the grass and wonder if some trick of slanted sunlight will bring the stone to life. At my feet a giant boulder is covered with symbols that I cannot read. They are incised deep and rough in the stone, dappled with grey lichen. Here, for all I know, are some of the twenty inscriptions said to survive at this site, from Tibetan, Persian, Old Turkic and Mongolian to the script of the Liao dynasty's ancestors. But I see only a jungle of densely clustered signs – tribal seals, perhaps – like a lost alphabet. Batmonkh thinks he recognizes images resembling the brands on nomad horses, and I imagine I detect, choked under the lichen, my White Horse's scar: a bisected circle.

We return to our UAZ with a rankling unease. Tochtor is asleep in the driver's seat, his belly ballooning comfortably between his shirt and trousers. He enjoys these journeys for their open air beyond the city, but sees no point in old stones. Nor, for a moment, do I. Almost three hundred carvings were identified on these scarps by Mongolian archaeologists as long as sixty years ago. Among the petroglyphs typical of the second millennium Bronze Age, I had imagined finding animals from a changed terrain (for this outcrop once lay above a lake) and I would make out the profile of a moose, maybe, whose voracious appetite for foliage would betray forest vegetation long ago. Perhaps I would even glimpse an outlying mammoth (they survived in the Altai to our west as recently as 1000 BC) or a leftover rhinoceros. Instead, as the great rock sinks from sight, I settle grumpily in the back of the jeep, knowing that a whole cavalcade of animals somewhere inhabits the stone, and that my eyes have lacked the acuity to resurrect them.

Forty miles beyond this solitary crag the ground rises and shadows into an outcrop of pine trees. You might wander its sandy soil and wonder only why the earth seems so ruffled and worn, like the site of a vanished village, or why some rocks have been curiously aligned. We climb low hillocks where the trees took hold long ago, and once I discern the outline of a buried entrance shaft in the powdery earth. For here, at Duurilag Nars, is the royal necropolis of an elusive nomad people, the Xiongnu, whose empire two thousand years ago had spread deep into Siberia, and beaten against the Great Wall of China. They left no written record of themselves, and are refracted into history only through the lens of the horrified Chinese, who recorded them a plague of faceless barbarians. Ten years ago, when archaeologists probed the ground where we walk, the bodies that lay strewn and decapitated in their looted chambers were imagined a mixed Caucasian and east Asian race. Many scholars have thought them the ancestors of the Huns, who invaded Europe around the time that the Xiongnu themselves fade from history.

In this cemetery of two hundred graves, only five have been excavated. Somewhere beneath our feet a large stone slab had opened into three tiers of wood-lined chambers tilting and half caved in after the intrusion of robbers. In its lowest chamber the red-laquered coffin had disintegrated, but the tracery of its gold-foil lining still patterned the earth, with studs of golden flowers. Fragments from the finery that once adorned the corpse's chest shone among the debris: bird-shaped ornaments in lapis lazuli, gold and amber beads, drops of tear-shaped turquoise and little horses of gilded bronze.

Horses haunt these graves. Close above the tomb chamber had lain a tangle of harness – snaffle bits and cheekpieces – and the skeletons of twelve sacrificed horses, their legs bent as if walking, ready to escort the spirit into the steppeland beyond death. In other graves stood jars filled with horse bones. For this was an empire of the horse. The Chinese recorded with astonishment how small Xiongnu children, before they could mount a pony, would ride on sheep and shoot at birds and field mice. In their endless wars the Xiongnu – a loose confederacy – could send several hundred thousand mounted warriors against the great Han dynasty, whose infantry sometimes campaigned on horseback in order to keep pace with them, before dismounting to fight, never feeling their equal as cavalry.

In times of uneasy peace the two empires gave or received tribute according to which was ascendant. The Xiongnu would send their princes as hostages. The Chinese submitted their princesses in marriage – contemporary poetry is filled with their sorrow – along with envoys whose submission was tattooed on their faces. Among the funerary gifts in the richest grave – ceramic bowls, silks, bronze cauldrons and kettles – a black-laquered chariot, imported complete from China, had left behind an axle from its high wheels, with the panels of its carriage-box and the fitting for a parasol above. Perhaps fear of the tomb's darkness lingered in the gift of a triple lamp, and of a Chinese mirror believed to emit light and deflect demons.

In the quiet dusk our footfalls crackle like gunshot over fallen pine cones, and tiny bats come darting from the trees. We wonder if any grave among these hundreds has escaped defilement, and what may remain under our feet. Often it is hard to tell if the smashing of funerary artefacts was the work of robbers or of mourners, for even now the custom of breaking such offerings endures among remote Siberian peoples. The afterlife, they conceive, is the reverse of this one, so that what is broken here is intact over there, and the wreckage attending the dead is waiting, as they are, to be whole again.

As it winds through the soft earth, the Onon brims with flood-water. It is a hundred yards across now and flows fast, without glitter. When I clamber down to drink from it, the banks crumble away. Its current comes cold to my fingers.

An old man calls the river 'Onon Queen Mother', as the Buryats do, who conceive it as a woman. You must not pluck the shrubs or trees along the Onon's banks, he says, let alone relieve yourself there. The river has already been polluted by gold-mining near Batshireet, and the waters sullied. Pull a taimen salmon from her depths – as local people are learning to do – and the Onon will grow angry and burst her banks. He does not know that far downriver she becomes the great Amur, dividing Russia from China, or quite where she ends. For him, after the Onon crosses the border into Siberia, she departs into a mist of unmeaning.

East of Binder, where the little Hurhin tributary joins her, some have imagined the birthplace of Genghis Khan. The Onon rustles faintly as the rivers meet. The current splits around waterlogged islands plumed with willows, and carves out banks of pebbles and fallen birch trees. According to *The Secret History*, Genghis Khan was born on the Onon near an enigmatic 'Spleen Hillock', and the surrounding grasslands here, suited to a nomad camp, with the rise of a nearby hill, have fed the national craving for a site of worship, scattering the slope with *ovoos*.

Still greater controversy attends the conqueror's grave. He died in 1227 while on campaign a thousand miles from the Mongol heartland, and his cortège, it seems, returned him to the Khenti mountains. Almost at once wild rumours spread of his tomb's whereabouts. The returning cortège became a secret and terrifying cavalcade. Every living creature that witnessed it was slaughtered. Forty young women were incarcerated in the khan's sepulchre, and the slaves and soldiers who built or guarded it were executed, until nobody was left who knew its location.

The closer the record to Genghis's date of death, the vaguer it becomes. Within nine years two Chinese ambassadors, eager to visit the place, were led to the guarded border of the Great Forbidden Precinct in the Khenti mountains, and saw no sign of it.

Ever since the 1870s many hopeless expeditions have set out to discover it. Most scholars imagine the grave to lie on the southern slope of Mount Khenti, believed to be Burkhan Khaldun, but this is uncertain. The mountain spreads for some four hundred square miles of hard terrain, where glaciated rocks give an illusion of human artifice, and no grave has been found. Many Mongolians prefer that it remain so.

The mystique of his unknown tomb may enhance the illusion that Genghis Khan is still alive, and now, after a seventy-year Soviet embargo, the emperor has re-emerged to overawe his people. With the dawn of independence in 1990, the floodgates opened. Soviet names changed overnight. Genghis Khan airport appeared, Genghis Khan University, a Genghis Khan luxury hotel, an institute for Genghis Khan studies. Every other newborn boy was named Genghis or Temujin (the khan's birth name). Even in the provinces people were drinking Genghis Khan beer, listening to the Genghis Khan pop group and downing shots of Genghis vodka. In the capital's main square a Moscow-inspired mausoleum holding the embalmed bodies of Sükhbaatar and Choibalsan, the nation's revolutionary heroes, was demolished to make way for the giant Genghis Khan memorial, and a revived shamanism claimed access to his spirit.

Meanwhile, over the border in China's Inner Mongolia, at an alternative site for Genghis's burial, his worship has flowered into a quasi-religion of universal peace, bringing with it a dark irony. Since Genghis's conquering grandson Kublai Khan founded the Chinese Yuan dynasty, Mongolia could lay claim to China itself; on the other, grimmer hand, China, citing the same united empire, may contemplate a historic claim to Mongolia.

*

The way to Dadal, the Buryats' little capital, follows a tangle of bone-jarring tracks, where we steer by compass point. Here and there a solitary *ger* leaves a grey dome under the hills. We cross the Onon with our jeep on a pontoon raft, hauled by a fixed cable and a silent boatman. The water under us seethes with troughs and eddies, as if from some hidden disturbance. Copper-skinned children are laughing in its shallows. The moment we regain our track the river drops from sight, the steppe returns to its naked calm, and we are alone again.

After an hour a line of telegraph poles crosses the skyline, then Dadal appears. It is a sprawled village of stockaded cottages, some dressed up with dormer windows and filigreed eaves. Motor scooters have displaced its horses, and satellite dishes hang from the walls. But the few people about look uniformly poor. Some stout, cheery women with the flushed cheeks of Tibetans are consulting a mobile phone, and rugged men in *deel*s and heavy boots sit in the cold sunlight. The mud streets seem to lead nowhere. The fences that trim them are breached or sagging, and old Korean trucks stand in the puddles.

Dadal is another, groundless site for the birthplace of Genghis Khan, and a jagged slab of memorial stone, carved in gold with his angry image, has survived since 1962, when it was raised against a rival claim in China. It stands now in a near-devastated trekkers' camp. Above, on a steep hill, which I climb with aching ribs, a celebratory *ovoo* flutters with multicoloured scarves – red for fire (says Batmonkh), yellow for the sun, green for earth, white for purity, blue for the Eternal Sky – with rotted prayer flags hung up by monks, and some votive vodka bottles.

These politically inspired landmarks merge with the timeless animism all about them, beliefs so diffuse and ingrained that even the mass deracination suffered in the early twentieth century could not erase them. Rather it was the ensuing assault on Buryats in the 1930s that severed whole communities, and left some people with no compass to their past.

In a quiet Dadal street of prettier dwellings than most, an old man is defying Time. Chiment lives with his wife a foot or two above the ground, in a log cottage moored on wooden blocks against the permafrost. At eighty-five he emanates an odd, hardy sweetness. He is still sturdy and smooth-skinned.

'I think I am the third oldest person in Dadal. There are three of us left, very old.' He smiles faintly: 'I am the youngest.' We sit side by side in his kitchen, while Batmonkh interprets out of the deep, hard Buryat accent. 'We call ourselves the "direct memory people" because we experienced what the others only heard of. We are the last.' He wants to talk to me, I realize, because he feels his past sliding away, like a language that soon nobody will speak. A little didactic, he pauses for long seconds between speech, as if recovering images before they go missing.

'I don't know where my people came from, but from somewhere in Russia during the Civil War. We Buryats fought alongside the White Russians against the Reds, and after they lost my family fled into Mongolia. They thought it was empty.'

More than 40,000 Buryats flooded south at the time, but the easy drift of pastoral nomads between Siberia and Mongolia was soon only a memory, and by the time of Chiment's birth the frontier was sealed. Fugitives then looked back at their homeland with the dread of dying in exile, and sometimes with the bitter wonder of knowing that their relatives were only a few miles away inside Russia – within range of a dog's bark, they would say. Unwilling to leave their bodies in foreign soil, some refugees chose to be cremated rather than buried, so that the wind might carry back their soul. At lunar New Year especially, they ached to return to their families, and are even said to have crossed the snowfields of the frontier wearing their shoes reversed or fitted with deer hooves to outwit border patrols.

But to Chiment, whose ancestry was severed, even this was useless. 'My father and mother were executed in the 1930s, I do not remember them. Then I was adopted. That's what happened in those days. Adoption was a way of protecting people, children. Everywhere families were splitting up and people divorcing. I remember liking my adoptive parents, but that is all. The father was captured and executed too. Thousands of us were. And our herds were taken away. They say my own father once had fifty or sixty horses, which were our life.'

He turns a gaze of mild appraisal on me – anxious that I am listening – and it is easy to imagine suffering in his sloping eyes and thin-set mouth. But I sense instead a hard-won tranquillity. 'After that,' he says, 'I was sent to a little settlement in the north, to be looked after by an old couple. There were eighteen families of us, all orphaned or separated. Then the war came and the propaganda to send our goods north to Russia, although I don't know what we could do for Russia, small as we were. And I was just a boy. But it was here that I found my wife.'

She is sitting by the stove, swatting at flies with a plastic swatter: a tiny, simian woman in a billowing skirt, who seems not to hear us. She looks a generation older than him. Chiment says: 'We were married very young. We were both eighteen. Her father had been executed too.'

She turns her elfin face to us from the stove, but her eyes are shut. She and Chiment had emerged from the terrible years of Choibalsan together, only to suffer the bewilderment of forced collectivization. Yet she had borne him ten children, and only one of them died. They could not afford despair. After the death of Stalin they had openly protested against a ruthless interrogator named Danzan when he returned to Dadal from Ulaanbaatar. Quickly the protests spread, as if a great darkness was lifting. Danzan took poison.

'Even in Dadal', Chiment says, 'everything changed. We had a corrupt Party committee here, prosecuting whoever they wanted. On the death of Stalin one of its members went mad, I think. Or perhaps he was drunk. During the national mourning he ran wild about the village crying, "Arrest me! I'm happy! Happy Stalin's gone! Why isn't anyone arresting me?"' He winced at the memory. 'But nobody did.'

My eyes wander round his home. His kitchen is open on a big, carpeted sitting room, with a cabinet of china. He has a television, a new fridge. I see no prayer wheel or incense burner. Did Buddhism ever help, I ask, or shamanism? His expression does not change. 'No. Nothing helped. All those things were cleaned out of us. Our minds were emptied.'

In the end he had made a living by cattle farming, he says, and in local administration after times improved. The wall behind me is covered with old calendars and a constellation of photographs – children, grandchildren, great-grandchildren – a whole warm and complicated family, fathered by the orphan who was born into none. I wonder if he ever imagined his home in infancy, a pasture of lost horses. But he only says: 'I am just here.'

Whatever he has achieved he has done by native acuity: the Buryat intelligence that is still resented by the country's dominant Khalkha Mongolians, together with the Buryats' perceived collusion with Russia in the 1920s. Chiment is too wary or courteous to complain of this prejudice in front of

Batmonkh, but he says before we leave: 'You can read in histories about what happened here, but often they are wrong. I tell you this: it is people, not regimes or doctrines, that do these things. Half of all that happened was not political at all. It was about personal feelings: jealousies and anger, old feuds . . .'

I ask: 'Do many remember this?'

'There are too few who share my past. Young people cannot understand it at all. They live in a different world. They even admire Choibalsan. They say he was a great strategist and statesman. I say he was a monster. I experienced him. They didn't.'

Perhaps it was true that the psychic wounds of the old diaspora were fading. The younger generations that could not understand Chiment were finding their identity not in the Russified lands of their origin, but here in the Mongolian homeland and their native tongue.

When Batmonkh and I find a ramshackle restaurant for lunch, an old black-and-white propaganda film is playing on the television above us. Three listless young men and a little girl are gazing up at a magisterial Stalin conferring with an obsequious Choibalsan, whose chest is smeared with medals. The film endows both tyrants with sombre gravitas, as they move and orate not in the human world of Chiment but in the rival land of manipulated history. The bored men get up and leave, while the small girl's eyes swivel shyly between the television and the outlandish foreigner.

Batmonkh has ignored the screen while eating his noodles. But now he says: 'I think 15 per cent of our people were killed at that time. The family histories of almost everyone I meet turn blurry in the 1930s. Nobody knows anything any more . . .'

I ask: 'Your mother's too?'

'She was raised in another family. Her real grandfather disappeared, killed, I suppose. He'd become a monk, and he was betrayed.'

'Who betrayed him?'

'His younger brother. He denounced and arrested him himself.'

I had seen no signs of Buddhism since leaving Ulaanbaatar. Everywhere we went I was on the lookout for monasteries, but in these remote regions hardly one remained. The faith, it seemed, had never recovered from its ferocious repression in the 1930s. In Binder the solitary lama was ill; in Batshireet the monastery stood in ruins; and in Bayan-Uul, the last settlement before the Onon entered Russia, the lama had left to preside at a funeral.

The Tibetan Buddhism that spread through the country in the seventeenth century did its own share of persecuting. Sometimes it took over shamanic rites and spirits under other names, even the worship of Genghis Khan, and lamas officiated with local chiefs in grand *ovoo* ceremonies; at other times the shamans were arraigned and executed. By 1920, on the brink of disaster, the hegemony of the Buddhist church enveloped the whole land in a suffocating shroud. One third of the populace were monks or monastic dependants, and travellers wrote with repugnance of their indolence and debauchery. It took the Soviet-backed republic almost twenty years to undo this becalmed theocracy, levelling most of its three thousand monasteries and temples, and secularizing or slaughtering their monks.

One last time we travel over a near-trackless steppeland towards a monastery that Batmonkh hopes may still exist. When we cross the Onon again, its waters are slicing steep banks through the yielding earth. We find a dosshouse where we sleep fitfully in a narrow room with one light bulb and no water. Next morning we wind across grasslands into a hidden valley and an empty campsite. A little bridge and a path of sunken stones lead into the monastery courtyard. It has been overgrown for eighty years, and the temple mouldering into ruin. Some 120 monks had once lived here, the camp caretaker says, but they were massacred in the 1930s. Recently someone had brought in a shaman to invest the place with a benign spirit. The shaman said he could feel blood and violence here, beyond his power to exorcize. Now, when I peer through the clouded windows, I glimpse only a disintegrating prayer hall, and the advance of swarming fungus.

We make for the Russian frontier through thickets of pine and silver birch, until the land opens and mountains rear up, stark beyond the steppeland. At the makeshift border post a portly commander takes us to where the river passes out of his country and into Siberia. But we cannot cross the frontier here. The nearest border post for foreigners is over a hundred miles to the east, at Ereentsav. But he drives us down an overgrown track to a broken iron gate signed 'Russian border 200 metres'. Then he leads us round it on foot to the bank of the Onon, running steely and fast towards the north and the faded mountains.

'That's Russia,' he says. 'People have drowned trying to cross the Onon here.' But he does not say which way, or why.

Batmonkh asks: 'May we take a photo?'

The commander laughs. 'You may. But don't put it on the internet.'

It is another two days before we reach Ereentsav across an empty land. Batmonkh and Tochtor are quietly worried at my leaving them. Where will I stay? How will I go? I don't know, of course. The solicitude in Batmonkh's face gives me a pang of apprehension. Perhaps I have come to rely on his resourcefulness too much, and on a kind of reticent concern. Now he asks me to write to him, and perhaps send him something to read. I will, of course, with the story of our journey, if it sees the light. We embrace in a clumsy bear hug. Then I am walking to the Russian frontier with new excitement and a tinge of fear.

3

The Treaty

Through a deserted country, fringed by new mountains, only the Onon makes a glitter of movement. Its current gives an illusion of purpose, and in the way of great rivers its source, for local people, can exert a near-mystic allure, as if it held the secret of generation, while its oceanic end evokes death. To most Buryats who occupy the Onon north into Siberia, it is enough that the river emerges from the sacred Khenti mountains and departs into who knows where. Strange to European eyes, its shores are empty of human life; the cattle breeders' preference for meat over fish has intensified its solitude. Its banks seem bare not from neglect but from native reverence. You may not clean yourself in its waters, but if you scoop them out for washing, the river itself remains inviolate. Its magic lies in its elemental flow.

Its future catches the heart. Ahead of me, for over 300 miles its northward course meanders and delays through remote valleys until it meets the Trans-Siberian Railway and veers east under the Russian name of Shilka. For another 350 miles it plunges through wild mountains towards China. It is then only 1,000 feet above sea level, but still far from any sea, and Siberia's boreal taiga, the largest forest region on earth, comes crowding to its banks. For over 1,000 more miles, now renamed, the huge flood of the Amur defines the border between the imperia of China and Russia, whose mutual suspicion has aborted any breakwater or almost any bridge between them. At last beside Khabarovsk, its largest city, the Amur turns north and dilates into a labyrinth of shifting channels and islands, a navigator's nightmare, as it makes for the lonely Okhotsk Sea and the Pacific.

I stand beside the Onon now with my back to the high watchtower of the Russian frontier. For five days I have circled round from Ereentsav to return here, hitchhiking a lift from a Mongolian family, and then by a Russian bus north-west. One fading afternoon I had seen a column of trailer-borne tanks moving the other way, with army lorries full of lethargic soldiers, and counted fifteen armoured cars lined up in a field. I didn't think much about this. I imagined only that some border battalions were relocating. I had found a small hotel in the regional capital of Aginskoye, and slept in the sudden luxury of an en-suite bedroom.

Now I sense the watchtower sentry's binoculars raking my back. I have reached here in an aged car with travellers met by chance. In the Buddhist monastery at Aginskoye a gentle monk – not Buryat, but Russian – had been departing with an old friend down the desolate road back to the border. Dimitri and Slava had no interest in crossing to Mongolia, but planned to hike around a mountain nearby. Then they became intrigued by my journey along a river they barely knew. So we find ourselves gazing northward together into Siberia: the Buddhist monk Dimitri, small and cowled against the wind, and his big, hirsute friend Slava, who says only: 'Let's see how far our petrol takes us . . .'

The country before us sprawls north and east in miles of tall grassland. This is the Daurian depression whose earlier inhabitants migrated to Inner Mongolia, where their descendants remain. The mountains gather on each side as we go, starker than those to the south. To our west the Yablonovy massif leaves a long profile across a greying sky, while milder ranges move obliquely east towards China. The Onon draws a line of woodland at the mountains' feet, and ashen regiments of dead birch trees descend above its banks. This whole region exudes something lost and eerie. The few villages look half-inhabited, their fences falling, their roofs breached. The gaily coloured housetops of Mongolia have gone, and these ones are tiled in fibre cement and shelter homes of old fragility. Here and there a broken-down tractor rusts in an overgrown field. We glimpse a few villagers: Buryat and Russian intermingled. They look slow and depleted.

Slava and Dimitri sit in the back of the car and never stop talking, while the driver, Dorje, a teacher of Buddhist physics in Dimitri's monastery, keeps an old and peaceful silence, gazing through his splintered windscreen as he meanders the potholed road. His second-hand Toyota has its steering wheel on the wrong side for Russia – it has spent five years in Japan, twenty with Dorje – but even old Japanese cars, Slava says, are more reliable than new Russian ones, and this one will never be sold. A miniature Buddhist prayer wheel turns on its dashboard but Dorje, as we crest every rise, raises his hand in greeting to the pagan land spirits.

Near the village of Narasun a light rain is falling. Sometimes the Onon winds among marshy inlets choked with willow, at others it thrusts a path through naked hills. Ahead of us, from end to end, the underbelly of the sky has turned to thunder, with massed banks of cumulus billowing up from the horizon, as if from volcanoes.

In a sleepy village a dapper but drunk Buryat hotelier assigns us two rooms whose outdoor lavatory stands in a thicket of snarling dogs. The sky is pouring. We settle to carve up the Uzbek melon which Slava brought from Moscow two days before, but his salted fish is a month beyond its sell-by date, and it stinks. We laugh together, and he and Dimitri bandy jokes which my Russian is too poor to understand.

Theirs is a friendship of seeming opposites. Slava owns his own trading company, centred in Moscow, and he had once employed Dimitri as his agent in China, extracting silicon. They worked for years together. But Dimitri lost interest in silicon. He learnt Chinese, then Tibetan, then started to study Sanskrit and to travel among monasteries. So he left commerce and became a monk. But every year Slava travels from Moscow to see him – Dimitri is his only friend, he says – and pulls him from his studies to go trekking. Dimitri, who is slight and quiet, complains of being too old for this, although like Slava he is only forty-five. While Slava shoulders a mountainous backpack, Dimitri carries a little satchel. Slava has a second wife and teenage son back in Moscow. Dimitri, of course, is celibate.

But Slava hates Moscow. He craves quietude, as Dimitri does, and needs to walk in wilderness. His wife, he says, is addicted to the capital, but he rarely visits her. Instead he travels and works compulsively from his computer. His computer makes him free. Yet he admires and even envies Dimitri, who has entered a different freedom. He cannot follow Dimitri through the maze of Buddhist teachings, but he too is retreating from urban life. He tells me quietly: 'Dimitri could have made a fortune in business, or he might have lived well just by translating Chinese. But he didn't want it. He wanted to live simply. He earns the equivalent of thirty dollars a month, plus his meals from the monastery kitchen.'

'Did he never want family?'

'There was some sadness with a Chinese woman,' Slava says. 'I cannot ask him. Something went wrong, and he decided that family life was not for him.'

So Dimitri had built a two-room home within the walls of the remote monastery where I met him, and was teaching the Tibetan canon. Among the Buryat monks his pale Slavic face, fringed by a dust of ginger beard, might have carried a shock of strangeness, but he was long known here. Every day a lonely passion took him to the library, a dark chamber banked floor to ceiling with boxes – crimson, scarlet, blue and green – where the precious Tibetan texts lay, printed by woodblock on separate strips of paper. Once the printing press of this Aginskoye monastery had turned out the sacred Kangyur and Tengyur scriptures in painstaking and beautiful versions – Tibetan and Mongolian – but during the Stalinist persecution they had been seized or destroyed, along with the monks. The Russian ethnographer Nikolai Poppe, who later fled to the United States, recorded how he pleaded in vain for just one monastery to be saved, and how during the filming of Vsevolod Pudovkin's *The Heir of Genghis Khan* in 1928, the monks circled their monastery for the camera with the sacred texts held above them, and were then forced to throw them all into a ditch.

Dimitri says: 'Many books were taken off to St Petersburg – three train-wagon loads of them from this district alone – and others were hidden or scattered.' His mission now was to reassemble all the surviving treatises that his monastery had printed. 'Lamas still give us those their families hid. Often they cannot understand the Tibetan words, but they know how to chant them. They give them to us before they die.' So he sat day after day at a low table, with his back to the window, planning and cataloguing. It would be another five years, he thought, before he was finished. Bare light bulbs hung unlit from the ceiling, and his eyes ached. Ever since fire from a short circuit had destroyed the main temple four years ago, all electricity had been cut off. But Dimitri did not mind.

He'd had a nightmare in which his reassembled library went up in flames.

Overnight the storm has swept the sky clean, and we turn from the hamlet of Aksha down a wide track where the forest no longer belongs to the coniferous darkness of Mongolia. Sometimes, beyond the river, distant village roofs give an illusion of pastoral peace, and a lightness of birch and oak is seeping into the woods. The settlements we pass are all tiny and sprawling. Buryats and Russians intermingle. Their mud streets keep old Soviet names – Karl Marx, Komsomol – and there is a hamlet called Bolshevik. But the villages veer between recovery and decay, as if they had either outlasted or surrendered to some old misfortune. Some look brightly enduring, their cottages daubed turquoise or magenta, and their gardens thronged with sunflowers and chrysanthemums. Mongol women and young Slavic mothers, their abundant hair tied back, converse together on the streets, and their schools and culture palaces stand intact. In other settlements the only colours flare from synthetic flowers in the Orthodox graveyards, and the houses are in ruins. Yet street lamps stretch clean through them, stopping only at the last, straggling cottage, and larch-wood telegraph poles connect them in wobbling lines, raised on concrete stilts against the rot of the moist earth.

But even in decay the wooden houses look hardier than the collective farms, whose ranges of plastered brick gape with shattered doors and windows, and roofs crashed in. They have been abandoned for years, and their fields parcelled out. In his home village, Dorje says, he had been allocated eight hectares of barren fields, and no water. He says he has left them fallow.

Ahead of us now, through mild hills, the Onon holds a greenish darkness. The woods break apart around its valleys and skirt slopes still starred with the violet asters of the Mongolian steppe. From my large-scale map, where villages are dotted along the river, I had imagined finding fishing communities. But instead their inhabitants survive on subsistence farming and illicit hunting. In every settlement a tattered notice is scrawled with a telephone number and a demand for deer antlers. So the river winds solitary and untouched. The unkempt pastures and potato fields peter out two hundred yards short of it, and a disused track – perhaps from the time of state farming – straggles alongside. We stop and walk a while where the current divides among islands, its banks crumbling when I descend them, and we hear the cries of quarrelling ducks downriver, and we are wandering quite alone.

Towards evening, as we near a main road, an unfinished hotel appears high above the river, and beside it a modern shrine to 'Holy Mother Onon'. This coupling must be the enterprise of some local entrepreneur: an aborted union of commerce and folk belief. Inside her temple the incarnate Onon sits crudely painted in full Mongol rig, with a high, cylindrical headdress and earrings dripping to her waist, presiding over waters where a giant fish gasps. But outside, far below her tacky shrine, the Onon itself forks and reunites in a cascade of molten silver, and a boulder shimmers with the azure scarves of pagan pilgrims.

We are nearing the limits of the Mongol world. Nothing in the pasturelands reflects this: no geographical feature to break the distances that drew the Cossacks east and south three centuries ago into the fragmented lands of Buryat herdsmen. But as we move along the Onon at dusk through the village of Tsugol, a huge monastery emerges from the unlit streets. This, perhaps, is the last vestige of Buddhism along the river. Behind its walls a temple looms over a scatter of shacks and lesser shrines. A century ago, says Dimitri, this monastery of Dashi Choypelling, the Country of Happy Teachings, founded in 1801, was a powerhouse of Buddhist dialectic and linguistics. Its printing press rivalled that of Aginskoye, its library stacked with illuminated scrolls, and it ran a famous medical school.

Dimitri knows its solitary ordained monk, who opens its creaking doors and ushers us to his refectory table. It is spread with stale biscuits, jellied sweets and slivers of discoloured meat. The monk picks at them unspeaking. His eyes flicker over me. They are faintly unnerving. His face is that of an immense and enigmatic child: a perfect oval. From time to time he emits a high-pitched titter about something privately funny. Perhaps it is me. I think it is this giggle that makes me mistake him for stupid.

I want to ask him questions about his calling, but his replies are all bland, evasive, as if enquiry were irrelevant. Dimitri sits quiet, and eats nothing. Slava is reading on his computer. I am wondering at the monk's solitude. Apart from five part-time lamas, who return to their families at night, he is alone.

A century ago the Buryat lands of the young Soviet Union held 47 monasteries with 15,000 lamas. But as in Mongolia, Stalin's Terror saw the monks sent to death or the Gulag, and their monasteries levelled.

I ask tentatively: 'What happened here?'

The monk spears a scrap of meat, breaks his silence. 'The young ones escaped. Those able to work were sent to the camps. The old were taken out and shot. Down there, by the river.' He waves an arm to the east. 'This monastery was turned into an arsenal and stables. That's how it survived.'

'And the ordinary people, those who had believed . . . ?'

'They kept secret images and remembered prayers. But when freedom came they found their children couldn't

54

understand their funny chanting and weird prostrations.' He gives his shrill titter.

There was much else to alienate them, I thought. By the time the Soviet Union disintegrated, the rural fabric of the country had transformed: collectivization restructured village life, and organized faith had all but vanished. Five lamas who had fled this monastery to China returned after 1995. 'But they were already very old,' the monk says, 'and they are dead.' And now, with state repression lifted, the impact of the past became clear. He might have imagined these halls resounding again with the chant of their hundred lamas and the clamour of teaching. Instead there is only his own silence. This, in its way, seems sadder and more final than repression; but I cannot find the words tactfully to ask him any more, and he goes on sitting opposite me, smiling a little, munching biscuits. His stocky build and swaddling monastic boiler suit lend him a childish pomp.

He repeats: 'Their children were estranged, but sometimes their grandchildren become interested. This is their past after all . . .'

'Was it like that for you?'

'No. That was not my way. My parents were indifferent.' But he does not continue about this. He brushes the flies from the meat. He had studied Buddhist philosophy for four years in Karnataka, he says. 'But I never finished, because I was lazy.' Titter. 'And India is hot. And I came here . . .'

He throws a muslin cloth over the stale food and its flies, and we all get up and tramp to the monastic guesthouse in the dark. As we go, almost insensibly I become aware of something echoing far away. The noise is strident and hollow, as if a great edifice were being built or demolished beyond the river. But the others say nothing. Our guesthouse is a gaunt room, asthmatic with dust. The beds that line the walls hold a few threadbare blankets and their mattresses are soiled with overlapping stains of urine. Some filmy water stands in a plastic tub. In my leftover weakness I wade through grass and scrub to the outside latrine with my arms outstretched like a tightrope walker in the night. Dorje sees my discoloured ankle on my return, and bends down with sudden tenderness to lay his palms on it. 'Do you feel the heat? Do you feel it flow?' Batmonkh had once suggested painkillers and a bandage; Dimitri had prescribed Tibetan oils; and now this shy monk is stooped beside me, transmitting his healing energy. Yes, I lie, I feel it. Everything is better.

Dimitri says: 'The monastery will have medicines. We'll ask the monk tomorrow.' He senses my hesitation, then says: 'The monk may seem strange, but he's very intelligent. When he calls himself lazy, that's modesty. He knows different languages, including Sanskrit and medieval Tibetan, and he understands more English than you'd think.'

I feel ashamed. The monk's girlish laugh and baby face had misdirected me. Perhaps he liked it that way. Dimitri perches gingerly on the edge of my mattress. He says: 'I don't know how he came to Buddhism. He says his parents were atheists.' He smiles faintly. 'But then mine were too . . .'

'Always?' He so rarely talks about himself.

'Yes, always.' His voice detaches, as if talking about something long ago. 'My father was an official in the Komsomol, the Communist youth organization. He worked in the Crimea – I was born there – and in Uzbekistan. But nobody much believed.' He laughs in wonderment. The cowl has slipped from his shaven head.

'And you?' I ask.

'I worked a long time for Slava in China. The East always drew me. I travelled a lot, and always alone, like you. Then one day I came to Sichuan province, to where it nears Tibet. If you go west from Chengdu, a long way, you reach a mountain pass, and it's very beautiful. I remember as I crossed, I seemed to be going from one consciousness to another . . . and something happened to me . . .' He smoothes a piece of crumpled paper and sketches out for me: Chengdu–Kangding–Litong–Daochen. He writes this as if it were holy land. I must go before I die. 'There are monasteries everywhere. It was a changed world. And I felt that people were living in a different way, by different codes. There's a three-peaked mountain there called Yading' – he touches it onto the paper – 'I walked round it with Tibetan pilgrims, and it was somehow very pure. But there was nothing mystical. Those people are very tough, very direct. I couldn't talk with them, or with the monks. I still don't quite understand . . . I was thirty-five, not young. I don't understand how it changed me. And it was just the beginning. It took years before I looked back, and realized . . .' He gets up and goes to his bed against the far wall. Some teacher's authority enters his voice. 'But it's not reincarnation that drew me, or anything mysterious. It's the moral principles: that these are values to trust.'

I lay a blanket over my soiled mattress, but cannot sleep. The only light comes from Slava's computer. He primes his mobile phone for me, and I go outside in the starlight and call my wife. She has been following my journey on a map. Am I in a place called Tsugol? she asks. Even over this shaky connection I can hear her alarm. She says I am at the epicentre of an immense Russian–Chinese military exercise. It's in all the papers: the biggest such event for nearly forty years, with 300,000 soldiers . . . As she speaks, I can hear heavy vehicles grinding past the monastery walls.

I try to sleep. But every hour, it seems, Dorje gropes his way outside to smoke; and once Slava embarks on a long routine of yoga exercises, so that I wake to see his enormous torso upside down beside my bed, and his feet where his head should be, or curved behind him to the floor. Much later, my sleep is broken by army lorries moving nose-to-tail outside. Their orange lights blink in our curtainless windows, and when I wake two hours later they are still passing.

In the perfect oval of the monk's face all stress has been smoothed away. He becomes a genial doll. 'You've travelled from Mongolia? You know they worship Genghis Khan there. That is because they are very poor and have nothing else to do . . .' Then comes his tormenting giggle. Yesterday I underestimated him. Today I search his words for esoteric wisdom.

He takes us round the monastic shrines at dawn, while gunfire sounds in the distance. Above us the main temple ascends in triple storeys of vermilion and gold. From its winged columns, sheathed in multicoloured stones, the tiered roofs swim out in a peaceful symmetry of upswept eaves and finials dangling tiny bells. All around its walls shine discs of dull gold for deflecting demons.

The monk says the temple burnt to the ground in 1991 and then was faithfully rebuilt. He pulls an iPhone from his robes to show a wrinkled photograph, dating from 1890. In its faded monochrome the lamas are assembled in dense ranks for the White Elephant festival. Even its flanking stairways are thronged with worshippers.

We go inside through a blaze of crimson pillars and rainbow hangings towards an altar white with polyester flowers. The golden figure that glimmers here is not of the Buddha but of the revered teacher Tsongkhapa, whose statue is replicated around him in banked shelves of over a thousand tiny statuettes. The monk says: 'When you worship here, the more of him there are, the more merit you get!' His snicker sounds shrill, I imagine with disbelief. I glance at his unreadable face. But maybe the trilling sound means something else. Perhaps it does not translate. Near the altar a solitary, mahogany-faced lama is chanting softly, and the monk is moving on.

The monastery's precious 108 handpainted scrolls, once feared lost, have been recovered, he says, all except the first one. And now Dimitri beside me whispers: 'Actually, that one is in my library at Aginskoye. I've never told him.' He relishes this arcane competition. 'But I suspect he knows.'

Now the monk is guiding us towards a last temple, sacred to Maitreya, the Buddha of the Future, who will one day usher in a nobler age. The doors open on a standing colossus. His naked body is dusted in jewels. It swells to a golden torso, where his elongated fingers are lifted towards his face as if to apply makeup, but are touched together in a sacred sign of unity. Over twenty feet above us, under a tiara of semi-precious stones, his face is a shining ellipse, like the monk's, and gazes far beyond eye-contact, dreaming.

'He will arrive after 5,000 years of the First Buddha,' says Dimitri, unsmiling. 'That is, in 2,500 years' time.' But he can't help adding: 'Our statue at Aginskoye is bigger.'

Now it is Slava who whispers to me: 'I don't think the historical Buddha ever existed . . .'

But the monk is declaiming: 'His kingdom will come after a terrible war, when the rule of our Buddha will end. Then it will be a time of decadence! Humans will have shrunk to dwarfs, and they'll be shooting one another' – he mimics a child firing a water pistol – '*Tee-hee*. Then the Maitreya will arrive, towering above them – that is why he is portrayed so tall – and the new reign will begin . . .'

All the time he has been speaking, the explosions outside have intensified, as if the cataclysm he foretells had already started, and we emerge to see the whole valley to our east pouring out smoke. A few villagers have assembled to stare. Dorje has already driven back towards Aginskoye, afraid, but the driver of an old Toyota will get us to the next town, the monk says. He looks at me with his opaque calm. 'If they hear you speak English,' he titters, 'you will end up in prison.'

We cram into the car. Its driver looks tough and able. A jet fighter bends out of the sky. As we leave, the monk pokes his head through the window: 'Which is your favourite football team?' he asks. 'I like Arsenal . . .'

We descend towards the river. There is no other track. In front sounds the long, continuous rumble of artillery. But the windows of the Toyota are so blistered that its passengers must be all but invisible, and in its front seat the bulk of Slava obscures me. No sooner do we reach the Onon than we run into a roadblock, and my breath goes cold. But we reverse out of it and cross the river by another bridge. Smoke is cascading from the valley just below, but we drive up the slopes beyond. On the ridge beside us, two self-propelling guns wait un-manned. When we come upon the army camps, we find them deserted. The Russian tents stand in massed rows, their lorries aligned beside them. A little farther on we reach the Chinese bivouac. For hundreds of yards the soldiers' tents are no more than half-open shelters of coarse canvas strung over wooden frames. There is no sentry in sight. And of the five hundred military police reportedly patrolling this zone on horseback, we see none.

Even as we climb out of this fake inferno, I imagine this is less a military exercise than a political warning to the West. Slava and Dimitri have gone tactfully silent. The Chinese contribution, it seems, is important only as a symbol: a mere 3,200 men, based here under their flimsy canopies. There is even a token contingent from Mongolia. But soon the low booming in the valley dies away, the air clears, and we are travelling west on the road towards Aginskoye, free.

* * *

The thrill of solitude returns, like an exposed nerve. Now the comfort of companions has gone: the heavy certitude of Slava, Dimitri's gentleness. I left them at the railway station of Mogoytuy, beneath the war memorial of a T-34 tank blazoned 'Stalin'. They enfolded me in quick farewell. They'd found me a driver named Vladik, with a decrepit Lada, and now this impetuous youth and I clatter through the suburbs, making for the viaduct of the Trans-Siberian Railway. We dodge down a dirt-track alley, then squeeze between the piers of the railway overpass – every panel of Vladik's Lada is already dented – while an engine clanks above us, pulling seventy wagons south to China. I hear them overhead with boyish wonder. This Trans-Manchurian branch line, cutting clean across north China, was completed in 1902 when Russia forced a sickly Celestial Empire to concede its 900-mile short cut to Vladivostok: a line fraught with future trouble.

For a moment the rail and the road run parallel, then we are moving alone across a sunlit country, where the grasslands are yellowing into autumn. This is the north-west limit of Dauria, whose steppelands flow back south to the seasonal lakes and airways of a million migrating birds. Vladik drives as if he's angry with the world. From time to time a tributary of the Onon slides under our road. In a land once called the granary of the Amur, the villages are small and far between. But here and there a valley side is quilted with harvesting maize and in the pastures the hay is already scrolled into sodden wheels. They'll probably rot early, Vladik says, the sky had shitted all summer.

Now the Buryat cattle-lands have ebbed behind us, and where the Onon meets the Ingoda river descending from the west it loses its name and becomes the Shilka. Here, in more purely Russian country, it is no longer Holy Mother, but the Little Father of Russian endearment and respect, and as the Shilka it flows east for 350 miles to unite with the Argun at the Chinese border. There at last it becomes the Amur.

Vladik drops me off in the centre of Shilka, an early spa and gold-rush town. 'You watch out,' he says. 'It isn't like my home town Mogoytuy. Everyone gets on OK there – Russians, Buryats, immigrant Uzbeks, we even have Baptist chapels – but Shilka's a shit-heap.' He stubs out his cigarette on the dashboard, suddenly despondent. 'I don't think anywhere's much good now, except maybe America.' As he drives off he calls out: 'But we all hate the Chinese!'

For a while I imagine him right about Shilka. There are only two hotels here. In one I'm cursed out by a drunken owner; the other stands in a garage repair yard, and is locked. So I find a *marshrutka*, a shared taxi, which takes me the thirty-odd miles on to Nerchinsk. This, too, has an evil reputation. Vladik said it is full of thieves and ex-convicts. But I arrive at a rest house in a yard full of marigolds and chickens, and wander its corridors alone until a cleaner finds me a room, and I fall painlessly asleep.

* * *

In this limitless Siberia the average town is thin and sprawling. You walk down empty streets, no car or bus in sight, and arrive at a square where a few old men sit smoking. You ask: where is the town centre? But you are already there, in this dusty square, where some cars and trucks are lined up before shops whose windows show no goods.

Nerchinsk keeps the frail bone structure of a former dignity. Its restored cathedral, whose bell tower was destroyed long ago, overlooks a silent road near the town's heart. A portico of Doric columns crowns the derelict merchants' court nearby, and behind a classical façade the long-closed Hotel Dauria may have hosted Anton Chekhov on his journey east in 1890. 'Yesterday was in Nerchinsk,' he wrote laconically to his family; 'Not a knockout of a town,' and an air of depletion still pervades it. Tired-faced men and hefty women trudge its streets in nondescript dresses and anoraks sporting counterfeit logos. Half the inhabitants seem to be wearing Versace or Dolce & Gabbana, yet driving ancient Toyotas and crossing potholed streets lugging empty shopping bags.

It was mining that shaped the town's identity. In 1700 Peter the Great despatched Greek engineers to prospect the surrounding terrain, and within a few years they uncovered enormous seams of silver. Nerchinsk became the nerve centre of a landmass whose inhabitants – criminal and political convicts, indentured peasants – toiled underground from settlements dispersed over thousands of square miles. Perhaps these half-remembered centuries account for the criminal reputation that lingers, together with the explosions that convulsed the town in 2001 when Mafia ignited its arsenal by mistake.

Nerchinsk has been in decline ever since the Trans-Siberian Railway bypassed it at the end of the nineteenth century. Its distant silver mines are long worked out, its factories failed. A palisaded prison spreads close to where the Nerva river joins the Shilka, and a military airfield lies abandoned on the outskirts. I search in vain for any memorial to the treaty signed here: an agreement whose breach and promise still resonate across three centuries.

The 1689 Treaty of Nerchinsk marked the first check to Russia's headlong conquest of Siberia. From the Ural mountains to the Pacific Ocean, over more than three thousand miles, Cossacks and soldiers had traversed the whole continent in less than sixty years. It was in the frozen governorate town of Yakutsk, six hundred miles from the still-unknown Amur, that rumours spread of a mighty river flowing through a paradise of harvest fields to the south. In 1643 a desperate, three-year expedition under Vasily Poyarkov descended from the starving settlement and ravaged the middle courses of the Amur, exacting a tribute of furs from the scattered Daur tribespeople, or slaughtering them. By the journey's end Poyarkov's mutinous force of 150 men was reduced to 20 by starvation, disease and fatal flogging – some he killed with his own hands – and he returned to Yakutsk with the first, tentative mapping of the Amur. In a pattern that would be repeated, Poyarkov was recalled for trial in Moscow, and vanishes from record.

Four years later a more terrible scourge was unleashed on the Amur by the buccaneer Yerofei Khabarov, who ravaged the riverine settlements for over five hundred miles. In one episode alone he boasted of the massacre of 661 Daur villagers 'with God's help', along with mass rape.

But now the native peoples appealed to the nominal suzerain of the region, China. Khabarov was withdrawn for trial in Moscow, and his eventual successor, with more than two hundred men, was blown to bits by Chinese cannon on the lower Amur. For thirty years afterwards the two great empires fought a shadow war of mutually ignorant diplomacy, while a flood of Russian peasants, Cossacks and criminals, beyond government control, poured into the Amur basin. It was after 1680, with their rule secure, that the Manchu Chinese at last lost patience. One by one the Russian forts were eliminated, and after the death of more than eight hundred besieged Cossacks in their last Amur stronghold, Moscow and Peking moved to negotiate a peace.

Nerchinsk by then had become Russia's gateway to the Amur, yet was little more than a stockaded fort with a few government and traders' dwellings. This wooden village would later be wrecked by the flooding river, and rebuilt more durably on higher ground; but in 1689 the waterside meadows became the venue for the first treaty China ever concluded with a European power. The two empires – the parvenu Russian and the ancient Chinese – were deeply strange to one another. Their delegates were well versed, but their rulers far away. Peter the Great, barely seventeen, was preoccupied with domestic turmoil, but his depleted Treasury was dreaming of trade with China. The Chinese emperor Kangxi, the most powerful and cultivated of his dynasty, was anxious above all to seal his frontiers against the incursions of these brutish northerners, and to prevent Russia from allying with a newly belligerent Mongol power pressing in the west.

The delegations agreed to meet in scrupulous equality, but China's two ambassadors, close relatives of the emperor, arrived from Peking with 1,500 soldiers and a fleet of supporting junks and barges, loaded with cannon, that converged on Nerchinsk along the river. Against this entourage of some 10,000 the Russians could muster barely 2,000 men. But issues of procedure and etiquette stifled all else. Noting the Russians dressed in cloth of gold and precious furs, the Chinese stripped off their blazoned brocades and moved to the conference in sombre dress under huge silk umbrellas. An identical number of guards attended each embassy: 260 men, who faced off at equal intervals and ceremonially frisked each other for hidden weapons. The Russian ambassador advanced behind a slow march of flute-players and trumpeters. The delegates dismounted in unison and entered their two tents simultaneously – tents that had been scrupulously merged so that no one would suffer the indignity of visiting the other first. The ambassadors sat down and shouted their greetings in concert. Only three Russian dignitaries took seats, and the Chinese mimicked them, leaving more than a hundred mandarins standing opposite their Russian counterparts during the first session. They remained in mutual incomprehension. The ambassadors shared no word of language. So the negotiations were conducted in Latin by two Jesuits attached to the Chinese court, and by an erudite Pole for the Russians.

Each ambassador began with outsize demands. The Russians claimed the Amur as their frontier, by virtue of their partial occupation and the adherence of local tribes. The Chinese responded by advancing their supposed suzerainty north to Lake Baikal and the Lena river, annexing half of east Siberia. They too cited the submission of natives, but the territorial rights of such peoples were entertained by neither party. Often the talks broke down. For ten days the two Jesuit fathers – the Portuguese Pereira and the Frenchman Gerbillon – shuttled between the sullen camps with new formulas and compromises. Among the suspicious mandarins, they were elevated by the favour of the emperor. He esteemed Gerbillon as a scientific scholar, while Pereira endeared himself by his musical talents: sometimes the emperor and the Jesuit were seen sitting side by side to play the harpsichord.

In the end, while the Russians secured the trade sanctions that their impoverished Treasury craved, the Chinese gained deeper concessions. Extending their frontier far north of the Amur, along the crest of the Stanovoy mountains, their sovereignty would now embrace the whole river and its tributaries from the Argun to the Pacific.

Solemnly the treaty was drawn up in Latin, Russian and Manchu. Both sides appear to have been pleased. More than a century later the Russians began fretting at its outcome, blaming Jesuit perfidy and the ambiguities of Latin and geography. But for the moment, in the words of the Chinese embassy: 'We made a common oath to live forever in harmony.'

In the desolation of today's Nerchinsk, where no memorial to this treaty survives, the streets uncoil over inexhaustible distances to buildings that dwindle before I reach them. Of course this is illusion, and somewhere near the town's centre comes a bizarre shock: an immaculate façade of pedimented doors and windows blazing white under high crenellations.

I circle its walls into a wild garden. Beds of dahlias, petunias and snapdragons are all flowering at once. The air is filled with their hybrid scent. Workshops and stables rise from the shrubbery in castellated blocks of splintering stucco and naked brick. Their roofs have crashed in and their floors rotted to earth. I might be entering the barbican of a ruined castle. Recently an enterprising journalist came upon a vast, shattered glasshouse here, and formal beds of castor-oil plants. Now this palace has become a museum, where I pay a pittance to enter, and find myself alone.

In its ballroom two sombre faces gaze out from oil paintings flanking a giant pier-glass. The Butin brothers were entrepreneurs who flourished while working for a Siberian tea-trader named Kandinsky, great-uncle of the future artist. Soon they acquired far-flung assets in gold, iron, salt and distilleries. Their steamboats sailed the Amur. Through the 1860s they transformed Nerchinsk with a telegraph station, a town library, pharmacies, printing shop and a free music school.

I stare back in wonder at their portraits. They built their palace in the late 1870s after endowing half the district with primary schools, and a year or two later their businesses started to unravel. They were themselves poorly educated, but their ostentatious rooms are redolent of music and books. Above the ballroom windows hang moulded panels of musical staves, lyres and trumpets, twined with the names of Mozart, Bach, Rossini, Glinka ... A sixty-air orchestrion had once played in the gallery where gilded cupids still pluck harps and clash cymbals. In the library, histories and encyclopedias survive in five languages and mildewed bindings.

Perhaps the faces that gaze out are troubled only in a viewer's foreboding. The older brother Nikolai rests behind a splayed and greying beard, but his brows have corrugated above pained eyes. He was an asthmatic who could not live in his own palace, but retired to an airy pavilion in its grounds. It was his younger brother Mikhail who became the firm's energy and brains. His honorary diplomas hang in their showcases, while on a nearby desk lies a business letter in his fluent hand, with a goose-feather quill alongside.

In their photographs the extended Butin family assembles for the camera as sombre and seemingly respectable as any Victorian clan. Here the melancholy Nikolai becomes more haggard, and Mikhail's first wife Sophia, in whose young memory he built a school for women, peers out unknowable from beneath a pretty bonnet.

Mikhail himself, more raw-boned and Tartar than his portrait, wrote books promoting commerce with China and the United States, where he travelled in search of ideas, lamenting Russia's backwardness. He envisioned the building of a continental railway twenty years before the Trans-Siberian was begun. But the Butin enterprises sank into receivership. Nikolai died in 1892, worn out by anxiety, and Mikhail gave their great home to Nerchinsk city, and died in Irkutsk, far away.

These resonant halls must be unique in Siberia. Marooned in a vast region of mines and empty hills, they survive in the awe of contemporary travellers before the Bolshevik Revolution gutted them. Tapestries, silk curtains and Flemish Old Masters once shone on the walls above marquetry floors;

and cream and gold furniture, upholstered in satin or draped with oriental rugs, spread into a conservatory brimming with orchids and lemon trees.

But the chief marvel remains the ballroom, whose vacant space is doubled by four prodigious mirrors. In a fit of hubris the Butins bought them at the Paris Exposition of 1878 – monstrous, 25-foot-high pier glasses – and shipped them halfway across the world to the mouth of the Amur, where a purpose-built barge carried them two thousand miles upriver to Nerchinsk. The greatest of them – the world's largest pier-glass in its day – faces the ballroom doorway, and dwarfs whoever enters in a reflecting archway topped by lounging cherubs.

I go outside into the blazing light. On a nearby railing a noticeboard pictures luminaries who have visited Nerchinsk in the last two hundred years. Alongside Chekhov, I see the lugubrious profile and drooping moustaches of the American George Kennan, who travelled Siberia in the late nineteenth century and exposed the czarist penal regime in his grimly revealing two-volume *Siberia and the Exile System*. His earlier writing had persuaded the Russian authorities to trust him, and for over a year, in deepening disillusion, he explored the convict mines and prisons of eastern Siberia, outraged, above all, by his encounters with innocent victims of conscience. Ever since the incompetent Decembrist uprising against Czar Nicholas I in 1825, and the violently suppressed Polish insurrection of 1863–4, political dissidents had been exiled to the innocuously named Nerchinsk Silver-Mining District, whose wilderness extended thousands of square miles southeast. By 1885 it was less the dangerous state of the mines that repelled Kennan than the insanitary prisons where inmates idled for months under apathetic and corrupt officials.

In Nerchinsk he arrived exhausted at the most disgusting hotel in his ample experience, and described with rueful humour the scuttling of its rats and cockroaches, the greenish washing-pan that had doubled as a toilet, and the absence of any bed or of a mirror in which to have 'the melancholy satisfaction of surveying my frost-bitten countenance'. But it is Kennan who left the fullest description of the Butin palace, then still pristine, applauding Mikhail Butin as 'half American in his ideas and sympathies'.

Back in the United States, over many years, Kennan lectured to more than a million Americans – sometimes clambering onto the stage dressed as a convict in leg-irons – and half a century later his great-nephew George Frost Kennan became an influential diplomat, historian and speaker on the Soviet Union, confronting an empire whose labour camps far outstripped in horror those reviled by his forebear.

In the wooden village of Kalinovo, a few miles south of Nerchinsk, a lonely church is rumoured to be the burial place of Yerofei Khabarov, the brutal pioneer of the Amur. Long before I reach the village, I glimpse blackened turrets that have toppled askew under their crosses. Giant fissures split the church façade from top to bottom. They give entry everywhere, and shrubs are pouring in. Where a grave or a memorial might be, the plastered bricks are tumbling from the foundations. Someone has hung a few icons in the sanctuary and set up a tin table as an altar.

'In the west of Russia they preserve their churches,' a village woman tells me bitterly. 'But here they just let ours fall to bits.' She teaches at the local school, and doesn't know what to tell the children. 'Our church has been turning into a ruin these last fifty years. Yes, there was once a monument of some sort, but it disappeared. No one remembers it.'

Another legend has it that it is Khabarov's brother Nikifor who was buried under the walls. But this Church of the Dormition was built in 1712 – almost the oldest masonry church in east Siberia – and the Khabarovs died decades before. Yerofei himself was recalled to Moscow to face trial for multiple crimes, then pardoned, and surfaces only sporadically in records afterwards. Where he died is unknown. Soviet historians reduced his atrocities to a mere footnote, and credited him with annexing the entire Amur basin for Russia, as if the Treaty of Nerchinsk had never existed.

A copy of the treaty was once on display at the Butin palace, but I could not find it. On enquiring, I was led to an upstairs office where a curator eased it from a red folder, and laid it quite tenderly in my lap. Nobody knew its age, and its triple scripts were unreadable to me: the Jesuits' Latin, the Manchu (with a handsome seal) and the early Cyrillic Russian, which gave an illusion, in its elaborate and beautiful precision, of being more enduring than the others.

4

The Shilka

My hotel is empty. Somebody feeds the chickens, someone else cleans the corridors, but I never see them. My room is large, and I gather blankets and pillows from its other beds to cushion my ribs and ankle before sleep. At night there is nothing to divert you from your pain. You wonder if you should return home, but know you will not. If you consider bypassing a place you'd planned to visit, it immediately torments you with its promise.

By morning I have become a little comical. I sit balefully on my bed, planning how to stand up. Bending forward – to tie a shoelace, retrieve something dropped – provokes gloomy circumspection. Crouching above the hole in the squat-latrine becomes a trembling hazard. In the street, I find myself taking tiny, frail steps as if after a stroke, and I remember old people from my youth with renewed sympathy. I am one of them now.

But a foolish pride remains. I hope my unsteady gait will not be construed as drunkenness. I try to lengthen my stride. Perhaps I will gain kudos as the victim of an industrial accident: I could even be taken for a veteran Hero of Socialist Labour (but there are no factories left in Nerchinsk). As I walk, the hurt ribs deflect attention from the throbbing ankle, as if I can entertain only one pain at a time. And after an hour, perhaps, if the surroundings are diverting enough, the last ache becomes absorbed into the body, sinking a little beneath consciousness, until it is all but forgotten.

So I turn east again in expectant spirits, and cross the 60-odd miles to Sretensk in a part-time taxi driven by a morose student who wants to live in London. The land around us is changing. On either side the shadow lines of hills begin to thicken and converge. The villages grow fewer, poorer. At Sretensk a side-track of the railway peters to a stub of stranded carriages on the far side of the Shilka. Here, where the mountains begin to squeeze the river on its descent towards China, the small town continues in a time warp. Sretensk was once the junction where overland traffic from the west met the navigable river flowing east, and for over half a century a fleet of steamers opened a lifeline between European Russia and the Pacific. But in 1916 the Trans-Siberian bypassed the little river-port, turning it obsolete, and now I enter a town of mellow tranquillity, where a road of wooden houses turns out to be the high street, and forested hills loom close, and nothing has overlaid the past. With their filigreed window frames and eaves and bright-painted shutters, the houses might be dwellings from Russian folk tale, inhabited by cannibal witches or holy simpletons, and some handsome buildings in plastered brick remain above the empty river.

There is only one hotel, immured in an ageing edifice of stucco mouldings and flaking whitewash, beside the lonely square that descends to the jetty. Inside, a stone stairway climbs past a Dutch stove into a den of time-polished timber. Once, in 1904, this was the Russo-Chinese Bank, but its massive iron doors now open on a fusty billiards room. The only person here is a sad-eyed receptionist gazing at her mobile phone. I go down a dark passage under ormolued lamps and little chandeliers that decorate it like makeup. A grandfather clock chimes at random, and a wind-up gramophone turns a 78rpm record of Maria Lukic singing 'Don't Fly Away'.

Perhaps it is the intimacy of the town, cradled in its hills and wrapped by the river, that sheds a gentle euphoria. My journey's urgency subsides, and a benign idleness seeps in. Even the town's monuments seem faded far back in time. A silver-painted Lenin waves from an overgrown park, and the only ship I see is a decommissioned patrol vessel set up on a memorial ramp. But I hear that twice a week a small passenger boat arrives from the town of Shilka and goes on to remote settlements downstream, where I see the river winding eastward towards China between hills massed with forest.

For three days I nurture this prospect, walking compulsively along the Shilka, up and down a potholed road, while the great river glistens alongside. A few old people work in their vegetable gardens, and cattle wander unchecked across the way. The river is barely wider than a week ago – perhaps four hundred yards across – but it flows differently beneath these constricting hills, its surface twisted into thick boils and eddies, like mercury. And its solitude continues. Nobody fishes or sails on it. The air is so quiet that you can hear people talking on the far side.

But for over half a century the quayside here – shrunk to a platform overhanging the water – was the nerve centre of a slovenly transit town. In a few surviving photographs migrants from west Russia and the Ukraine cover the dockside with their ragged children and bundled possessions, waiting for the steamer that might carry them to new promise. They look pathetically vulnerable. Shrouded women in calico skirts and sheepskin-swathed men already work-worn, they are on their way to the few acres assigned them, and to the lottery of floods and Manchurian bandits. Such families joined the Cossacks and garrisons of the Amur as farmers and traders. Many were

Old Believers, sectarians in flight from Orthodoxy, and their providence and industry at last created the region's modest wealth, until the peasants flooding in on the Trans-Siberian Railway, and the ravages of the Civil War, subsumed them.

The boats that carried them were ironclad paddle steamers built in the shipyards of Glasgow and Belgium. These double-decked edifices, girded with spindly funnels and ungainly wheels, were usually owned and run by foreigners: British, American, German, Japanese. Their shallow draught, as little as four feet, was designed to navigate the shifting sandbars that curse the Amur. Day and night a sailor in the bows would probe the riverbed with a ten-foot pole, and sing out warnings to the steersman. As the ships wound through the darkness, little oil lamps lit their way – red on the Chinese side, white on the Russian – and were replenished by solitary lamplighters from dugout canoes.

As early as 1866 the American Thomas Knox, voyaging round the world, was astonished by the human cargo encamped on the deck of the *Korsackoff*: a horde of ex-serfs and Cossacks, whose horses stamped all night above the ceiling of his flea-infested cabin. The missionary Francis Clark, travelling with his wife and small son in 1900, wrote that even on the *Baron Korff*, whose staterooms were handsomely furnished with 'a good German piano', the steerage passengers lay en masse on the iron floors with their naked children. The cabins were filthy. The ebullient British journalist John Foster Fraser awoke to cockroaches dropping from the ceiling and swarming all over him.

The food was universally accounted disgusting, and fastidious Western passengers baulked at the table manners. For lunch, laid over ragged oilcloths, Fraser shared a hash of unidentifiable meat and oil-smeared potatoes with a fur-trader, a chain-smoking army wife and a black-whiskered Tartar colonel. As their brandished forks and spoons sank into the communal pot, an orgy of chomping, salivating, snatching and finger-sucking broke out, completed by ten minutes of violent tooth-picking. This was the elite table. A French passenger threw his sugared cabbage out of the ship's window, plate and all, in a fit of outrage.

There were other craft sailing the river. Whole families of migrants floated downstream on tight-packed rafts with their wagons, horses, cattle and dogs crowded on board, sometimes on their way to Khabarovsk 1,400 miles distant on the middle Amur. Hundred-yard pontoons of timber floated the same way. A medley of native skiffs appeared – dugout canoes, even improvised paddle boats – along with convict barges pulled by the steamers, whose passengers would fraternize with the caged prisoners when they all ran aground.

In 1861 the anarchist Mikhail Bakunin, slipping away from Siberian exile, boarded a steamer at Sretensk on his eastward flight to America and Europe. In following years, in a ferment of revolutionary scheming and inflammatory rhetoric, this contradictory man became the challenger to Marx in the First International, and imagined an independent Siberia turned towards the Pacific and America, with the Amur river at its heart. Almost forty years later, exhausted after a two-month journey overland from Moscow, Anton Chekhov arrived at Sretensk on his way to Sakhalin island in the Okhotsk Sea. His steamship juddered downriver for a week and pitched so violently that he could barely compose letters. There were schoolchildren on board, with a group of convicts who were disembarked at the goldmines of Kara that had so distressed George Kennan. A tame fox commandeered the washroom.

Chekhov lost his unsentimental heart to the Amur river. His letters to family and friends ring with its wildness and solitude, with its multitudes of ducks, grebes, herons and 'all sorts of long-beaked rascals'. The opposing shores of Russia and China were as beautiful and savage as one another. 'I've seen a million gorgeous landscapes,' he wrote. 'I feel giddy with ecstasy.' Before leaving Moscow he had been diagnosed with tuberculosis, but truly now, he felt, he was not afraid of dying. 'And what liberalism! Oh, what liberalism!' The frankness of the inhabitants amazed him. So far from European Russia, they spoke their minds out loud. There was no one to arrest them, and nowhere to be exiled, since they were already in Siberia. Russia had forgotten the Amur, they said. The girls smoked cigarettes, the old women puffed on pipes. They ate meat in Holy Week. Escaped convicts moved about unbetrayed.

I sit on the deserted Sretensk quay, waiting for my own boat, and scan the vacant water upriver. On the far shore the reflected shell of a defunct collective farm glimmers in the current, alongside the beached carriages where the railway ends. Downriver the hills converge in a faded palisade where I hope to go. But I wonder, with vague foreboding, if I will be barred from embarking on a boat that noses towards the forbidden Chinese frontier.

Six or seven women and a silent couple come down to the jetty with their bags and trussed bundles, and wait. The buildings that once flanked the quayside are gone, and the long esplanade of rotting planks, with its patient hordes of peasantry, is only a photographic memory. Sretensk itself is no longer the quayside shanty town of travellers' disgust, sunk in shin-deep cattle dung. I wait with the old women for two hours, then three. At last a brusque official arrives and nails a notice to a nearby post. There will be no boat for another four days. The old women murmur together for a while, then one by one they pick up their bundles and trudge away.

It is after this that Sretensk begins to pall. Its public buildings, with their patchwork façades and random mouldings, start to seem crude and overweight. Sometimes their stucco has dropped away to reveal the timber frames that uphold them. At evening there is nowhere to go. By day I resort to the 'Café Hope', obscured in a compound of closed offices, where slow-smiling women serve black bread and *pelmeni*. Two lorry drivers are the only clientele. Next day a drunk falls from the post office steps and lies bleeding beside me. He is light and ghostly in my arms when I help him up. No one takes any notice. I imagine inhaling an insidious malaise from the town's air. In my hotel the only other guests are a brother and sister, half Cossack, half Chinese, who are searching for their grandmother's grave. She had been shot during the Revolution, as many Cossacks were. They have found their old family home; but others are living in it now, the man says, sounding annoyed. Its owner had invited them in, and offered them tea. Then childhood memories had flooded over him. He laughs with pleasure. His sister had wept.

At the outbreak of the First World War the barracks at Sretensk became a camp for prisoners. German, Austro-Hungarian and Turkish soldiers were interned here, as many as 11,000. The war had ended three years before they were released. By now they had been reduced by typhus and by the wayward artillery of Japanese troops fighting the Bolsheviks. But in a valley near the camp they had left behind a memorial inscribed in Hungarian to their comrades perished far from the motherland. I search for this, but can find no trace of it. Hunting for any record, I seek out the small, tired Sretensk museum. Inside its entrance, in a red-painted alcove, is a bust of Stalin.

I look in vain round the usual mounted animals and regalia from the Second World War, which Russians call the Great

Patriotic War, then find one of those curators who work for a pittance in the loneliness of these museums. Yes, there had once been a monument, she says. She even shows me a photograph of it: a whitewashed pyramid, encircled by chains. But it had been destroyed three years ago, she adds, and it was a mystery as to why.

I should have known something would happen. I have been too long here, too conspicuous in a place where foreigners never come. The knock on my door is not the shy tap of the cleaner, but a peremptory banging. When I open, three policemen are standing there.

'Come with us.'

At first I suppose this a routine check, but I glimpse the alarmed face of the receptionist as they lead me away. The police station is five hundred yards off, but I am ushered into a patrol car. Two of the men are in uniform, the third (the important one, I imagine) in plain clothes. The razor-wired police station stands above the river, and looks like the only office working in Sretensk.

Then my escorts disappear, and I find myself seated in a stark room where two other officers confront me across a bare table. One is cold-eyed, senior. He stands ten feet away from me, enforcing estrangement. The other is a hard-faced young woman who continually checks her computer. A local school-mistress has been summoned as interpreter, and sits nervously beside me. I realize, with sinking heart, that this is not a routine interview. There is nowhere for my gaze to rest except for a bank of filing cabinets and a tinted photograph of President Putin hanging above.

'Who do you know in our town?' It is the senior officer. His eyes have frozen.

'I don't know anybody.'

'Then why are you here? What are you doing?'

'I'm writing a book on the Amur river.'

'The Amur is not here. The Amur is to the east. This is the Shilka, in Zabaikalsky Krai.'

'The Shilka is an Amur tributary.'

The interpreter is stumbling. Her English is worse than my Russian, but her rendition gives me time to think. She looks downcast, and reticently sympathetic.

He says: 'You have been here five days.'

'I'm waiting for the boat. It didn't come.' Instantly I wish I hadn't said this. He will surely state that the boat is forbidden.

But he demands: 'Where have you been in Sretensk?'

I might answer that there is nowhere to go in Sretensk. But instead I hear myself talking about the waterfront and the river traffic in the nineteenth century; and seeing the cold eyes glaze in boredom, I enthuse on about Sretensk's past importance as a link between Europe and the Russian Pacific.

Soon he is looking at me with open hostility. 'Where did you learn all this? How do you know more than we do?' No glimmer of irony touches him.

'You can read this in history books,' I say. 'In England, in the State Library in Moscow [I'm guessing]. Anywhere.'

He pauses, picks up his mobile phone, lays it aside. Something is baffling him: the enigma of an old man who perhaps is only pretending to limp and speak poor Russian, but who is not equipped for spying – no hidden camera, no parabolic microphone (they have surely searched my room by now) – and who is travelling like a gypsy.

Then the younger officer swings away from her computer, whose screen I cannot see, and says: 'Your visa is wrong.' She holds up my passport. 'You have a business visa, when you should have a tourist visa.'

'I'm not a tourist. I'm writing . . .'

'If you have a business visa, you should be doing business. Were you in Moscow? Have you attended any symposia or conferences?' She lays my passport on her desk as if it were infected. She has long, turquoise-painted fingernails. Her slate-grey stare is for some reason more disconcerting than her colleague's. I imagine it turning suspects to stone, like the Medusa. I look back at her in confusion. I'd thought my visa foolproof. She goes on: 'Who is this host on your visa? Who is Azimut?'

'They own hotels,' I say. But I've no real idea who they are. Every business visa to Russia has a nominal host here. I add piously: 'It would be dishonest to pretend I'm a tourist.'

Medusa shakes her head. 'But you are not a businessman.'

Now the older officer barks out: 'We don't know who you are.' His questions at first are harshly formulaic. They arrive like hammer blows. How often have I been in Russia? When was I last here? Who did I know? Did I have relatives in Moscow? Then suddenly: 'What were you doing in Aginskoye?'

An alarm bell starts ringing in my head. Aginskoye was almost at the epicentre of the joint Russian–Chinese military exercise two weeks ago. I had booked into a hotel there, and they must have registered me. 'I was visiting the Buddhist monastery,' I say.

Medusa is glaring at her computer. 'Where did you go after Aginskoye?'

I have a fantasy that my whole life history is on her screen. Yet after Aginskoye I have surely disappeared from record. With Slava and Dimitri I had spent nights in places too poor to register. As if reading my thoughts, Medusa asks: 'How did you travel? Who did you see?' She pushes the stray locks from her face.

The policeman is glowering at me too. I am starting to feel sick. Suddenly I do not know Slava and Dimitri at all. I wipe them, innocent, from my mind. 'I saw nobody.'

A few moments later the two officers leave the room to talk on another telephone, the schoolteacher following. I am left to stare at Putin. I have no idea what they are thinking. In their few minutes' absence, my mind runs riot. It imagines trumped-up charges, prison . . . The tinted Putin stares dourly down. When the officers come back, they are both expressionless. It is the averted face of the schoolmistress that alarms me. Medusa sets out forms for me to sign. A tiny Orthodox cross is nestled at her throat. I read: 'Ranking No. 937033/5 of the Ministry of Central Affairs . . .' It details how I was apprehended and how my entering Russia is a civil misdeed, how my visa is not relevant to what I am doing. Medusa's fingernails alight on crucial paragraphs. I must pay 2,000–5,000 roubles. My visa is invalid and I may be expelled from Russia.

The fee is trivial. Two thousand roubles is half the price of a London parking ticket. But now the man says: 'You cannot return to this district. We are sending you to Chita. The immigration officials will decide what to do with you.'

I feel wretched. Chita is the provincial capital, two hundred miles away. My journey could be disrupted for weeks. The officer looks satisfied. He is smiling slightly to himself. I think I hate him. His chest pushes against his jacket, as if seeking medals, and I imagine he is hoping to see fear. I am ordered to a nearby room for fingerprinting, down a passageway past a pallid youth in handcuffs, waiting with his father. In this den an elderly woman lifts a big roller from an ink-pad, and seizes my right hand. She runs the roller over it like a builder whitewashing a wall, then forces my fingertips one by one over a triplicate form, squashing each one down. Next she inks and crushes my palm onto another form, where it prints out like a palmist's chart. I wonder bleakly what its fate line says. She repeats the same process with the left hand, unspeaking, then lumbers away.

Back in my interrogation room, the officers are talking about tomorrow. The interpreter looks tired. Medusa is hard to read. The snake-locks curtain her face. A car will be taking me to Chita at six o'clock in the morning, she says. She passes me a handwritten address. I will be met there. 'They may send you back to London.'

My spirits are ebbing away, leaving only resentment. A minute ago I was lamenting the upset of a deviation to Chita. Now, compared to my expulsion, such a detour seems wonderful.

For a long time the officers peer at computer screens I cannot read. Something is troubling Medusa. Her colleague disappears. Once again I am left alone. Three hours have gone by since my arrest. I try to reimagine my itinerary should I return next year. But suddenly it seems utopian to have conceived this journey at all. Of course it could not work. How foolish to have imagined otherwise . . .

Then everything changes. I never did discover why. Medusa returns after talking with the Chita authorities, I think. She says I am free to continue. She is very sorry for the nuisance caused. Her fingernails slide across another document, discard it. She smiles at me. I imagine ice cracking. I realize she is rather beautiful. 'Of course you may write about Sretensk, our history, our scenery. Everyone is honoured that somebody has come to our little town all the way from London.' I listen agape. She closes down her computer, and shakes my hand in farewell.

I return, shaken, to the river. It seems to move with conscious intent (I know I am overwrought) and carries the illusion that it is coming out of the past. At my feet – in the fleeting present – a few grasses bend towards the current, with some cigarette butts and a dead butterfly.

The schoolteacher believed that Medusa may have persuaded the Chita authorities to let me go. She had overheard her say I was a good man from England, visiting their town – the first time that anyone had taken notice of it. Or perhaps the Chita officials had gone online and discovered that I was a writer, as I'd said. She was not sure. But tomorrow was a Saturday, of course, and nobody in Chita, or anywhere else, wanted to work on weekends.

Behind the statue of Lenin in the small town square, beyond the jungle of its garden, spread the modest buildings of Sretensk secondary school. I have promised the teacher that I will speak next morning to her English class, which assembles in a wooden outbuilding, and she greets me with her reticent sadness, but says proudly that her college is more than a century old. Her pupils, in their mid-teens, come from all over this poor region.

They stand up hesitantly as I enter: fifteen shy faces, mostly girls. They are plainly dressed in jeans, in black, and have fringes and utilitarian topknots. They can hardly speak English at all. I talk slowly and clearly, but they do not understand. Nor, often, does the teacher. We revert to Russian, which she reinterprets into pidgin English. I ask them their ambitions: to go on to university, perhaps, to become engineers, doctors, nurses. But nobody answers. At last a stout, humorous boy – the class joker – says he wants to be a billionaire. They would have to pay for university, the teacher says, and their parents cannot. Maybe one or two will go part-time, while working. It will be very hard.

So what will they do after they leave? I ask. Blank silence, again. Several of them look wan and undernourished. One girl wears a surgical mask. The teacher answers that they might work in kindergartens one day. Then a gaunt youth pipes up: 'We boys must go into the army for a year.'

Of course. I had clean forgotten. And a year can seem very long. It lies like a trench between a teenager and any future.

I realize now that I have arrived as if from aerospace, with my talk of selecting one profession over another, or of getting to university. They come from poor villages, the teacher later tells me. They would be lucky to find jobs at all. Their parents are probably out of work. Even in Sretensk there is no work: just some administration, and the police. And of course their parents drink. I feel belatedly ashamed. I had imagined other lives for them. When I ask them, a little despairingly, if they'd like to go abroad, the faces go empty again. Only the stout boy says he was once in Georgia, in the high mountains, and by the sea. Nobody else has ever seen a sea.

He and one other – a red-haired youth with restless eyes – are trying to engage me. They scramble together some English from their mobile phones. Then they ask in chorus: 'Where are the prettiest girls?'

Perhaps I am trying to unsettle their thoughts a little, or divert nationalism, when I answer brusquely: 'India, Italy.'

The trickle of laughter that had started dies away. I sense a vague affront. The ginger-haired boy says: 'What about our Russian girls?'

I am not enjoying this. 'They are beautiful too,' I say. But when I stare around, I realize how cosmetic looks can be, and how beauty may be withheld by poverty, by diet. A minute later a pale girl gets up and excuses herself, because she has to feed her baby. She looks fifteen.

But I hear my own voice brighten with hope as I ask: 'What do you do in the evenings? On weekends?'

'I go for a walk sometimes,' says a thin-faced girl with freckles. She smiles dreamily. She likes animals, she says, she likes countryside. The land downstream to Ust-Karsk, where I am going, is beautiful. She has been there twice. The other girls say they listen to music – they name some Western pop groups which I don't recognize. Sometimes there is a disco in a local village, but this is rare. All their world seems to come through the internet, on the little phones they cradle in front of them: their music, their friends, their intermittent news.

The schoolteacher, in parting, is embarrassed for all of them. 'Occasionally a student arrives with better English,' she says, 'and it's always from the same village. There must be a good primary-school teacher, isolated out there.' She herself had studied at Chita University, but she was always shy, she says. Once two American teachers had visited and she could not understand them at all. Her whole class was struck dumb.

I feel I have done no better by her students. She says the world is letting them down. As for Sretensk, it is dead. There are mayoral elections today, and her husband, another policeman, is supervising a ballot out of town. But one mayor is like another.

Ruefully I start back to my hotel, circling through a hinterland of deserted flat-blocks. The town's population has halved in less than thirty years. Faded graffiti survive on the balconies of buildings ruined long ago. 'Beloved Larissa only you . . .' I pass the war memorial in Lenin's square, where the names of the dead, for so small a region, read in their terrible hundreds. In my hotel the smell of police lingers. This is the saddest after-effect of their coming: the revulsion or confusion in the gaze of others. The grey-eyed receptionist, so friendly before, no longer meets my eye. And the feeling dissipates only after time, that you are now the enemy. In the street you flinch at the sound of sirens, and become nervously aware of anybody walking behind you. You avert your face from police cars as they pass.

I want to leave now. I am relieved when the passenger boat appears next morning, small and distant on the river. I embark with the old women, unquestioned, and feel an old exhilaration as the boat reverses from the shore and points eastward. A cool autumn wind is blowing, and we settle in the seats below deck. I gaze out through clouded windows. High on the near bank, just under the police station, half concealed by trees, I glimpse a figure in dark blue, which tentatively raises its hand. I think it is Medusa.

5

The Lost Fortress

As it leaves the mild lands of Dauria, the Shilka enters a deep solitude. To the north the massif of the Yablonovy mountains stretches a thousand miles towards the Pacific, while low, broken ranges, shadowing the Chinese border, close in from the south. The roads along the river turn to tracks, then the tracks peter out. The Shilka becomes a deep, olive-green corridor. Its banks unfold in plunging curtains of forest, where the birch trees billow and turn gold, and larches blacken the skyline. It has a dense, hypnotic beauty. Sometimes the hills descend to the waterline in slabs of fissured granite, whitening as they reach the shore, and splashed with orange lichen.

The boat moves faster than the current. Its passengers are mostly sturdy women with worn luggage and sleepy children. From a raised cabin to the fore the captain follows the winding river under a thundery sky. Far off, where the surface flattens to dull silk under converging banks, the river gives the illusion of reaching an end, as if we were sailing an enclosed sea. Grey herons wait among the reeds, and flocks of cormorants fly fast along the shoreline, or settle on rocks to shake out their wings.

Once or twice we pass a log village where a path ascends towards some track back to Sretensk and the world. And once we grind our prow into the shore and a woman clambers overboard and heaves away her shopping bags to a near-deserted hamlet. Here and there the slopes open on a valley soft with trees, and I gaze into its wild beauty and understand the man beside me, who teaches drawing in the little settlement of Shilkinsky Zavod. His work is happy, he says; he is newly married. He would go nowhere else.

The captain notices a foreigner and beckons me to sit beside him. I stare out from the panoramic curve of his windscreen as it starts to speckle with rain. He is bluff and imperturbable. Yes, the river is fast-flowing and mined with shallows, he says, but he has been working it for thirty-eight years. 'I know my way by heart now.' The boat's draught is shallow, but from time to time he still crosses to the steeper shore. His co-skipper – a small, nervous man – interjects: 'It's very dangerous.'

'And what do people do in these villages?' I ask.

'They don't do anything.'

'Do they fish?' In all my journey I had seen no fishermen.

The captain laughs. 'Only the herons and cormorants go fishing.'

His dashboard looks half defunct, above a few simple gears. The ship's clock stopped long ago, and his prime possession is a Swiss watch. Every ten kilometres the black figures on white shoreside plaques tell our distance from the Chinese frontier. We are still two hundred miles away.

It must have been somewhere here, in 1692, that Ysbrants Ides, ambassador of Peter the Great to the Emperor of China, heard of a mysterious people who came annually from islands lying close offshore in an unnamed sea. They were a tall, bearded race, splendid in silks and fur overcoats, he wrote, and 'they come in small Barks to the Siberian Tartars, and buy girls and women of them, of which they are very fond, giving for them rich sables and black fox-skins.' But nothing was ever heard of these strangers again.

We are only 1,600 feet above sea level, yet still more than 2,000 river-miles from the Pacific. In a month's time, the captain says, the Shilka will start to freeze, and by January you can drive a truck along it. Soon his job will close down until late spring. The mid-winter temperature can drop to −40°F. 'Then what do we do? We just grow beards and carry on living as usual. It's no problem. People help one another here. It's not like in the cities.'

The yellowing clouds have broken now, and gusts of rain are splattering the windscreen in hard, bright beads. 'It rains like London,' the captain says. 'Just like London.' His knowledge comes from reading Dickens as a schoolboy. 'And fog.'

The river is misting to a white aisle in front of us, but closer at hand, scaling the hillsides, the silver birch trees still shine amber and green, and here and there a Siberian maple flames red. We are entering a region that was once less deserted than now. Over a century ago, where the cliffs recede at Shilkinsky Zavod, the huts had straggled several miles along the shore, and on the northern bank stood the grim hulks of smelting works, where barges could be built, with the offices of the imperial gold mines. It was a country of exiled convicts, criminal and political, who lived in plague-ridden prison barracks. The brutal mining regime closed down at the end of the nineteenth century, and now the deserted shores and ghost villages, dotting the waterway to a forbidden China, exist at the wrong end of history.

As the rain intensifies, the captain murmurs 'London, London' to himself. But he disdains even Moscow, where he has never been, along with any ideas of a metropolis. 'Why would I want to go?' He waves at the trees. 'These are my city.'

By evening the cliffs have paled from granite to limestone, and the northern shore is serried with the domes of low, shaven hills. We reach our end at the village of Ust-Karsk, where a youth hammers iron pinions into the earth, securing the boat for its return tomorrow, and the captain calls out, 'Goodbye, London!' and points me to a dim-lit café in the dusk.

At the hub of every Siberian village, in a bare canteen or hostel, there presides someone – generally a gruff matriarch – who commands a store of local knowledge and advice. And now Irina, raucous, blondish and benign, views me with momentary astonishment, then says there's no such thing as a hostel in the place, but she knows where there are beds. Her restaurant looks too big for its clientele: a gaunt void which a few habitués cross to buy vodka. But I accumulate a swarm of wondering young men, bellowing greetings, firing questions, shouting for drinks. There is a roguish one who declares himself my best friend, a baby-faced giant with a vodka bottle, a gangling enthusiast invisible under his moth-eaten aviator's cap, a hooligan with a limp, and a silent, long-faced youth, quieter than the rest. They wonder what a Westerner – the first they've met – can be doing here. Am I an American? Am I a gold-miner? A spy? Perhaps I am lost. They themselves want to leave. They have dead-end jobs, or none at all. They clamour for my email address (but they will never write). They pester me to send them books. They only release me when the restaurateur's teenage daughter arrives in a decrepit van to drive me away.

We crash down a rutted track for seeming miles. Our headlights waver over pools of recent rain. There is no other light. At a building in an overgrown orchard, a soft-spoken woman is waiting with a key, and I enter a dormitory of three iron beds. No one explains whose home this is, and I am too tired to ask. As the woman departs, I curl under threadbare blankets, and listen to the silence. The curtainless window frames a rectangle of darkness, hung with a sickle moon. I feel the engulfing solitude of where I am, and with it a sensation of lightness, as if I had sloughed a skin, while I drift into sleep.

But I wake near midnight to hear heavy feet tramping in the passageway. When I peer out, the woman with the key is dithering in the doorway of another room, and in the corridor, where a single light bulb hangs, an officer of the Federal Security Border Guards is facing me, his booted feet astride. His face is obscured under its peaked cap. It is a few seconds before he speaks, and in this blink of time, with sick recognition, I foresee my journey come to an end. Of course, I think, it was always a pipe dream. I stare at him with this bitter understanding. The woman gestures to the room beside mine, where he will stay. Tomorrow he will escort me back to Sretensk, I think, where Medusa has been overruled, and I will be transferred to Chita, then perhaps to England. I wonder how they traced me here. Perhaps one of the restaurant youths reported my presence – they who had cajoled me with requests for email and books. I suspect the silent one.

All this oversweeps my mind in the seconds before the border guard removes his cap. Then I see an elderly, dishevelled face with forlorn eyes. He looks a little drunk. His battledress is hopelessly crumpled.

He says: 'May I have a cup of tea?'

He is just another dormitory guest like me. The woman looks at me with mute apology. 'Do you mind?' He gropes his way into the room beside mine, and I go out to walk in the dying orchard, eased into silent laughter. A cold wind is blowing. Half the dogs of Ust-Karsk are competing with antiphonal howls, and the young moon is shining in the river. All night, in the room beside mine, the border guard watches the ancient television, and slouches away through the puddles at dawn, his cap askew on his head.

Now I realize that I have been sleeping in the annex to the village library. In a room beyond mine I glimpse the ageing books stacked up in lonely ranks. The librarian returns, and we sit beside them and share a breakfast of black bread and cherry jam. There are over two thousand volumes here, she says, with all the Russian classics. A photograph of Solzhenitsyn hangs on one wall. She is proud of her English editions in Russian translation: Walter Scott, Mark Twain, a stray copy of William Golding's *The Inheritors*, and a complete set of Dickens, published in Moscow in 1960. I wonder who ever comes here to peruse her tended shelves and little catalogues. 'Pensioners, mostly,' she replies, 'but sometimes a student too.' I wander up and down the stacks, astonished that they exist in this stricken backwater. They are survivors from the Soviet era, of course, and scarcely replenished since.

'Those were good times,' she says.

The river will carry me no farther. The Chinese frontier is barely fifty miles away as the crow flies. Beyond here a wildlife refuge seals off the Shilka from intrusion, sequestering its old-growth forest from Chinese logging, and preserving the Amur as the longest undammed river in the Eastern Hemisphere.

I find a man to drive me north along a mountain road towards the Trans-Siberian Railway, which converges on the river far to the east. In his shaky hybrid car – a Renault engine inside a Russian body – we leave Ust-Karsk over flooded tracks. This is still gold-bearing country, and the domes of a new-built church shed a gilded blaze over the colourless village. We climb into an autumn sea of bronze that rolls unbroken against the sky. Deep beneath us the swollen waters of the Kara tributary glitter and vanish. Our road has turned to mud. Once or twice, far below, we glimpse an antiquated structure that still thrusts its gold-panning shed into the torrent.

The stockaded prisons and convict huts that once scattered this valley have rotted away, but through most of the nineteenth century several thousand prisoners worked the goldfields that were the personal property of the Czar. The men's terms of imprisonment were hopelessly long, and even at their end they remained in forced exile, so that every decade, from this valley alone, up to four thousand ex-convicts were discharged into Siberia. Others would not wait so long. As in Stalin's vaster, more atrocious camps, the call of the cuckoo, announcing the start of spring, tempted men desperate to escape. But at Kara they were fleeing into an unpeopled wilderness, and few who joined 'the army of General Cuckoo' survived.

Now, for miles, we see no building at all, except a memorial to Red partisans killed in the Revolution: a solitary column in the forest valleys. It is two hours before we crest the Shilkinsky massif, and a new watershed begins. At the head of the pass a clump of birch trees flutters with votive rags. The driver delves into a packet that he keeps for the purpose, and throws some kopecks into the trees, murmuring a prayer for the safety of our journey. I wonder if this crossing place belongs to a leftover spirit, as in Buryatia, but the driver does not know. An Orthodox cross swings above his dashboard. This place has no name that he recalls, and no presiding saint or genie. He is praying to God.

We descend through woodlands shivering with ferns and purple undergrowth, and towards noon, bursting from a time warp, we hit the only road that crosses Siberia. Ten years ago the 1,700-mile stretch between Chita and Vladivostok – the last to be completed – was a bone-shaking gravel track, buckled by permafrost and swimming in mud. This, in turn, had replaced the centuries-old *Trakt*, which saw the pitiful shuffle eastward of convicts in chains, sometimes with their families trudging pathetically behind, along with travellers' horse-drawn carts, carriages and sledges that often came to grief. Now the new Amur Highway – a modest, two-lane artery – is almost empty of traffic. I see only army trucks and a few closed lorries that carry contraband from China, and drugs, the driver says. But he has become morose. He is angry with his wife for something I do not understand. After a while we see the slow giants of the Trans-Siberian Railway crossing the land to our north. At the first working station we eat a hefty meal of sausages and potatoes, and I embark at last for the town of Skovorodino.

Across all eastern Siberia the railway and the highway move in tandem, while the Amur shadows them to the south. Little inside the train has changed since my journeys twenty years ago: the same slippery berths, the jammed windows, the stench of urine, and the distinctive motion of the high carriages that gently, soporifically bounce. The sheets and towels, however, are no longer dispensed by the dragonish *provodnitsa* of my memory, but by a young attendant with pink-framed spectacles and encroaching smile-lines. In my compartment sit three young soldiers longing to finish their service on Sakhalin island and find civilian jobs. Sakhalin is brutal, they say, with snow six feet deep in winter, and roving bears. A soldier they knew was mauled to death. They look gaunt and delicate, with soft, tattooed arms.

Now the train settles to a hollow, rhythmic panting. Cantilever bridges carry us over the floods of new rain. In the September dusk the taiga drifts unchanging past our window at a slumbersome thirty miles per hour. The few carved-out pastures and vegetable patches look transient in this vast, breathing forest: one fifth of the earth's woodland. For a long time we follow the Uryum tributary flowing west as we climb the other way. Shallow ranges thrust against our track in walls of trees where nothing stirs. It will be dawn before we reach

Skovorodino, and we will have crossed the border between Siberia proper and the Russian Far East.

A slow night descends. Our compartment door fails to lock, and we become prey to the flotsam of bored youths who roam the corridors. For hours they barge in, begging cigarettes or the use of a mobile phone. The soldiers give in at first, then their faces close down. The most insistent intruder – a blond, bare-chested drunk – importunes me to join him drinking in the passage. 'Why will no one drink with me?' Long after I feign sleep he thrusts his head against mine. 'Why won't anyone . . . ?' Then he lurches away and we all fall into our interrupted dreams.

These are desultory nights. You wake to unlit platforms where the train has gone silent, and nobody gets on or off. Your companions mutter in their sleep. The Chinese border is moving up from the south. You feel it in the dark, like an incoming tide. Beyond the blackened mountains, forty miles away, in a long-prohibited zone, the Shilka meets the Argun river tracking in northward, and here they start flowing together as the Amur, and for over a thousand miles become the divide between Russia and China. In my half-sleep I anticipate crossing the border and travelling along the Chinese shore almost to the Pacific; but those unknown roads bring a now-familiar mingling of excitement and apprehension, and hours later I wake to the first light shining through the unchanged forest, and wonder where I will be stopped.

Skovorodino is not a lovely town. A short way off its drab main street, the roads wander into squalid suburbs and near silence. Behind its iron doors and pinched windows, only flaking shop signs – 'Ludmilla', 'Yulia' – tell that a food store may be open. Soviet slogans glorifying work are still set indelibly in its brickwork, and banners celebrating the anniversary of the end of the Great Patriotic War, hung up five months earlier, sag above municipal offices. The biggest buildings belong to the railway, for which the town was founded, and to the pump station that tunnels crude oil to China and the Pacific.

Two decades ago, in the declining Yeltsin years, I had left here on a side-track to the Chinese frontier, undetected. Now a draconian permit is required. When I apply brazenly to the Federal Security Service, descendant of the KGB, they promise a decision within an unspecified time, and no sure outcome. For an old paranoia haunts this frontier zone. A whole culture grew up around its defence. Enemy infiltrators were perceived to lurk everywhere. At first they were Japanese, then they became Chinese, until at last spies and saboteurs festered in the national psyche, the more insidious for being nameless. Only the vigilance of heroic border guards preserves the motherland from subversion. They have their own insignia, and sing their own anthem. And Stalin's fear survives in the longest fortified frontier on earth: 1,100 miles of barbed wire and raked soil.

The border village of Albazin, where I mean to go, holds a special place in this dark firmament. It was Russia's first, stubborn bulwark in the territory, staking out Moscow's earliest claim to the Amur. After the decimation of its Cossack defenders in 1686, its surrender was sealed at the Treaty of Nerchinsk, which confirmed China's possession of the Amur river for ever. For the few Russians who reach it, Albazin is heady with martyrdom and loss, eased by the triumph of eventual reconquest. But it is a reminder, too, of Russia's old fragility in the region. The humiliating Treaty of Nerchinsk is rarely spoken of, and in Russia commemorated nowhere.

For three days I wait in Skovorodino, in a seedy hotel run by two Armenian men. They keep to their national culture: sipping minute cups of coffee, smoking Ararat cigarettes, kissing one another at parting. My room is labelled 'luxe', although its washbasin leaks, the light bulb fails, and my window looks onto a junkyard of rusted furniture, where rats scuttle. In this cell, awaiting news that may not come, idleness grows more disheartening than hardship. I become more conscious of what may be forbidden, of my own injured body, of the coming cold. The sombre town seems more elusive than before. The surviving café where I sit is always empty. Attempted conversations peter out. Then I feel how little I understand where I am, and travel seems an exercise in failure.

But I walk at evening down the long main street, whose jaded stucco buildings start to appeal to me. The town is tranquil in its decline. Someone has planted shrubs under the boulevard trees, which glow with autumn berries. It is noon when the Security Service delivers my permit by hand to the hotel. My smile of relief startles the amiable officer. He wishes me a good journey. Two hours later, on the road to Albazin, where a mountain wall rises ahead of me, the road becomes a glacial avenue of mud. It shines smooth and perilous, and the taxi driver's hands too often leave the wheel. He has a blotched, dreamy face. He waves at the golden trees, drugged by autumn. He lives with his wife in a woodland *izba*, he says, while his daughters occupy a flat in suburban Skovorodino. He thinks them insane.

The next moment he has braked too suddenly, and the car is gliding noiselessly out of control down the glazed track. It performs a shuddering circle, then plunges us into a ditch. Our landing is so soft we might have sunk into treacle. The car is pitched forward on its front wheels. We clamber out unhurt, and stack larch branches under the chassis, but the car only sinks deeper.

'I've been on the road for thirty-one years,' the driver groans, 'and I've never had an accident before.' I suppress my surprise. He beats his forehead. But in half an hour a burly farmer appears in a giant tractor. He tows us back onto the road and drives away without a word. 'That's how things are here,' the cab driver says triumphantly. 'This is Siberia!'

A pair of gates – wonky frames of barbed wire twelve feet high – span the road a few miles on. The guards emerge from a blockhouse, grin at our mud-caked figures, then scrutinize my permit, return to their computers, and at last drag the shaking barrier apart. For half a mile an angry dog keeps pace with us. We drive on through the broken-looking village of Zhalinda, where no one is in sight. The sun shines for the first time in a week. And suddenly the Amur is below us, grown wider now, and on its far side, in a dense tapestry of forest, lies China. The birch trees burn in every shade of gold, red and emerald. The only sound is the graveyard clamour of crows, perched on the treetops like weathervanes, all looking south.

As we approach the scattered cottages of Albazin, I remember its half-abandoned fields and pastures, unchanged from twenty years ago. I remember too a woman of almost ninety, Agrippina Doroskova, who had come to embody, in her angry frailty, the region's Cossack memory and fading presence. In 1854 her grandfather had descended the Amur with the implacable governor Nikolai Muraviev, as he bloodlessly regained the river for Russia. She was composing a four-volume history of Albazin, she told me, in which the first years of Communism were a lost utopia, and even Stalin forgiven, whose Terror had all but liquidated the men of the town. Two black-framed government stars above her cottage doorway had honoured her brother and sister, killed in the Great Patriotic War. Surviving into the last Yeltsin years, she was obsessed by the threat of a ravening West poised to undermine her homeland, and raucously proclaimed the power of the proletariat to restore to Russia a near-mystical greatness.

I remember she had collected a hoard of local artefacts: old weapons, fishing tackle, domestic antiques, even some skeletons. She hoped they would one day be housed in a true museum, and now, to my astonishment, we find this in its own stockaded compound: a small palace of polished logs and new tiles, crowned by Russia's imperial eagle. On its wall hangs a plaque in Doroskova's honour – she had died in 2002 – from which her carved features gaze out with a benevolence I do not remember.

A short way beyond, high above the river, I come upon the semblance of a long-disused playing field. Its big quadrilateral is fringed by earthen banks now blurred in grass, and only a substratum of loose-laid stones betrays, here and there, that this was once a fortress. My driver has never heard of it. He was always poor at history, he says, before returning home.

I slide down the earthworks into the enclosure. Russet leaves are drifting from the surrounding oaks. If there is any structure underfoot, it is smoothed away under the grass. In this stark void, a mortuary chapel and a high black cross stand alone.

The two empires that clashed at this distant frontier, three years before the Treaty of Nerchinsk, were profoundly alien to one another. The Cossacks who manned Albazin, like Yerofei Khabarov's freebooters before them, were anarchic frontiersmen whom the horrified Manchu Chinese described as cannibal demons. They were so far from Moscow that a message might take a year en route. The Manchus colonized the Amur as earlier Chinese dynasties had done, less by military occupation than by exacting tribute from local tribes to a distant emperor. Peking lay closer to Albazin than Moscow did, yet it was still a thousand miles across wild country, and the Manchus advanced to the siege cautiously, extinguishing the smaller Cossack outposts along the Amur until only Albazin remained.

Their forces so vastly outnumbered the Russians that the Cossack leader, Alexis Tolbuzin, was forced to surrender. The Chinese permitted his garrison's departure with their families and possessions, but within two months the Cossacks broke faith, returned and rebuilt their fort more strongly than before. Its earthwork of compacted loam and tree roots rose twenty feet high above hidden pits mined with iron spikes. Artillery mounted on a raised platform pivoted in any direction, and bags of resin, hung above the ramparts, could be lit against night attack.

In July 1686 the enraged Manchu reappeared beneath the walls. They arrived in 150 barges up the Amur, towing 8 others stacked with cannon and ammunition. Methodically they circled the fort in a triple rampart of artillery. Tolbuzin faced them with 826 fighters, 12 cannon and a heavy arsenal of powder and hand grenades. Six times the Manchu charged the walls in a storm of cannonfire and incendiary arrows, wheeling huge, leather-bound shields to the palisades, where they piled firewood and inflammatory resin. Each time they were beaten back.

But no relief came. The river swarmed with Chinese craft, and a Manchu command post, circled in its own walls, was set up on the island whose willow-choked shores I could see through the mist. Twenty years ago in winter, as I probed the fort rampart with frozen fingers, a fragment of burnt wood had trickled into my hands with a musket ball that had missed its mark. Now I find nothing.

It was less the Manchu attacks, in the end, that subjugated Albazin, than the disease that raged through its garrison. Once, mockingly, the Cossacks sent out to the Manchu a giant meat pie, to persuade them that no one was starving. But in reality, by November, there were only 66 Cossacks left alive, Tolbuzin was dead, and half the survivors would soon perish of fever and starvation. The Kangxi emperor had never truly understood why these red-bearded barbarians clung so stubbornly to what was not theirs, and when Russian envoys reached Peking, opening the way to peace, he ordered his generals to hold back. During a six-month stand-off, scurvy and dysentery ravaged both camps. The doctors whom Kangxi sent out treated Russians and his own men alike. But by the time the Manchu returned, scarcely twenty defenders remained, and Albazin itself, after the Treaty of Nerchinsk, was levelled to the ground.

Inside the mortuary chapel I see two long mounds of earth, edged with stones. Above rows of withered carnations, an inscription salutes the nameless defenders beneath. The bones that had been reburied here three years before were discovered in dug-outs beyond the walls: mass graves where the dead sometimes lay in tiers, with iron crosses still on their chests. But most, it seems, had died without Orthodox rites. No priest survived the final siege. Eight years earlier, after makeshift graves were first uncovered, pilgrims from outlying villages had come on foot to witness the belated benediction of priests over the corpses in an all-night vigil. The bodies were buried under the stark black cross, along with those skeletons that had been lying around in Doroskova's hoard. But for several years afterwards the ground went on yielding up its dead. At last they were heaped together, many skeletons to a coffin – too late, now, to discriminate between them. Bishops and priests in sky-blue dalmatics lifted above them the icon of the Madonna they had revered. Then a Cossack guard of honour shouldered them to their long-delayed rest in the little chapel where I stood. Meanwhile an obsessed Cossack patriot constructed a raft complete with cannon, and floated it hundreds of miles down the Ingoda and along the Amur, stopping to honour every site where a Cossack fort had stood, and ending at Albazin.

From the vanished fort you might imagine this frontier war continued. The whole border with China is hermetically sealed. The steel watchtower above me stands empty, but when I look south I see, mile after mile, the gibbet-like posts linked in barbed wire, with their ribbon of raked earth to betray footprints, snaking into the distance. Along the Amur this 'control tracking lane' moves for over a thousand miles. Only where the bank steepens and the river flows a hundred yards below, do I walk over a debris of rusted wires whose posts have tilted askew or fallen. Their white insulators scatter the undergrowth, long defunct. At this height, under the village, the fence has been left to decay. On the far shore, deep into its hills, rise the domes of a Chinese oil refinery, linked to a pipeline that travels beneath the river.

I turn back to where the museum dreamed by Agrippina Doroskova stands among fallen leaves. In its grounds are a reconstructed Cossack farmstead, a Cossack chapel, a flour mill and a cosy *izba*, with a child's cot and toys, a samovar and pretty pictures, evoking a life from which all brutality and dirt have been airbrushed. But inside, the museum becomes an anthem to Cossack heroism. Its entrance blazes with a violent and romantic picture of the siege during some imaginary last day, in which the hirsute warriors, with their Madonna's icon held aloft, battle like gods under the flaming turrets of their doomed fort. In nearby showcases lie the leftovers of their war and burial: a scorched powder-horn, an axe head, some shredded belts, many little pectoral crosses, and the half-rotted plaits from the tight-bound hair of their women.

The curator is proud and solicitous. I am alone here – her first Westerner in months – but I am making obscure requests. From her archives she finds a snapshot of Chinese visitors: six businessmen whose wives are cowled in Orthodox headscarves.

They have Russian names, and one is holding an icon. Yet they look entirely Chinese. They are the descendants of Cossack defectors at the time of the siege, the curator says; they opted to join the Manchus rather than go back home. Why they did so is unsure. Perhaps they feared reprisal for crimes, or wanted to keep the native wives who might have been denied them in Russia.

The return of these 'Peking Albazinians' – their yearning for some long-past belonging – touches the curator with confusion. Some of their ancestors were prisoners, but most had deserted. They may have numbered a hundred or more. In Peking they became the nucleus of a separate company in the Imperial Bodyguard. They lived in the old city near the Eastern Gate, and were given female criminals to marry. They had a Russian priest and consecrated their own church, once a Lamaist temple, which they furnished with salvaged icons. With time and intermarriage, they lost their Russian looks and language. Travellers described them as godless drunkards. Yet the memory of their origins lingered. Their church transformed into an Orthodox mission that lasted into the twentieth century – as late as the 1920s it held Albazinian nuns – until other pieties – Bolshevism, Maoism – swept it away. Then the church became the garage of the Soviet embassy, before reverting to a tiny congregation.

The curator shows me the photo of a pretty young Chinese woman gazing at a showcase whose artefacts I cannot make out. 'She came a few months ago.' The young woman's expression is so passive – the ghost of a frown – that I cannot tell if it hides fascination or puzzlement. What can it mean to encounter these objects so estranged from her own: the illegible script, the fire-blackened grains of barley, the musket dropped in death by some far-distant relative?

With its sabres and medals from later centuries, the museum's history then departs altogether from her own. On one wall I come upon the prison photographs of Cossacks killed under Stalin. They face the camera in convicts' clothes with number tags. They look wretched and bewildered. Some have already been tortured. Doroskova had described these haggard innocents to me as ordinary villagers – farmers and tradesmen – yet their execution as somehow pardonable. And nearby is a cabinet devoted to her work: her typewriter, her manuscript, and a single yellowing treatise which is all that was published – I feel a writer's pang – of the four volumes she was planning.

Outside the museum Doroskova's grandson Alexei sits in the sun. He must have heard that a foreigner has come, and he has rigged himself up in the ceremonial uniform of the Amur Cossacks: an olive-green jacket with silver shoulder tabs, yellow-striped breeches and a toppling sheepskin hat. Even before I reach him, he calls out the Cossack greeting, *'Slava Bogu!'*, 'Glory to God!' I clasp a big, soft hand. His pinprick grey eyes are stranded in a huge, circular face, and his neck and chins overlap his military collar in serried folds. He might have stepped out of pantomime. 'So you knew Agrippina Nikolaevna!' He is aflame with pride. He speaks of his grandmother as if she were a ferocious saint, and when he says 'The Cossacks are coming back!' his voice is the echo of hers.

'Things are returning to where they should be.' He glances at the sky, as if God had organized this. 'For a long time our people have been forgotten. But we are strong, we will always return. Did you see the head in the museum? The reconstructed Cossack head? We were once immense people! Giants!'

'I saw it.' The plastic head was of average size, I thought, but oddly idealized. It resembled a Greek philosopher.

'They got that from studying Cossack skulls. Many were dug up. And in the end the skeletons were buried again in glory! Three years ago we had a ceremony here . . .'

Yes, I had seen the photographs in the museum: the Cossack guard bearing immense coffins, the gold-embroidered bishop in his globular mitre, and Alexei too, clutching a banner with the Russian tricolour against his sloping stomach beside a wobbly rank of child cadets.

'We must never forget! And now our schoolchildren are learning their traditions again. I am the Cossack ataman for this district, and I am teaching them. Even the girls are learning to cook porridges and fish soup like our soldiers did.' He caresses his stomach. 'Our farms too – the soil is already rich here. We're forming collectives, making plans . . .'

Yet I had seen only overgrown fields and ramshackle homesteads. Even in the nineteenth century the Cossacks had been reckoned poor farmers.

But Alexei is rushing on. 'We must repopulate our Amur villages, because our country may call on us again. What do we know of China? We must honour our dead, who fought them, and all the fighters who brought Russia to the Amur. Those were great days, great men. We were born warriors!' He will never acknowledge their atrocities, of course. Instead they are the heroes of a God-ordained empire. 'Soon we'll rebuild our fort here, just as it was. And we'll be patrolling our borders again. Those frontier guards are not enough. Russia needs us!' He thrusts out his enormous chest. It is speckled with the medals that the Cossacks bestow on each other. He fingers them one by one: the order of the Albazin Madonna from a local bishop (awarded for attending jubilees), the Order of the Cossack cavalry general Platonov, various papery decorations printed with horses and crosses, and a black and orange ribbon to celebrate the Great Patriotic War, which he pins on me.

'Even Stalin feared us. He was more scared of us than he was of Hitler! And rightly. We were stronger, braver. And older than Communism.'

A pair of gardeners wanders past to tend the museum grounds. '*Slava Bogu!*' he shouts. They respond with cursory nods. 'People ask if we can guard our borders, but every Cossack does it without thinking. Those men, and the whole village, they will have taken note of you, even if you didn't see them.'

I want to soften him now, try a joke. Perhaps he will suddenly laugh. In that blustering face I find no hint of his grandmother's manic force and anger. He looks oddly innocent.

'The borders don't need guarding now,' I say, unsure. 'Russia and China are at peace.'

His fists clench. 'But we have to be prepared. Always! The Chinese can't be trusted.' Patrolling the frontier has become a need in itself. Peace threatens it. 'We can never be sure.' His face quivers under its black fleece. The papery medals shake. 'Never.'

Yet Russia's rulers have always been wary of the Cossacks, whose semi-independence carried threat. They were not an ethnically separate people, but a far-flung network of militarized frontiersmen, bandits and fugitives, free of authority. They came to compose some of the most ruthless regiments in the imperial armies, and many sided with White forces during the Revolution, and were later broken by Stalin. Now President Putin was using them cautiously, as paramilitaries on Russia's western borders, and as keepers of order.

Alexei is hoping for a revival on his border too. He drives me about Albazin in his Lada, honking and waving, and it is hard to tell if the stray pedestrians, wanly responding, find him genially patriotic or a little ridiculous. He drives me a mile upriver to an empty clearing in the silver birch forest. Only a commemorative cross marks the place of a church. He takes off his hat in veneration. Beneath its shaggy mass he is completely bald.

'There was once a huge basilica here,' he says. 'I've seen photographs. Nothing left now except a few stones. But it was magnificent. Look.' He strides across the clearing and turns to face a vanished apse. His new, shining head transforms him. 'Imagine!' He lifts his arms and conjures a cathedral from the undergrowth. 'The sanctuary was over there. Christ Pantocrator in the dome above. And it was magnificent. Destroyed in the Revolution that should never have happened. Pilgrims would stop to pray here on their way to Albazin.' Then he crosses himself fervently, this quixotic man, and speaks about a custom of remembrance in which you caress a nearby tree and pray for someone you love. I embrace a pine to please him, and he takes me on to a viewpoint above the river.

On a big boulder, gashed with pink veins, a plaque inscribed in an old Cyrillic script gives thanks for the 1858 Treaty of Aigun, confirming Russian power on the Amur. Alexei loves this place, and the great river winding below. A track descends to its bank where the barbed wire has parted. This was the path, he says, by which disembarking passengers once climbed to Albazin. Nicholas II, the last czar, had arrived here in 1891 as heir to the throne, during his journey across the Russian Far East.

'Everyone here inherited memories of that day. The entire populace lined the route to greet him. He climbed to us on a carpet of flowers!' Alexei, of course, is a royalist. 'That whole Revolution was wrong. A disaster. It should never have happened.' His grandmother, to whom Lenin was a god, would have been appalled. 'Things should have evolved more slowly. But instead . . .'

Beneath us a herd of chestnut horses is bathing in the river. They are not the stocky beasts of Mongolia, but beautiful, long-legged creatures, glistening in the fading light. They seem to soften Alexei. He gives a rueful smile. 'There aren't so many horses as before. Young people ride motorbikes now.'

We are still standing by the Aigun memorial stone when they ascend the Czar's track and canter, untended, away. I stoop to read the inscription again. The stone had been installed only five years earlier, as if in nervous assertion of something contested. Its Church Slavonic script gives it an illusion of early authority. 'That stone confirms our right to be here!'

His head is massive in its sheepskin hat again. For the first time he lets out a laugh: a curt, gruff concession. 'We took the Amur in 1858 when China was weak. Everyone was taking bits of China at that time – the French, the Americans, and you British especially.' He is grinning.

I say: 'The Chinese still believe that the Aigun treaty was forced on them.'

By the mid-nineteenth century the Manchu dynasty was no longer the power that had concluded the Treaty of Nerchinsk almost two centuries before. Predatory Western nations were wrenching concessions from a country ravaged by civil war, and Russia began dreaming of an imperial destiny to the east. After the outbreak of the Crimean War, the belligerent governor-general of East Siberia, soon to be dubbed Count Muraviev-Amursky, convinced a cautious Czar Nicholas I of the Amur's strategic value. An Anglo-French fleet was cruising near the river's mouth in the north-west Pacific.

In May 1854 Muraviev moved downriver from Sretensk with a mile-long flotilla of armed barges and rafts. He went in the *Argun*, the first steamship to sail the Amur, with eight hundred Cossacks and a battery of mountain guns, and he carried with him the rescued icon of the Albazin Madonna. As the flotilla came in sight of the desolate fort, the soldiers fell silent, the band struck up hymns, and Muraviev stepped ashore to pray in the overgrown ruins.

The Chinese outposts on the Amur could only report helplessly to a distant Peking as the fleet passed by. Muraviev was commandeering a river that had been Chinese by treaty for more than a century and a half. For four more years the intrusions continued, building up Russian strength unopposed, and by the time Muraviev forced the Chinese to the negotiating table at Aigun in 1858, the occupation of the river was a fait accompli. The Treaty of Nerchinsk was reversed. The Chinese were compelled to concede all their territory to the river's north, turning the Amur into the border between two vast but ailing empires.

By lavish promises and threatened coercion, Muraviev flailed Cossack settlements forward along the river. Often he sited and named them himself. Within a few years 120 villages emerged whose families each owned almost half a square mile of land. Muraviev became a national hero. But the cost was sometimes fearful. A Cossack officer still remembered in old age the precarious provisioning of these scattered outposts. On a relief mission east of Albazin in 1856 he encountered frost-blackened spectres of men walking in temperatures of $-47°F$, still carrying their rifles. Beyond lay the stiffened corpses of the starved, their buttocks cut away where their comrades had eaten them. Sick of tasting the dead, they had cast lots to kill and eat the living.

Once the flail of Muraviev had lifted, the Cossack settlements seldom flourished. Often their land lay fallow. They preferred soldiering and other duties. By the century's end their settlements had dwindled to forty-five. Only in Alexei's vivid certitude can I imagine their revival. Here at

Albazin, in their nostalgic heart, it is not the Cossacks but the border guards who manage things. The museum curator looks embarrassed when I mention this. 'Well, yes, there are hardly any Cossacks left in this village now. No real ones.' She laughs. 'Alexei is the leader of people who don't exist . . .'

I am offered a bed in the erstwhile Soviet House of Culture. The place is big for a village so small, and is muraled in the vision of a time that seems long ago: high-hearted workers and soldiers, wholesome women harvesting. On another wall, Cossack boats like Viking longships are weighing anchor under Albazin fort, while inscriptions praise their heroism and assign the land inalienably to Russia.

Sometimes the Culture House does duty as a school. On its miniature stage, against a backdrop of dawn rising over the Amur, I come upon small children dancing and reciting poetry, under patient tuition. Irina is the kind of teacher with whom children fall in love. She apologises for the poor accommodation here (she can't know where I've been) and I stretch out at night on the clean fold-out sofa under the clean duvet, and fall asleep beneath a notice warning children about the river ice and fireworks on New Year's Day.

Towards midnight I wake with a tingle of wonder at where I am, and appease a transient hunger with sausage and black bread from my rucksack, then wander restless into the village. The stars are shining above the miles of barbed wire tracking lane, and China rises in silhouette beyond. A solitary dog is howling. In the curtainless cottage windows the only lights are those left on from habit, or the candles that gutter beneath an icon. The Amur lies in a pale thread below. Cattle barge across my path in the dark.

On the far side of the river, where China sheds no light, I imagine little but emptiness. To the south the massif of the

Greater Khingan mountains is starting to release the Amur eastward. For over two centuries until 1906 the Manchu rulers, to whom all this region was ancestral home, had tried to prevent their Chinese subjects immigrating from the south. Beyond their guard-posts the forested valleys were home only to the Orochen tribespeople, to stray bandits and to outbreaks of illicit gold-mining.

In 1883, on a tributary across the river from Albazin, an Orochen native, digging his mother's grave, came upon seams of gold. A horde of adventurers and ex-convicts rushed in – Chinese, Russians, Germans, Poles, French, soon mounting to ten thousand – and escaped anarchy by appointing their own despotic ruler, who proclaimed them the Zheltuga Republic. They designed their own flag, printed their own currency. They built a casino and music theatre, and a free hospital. Draconian punishments coerced them: 100 lashes for drunkenness, 200 for revelling too loudly at night, 500 strokes of a whip with nails for homosexuality. A rare photograph shows a street of tall wooden shops where men walk unsmiling in Western hats and Chinese slippers.

Peking reacted late, brutally. Its soldiers expelled all foreigners, but treated the Chinese as traitors. The Russians tried to save them, in vain. Somewhere in the darkness beyond me, the town went up in flames, the rivers filled with decapitated corpses, and the four-year Zheltuga Republic ended, returning the Amur to its lonely peace.

6

The City of Annunciation

From Skovorodino the Trans-Siberian Railway follows the Amur in an immense arc south-eastward. Hour after hour you gaze out on billowing ridges of birch, oak and larch. In the alluvial soil the ancient print of elm and ginko trees betrays that the flora here was richer once, closer to that of China or Japan: vegetation that may one day return. Somewhere you cross the invisible border of permafrost in slow retreat. Huge, undrained swamplands start to encroach. Begun in 1908 under the threat of Japanese invasion, this stretch of the 6,000-mile railway was the last, and one of the hardest, to complete. The use of cheap Chinese and Korean labour was abandoned, and Russian labourers were drafted, in the hope that they would colonize the territory afterwards. The railway transformed the whole populace of the river basin. The sparse habitations of early settlers, who had created a thriving rural economy, were drowned in successive waves of poorer immigrants which continued through the disruptions of civil war, famine and collectivization.

The belching steam-engines and cattle-trucks – forerunners of the behemoth that carries me from Skovorodino – were crammed with a haggard and hopeful peasantry to whom Siberia's notorious self-reliance and disdain for bureaucracy might be welcome. Even now it is easy to imagine that the spirit of early hunters and prospectors, ex-serfs and ex-convicts, survives in the boisterous friendliness and occasional threat that barges down the train corridors in string vests and drained vodka bottles.

I share my compartment only with a slight sixteen-year-old girl whose plaited hair coils discreetly into her dressing gown. In the darkness, huddled under blankets with her mobile phone, she whispers: 'Hello, Mama. It's Alena . . . No, I'm not . . . I'll be OK . . . some sort of foreigner . . .' And in the morning she addresses me in a tiny voice: 'Could you please leave the compartment? I have to change my clothes.'

We have woken to a waterland from which the autumn lustre is fading. Across its interlacing swamp and rivers, the forests have vanished, and telegraph poles march across a louring skyline. Towards noon we approach the Zeya, the Amur's great northern tributary. Descending eight hundred miles out of the Stanovoy mountains, this was the waterway that funnelled the first Cossack invaders south, and its gentle summers, its fertile black earth and deciduous forests nourished the rumours of a rural paradise.

And here a change is beginning. Ahead of us, for some two hundred miles, the hills retreat, the meadowlands spread out, and the Amur itself starts to thicken into reefs and islands before the Lesser Khingan mountains, barging in from China, pull it tighter for another hundred miles.

Alena photographs the Zeya through our clouded windows. We are both bound for Blagoveshchensk, the second city on the Amur, and it is the first time she has been there. As we draw nearer, she grows anxious. She wants to remember everything, she says. How will she ever remember so much? Even as our train lumbers into the station, she is photographing the compartment, her bunk, the *provodnitsa*, the passageway and me – 'My first foreigner!' – so that her innocent high spirits become infectious, and I carry her excitement into the streets of Blagoveshchensk.

By Siberian standards the city is old. Founded in 1856, its population mushroomed with the discovery of gold on the Zeya, and by the turn of the century mercantile palaces were going up alongside the *izba*s. The cost of living here, wrote a British traveller in 1900, was three times that of London. For almost two months I have seen no building of architectural beauty, or any structure much older than I am. Now I walk the river promenade and streets in starved euphoria. It is as if I had known the place for a long time, although previous journeys never took me here. Stuccoed mansions in pastel colours – eggshell blue, champagne yellow – have been turned into sleepy offices, university faculties, restaurants. They stand serenely in quiet streets. Some have weathered to an Italian warmth, and make play with classical architecture in turret-capped columns and free-floating pediments. They bring a capricious pleasure. Here and there a rooftop sports an urn or statuette.

Above the river a handsome esplanade stretches for seeming miles. Its granite walls swing out under airy terraces and pavilions, and every few yards, in its wrought-iron balustrades, the twin-headed Russian eagle splays its golden wings. All is mellowness and seeming age. The parks are adrift with fallen leaves. The pavements spread a pink and grey patina underfoot, and beds of petunias are flowering in mid-autumn.

The river is less than half a mile across, and on the far side, shining like a mirage or a torment, rises the Chinese city of Heihe. In the stillness of its distance it might have been painted there. Its stark geometry gleams with the future. Here and there, out of its Cubist forest, fanciful spires and crenellations give a hint of hedonism, and the upthrust of skyscrapers – thirty, forty storeys high, still topped by cranes – seems to swell with an obsessed energy and impatience. A giant ferris wheel is twice the size of the Russian one in the park where I stand.

Thirty years ago Heihe was a small village. Today its population has overtaken Blagoveshchensk's 200,000. Yet a thick, unending parapet of trees hides any human life or traffic there. This, and the wide river, seem to seal it in its own world: less a city than a distant apparition of prosperity. At night its nearer buildings shed multicoloured curtains of light over the water, and sometimes the amplified lilt of music sounds, as if all its inhabitants were dancing.

The dawn is thin and silvery. Beside my hotel – a gaunt survivor from Soviet days – a few anglers are dangling hopeful lines from the river esplanade. Near its eastern end, beyond a park teeming with black squirrels, the broad torrent of the Zeya pours into the Amur; at its west a watchtower looms. In between, for two miles, the scattered monuments are alternately imperious and playful. There are sculpted bronze dogs that peer at China over the balustrades or stretch comically in the municipal flowerbeds. A big, scrap-metal bull straddles my path. The statue of a border guard gazes south with fixed bayonet, but his dog has been worn shiny by the caress of children. Farther on, the towering figure of Count Muraviev-Amursky, scrolled map in hand, stares across at the Chinese ferris wheel, and a rebuilt ceremonial arch, torn down under Communism, celebrates again the visit of the last czar.

A Chinese tour group assembles beneath it. They cannot read the old Cyrillic inscription along its border: 'The Amur was, is, and will always be Russian.' They are busy taking selfies against a backdrop not of Blagoveshchensk, but of their own new city over the water. A sprightly old man, here for the first time, exclaims: 'This isn't much of a place, is it? Poor, very poor.' He gestures at Heihe behind him. 'But look at us!'

For the first time the solitude of the river, where I have seen one boat in 1,400 miles, is rudely broken. It has become a human waterway. The police sloops of both nations are skimming back and forth, and Chinese patrol boats, their guns shrouded in tarpaulin fore and aft, growl closer to the Russian shore than theirs. I watch transfixed. A slow barge traffic, mostly flying Chinese flags, is carrying crates and lorries downriver, and the Heihe pleasure boats are sailing past in a cloud of music, while their loudspeakers declaim the history, indistinguishably, of the shore that was once theirs. After 1858 the Russians treated the Amur as their own, confining the Chinese to its southern bank. Only in 1986 did Gorbachev's speech at Vladivostok – a landmark of conciliation – affirm the international norm of riverine frontiers, by which the border became neither the Russian nor the Chinese shore, but the Amur's navigable channel between.

The Chinese call the Amur the Heilongjiang, Black Dragon River, for the dragon's imperial grandeur – this was the emperor's beast – and for its ancient rule over storms and floods. In years of dragonish anger or neglect, melted snows and summer monsoons inundated thousands of square miles, plunging whole communities underwater in both China and Russia, with mass evacuations and hundreds drowned.

As for the Russian name 'Amur', its origin is uncertain, except that it is not Russian at all. It survives, it seems, from the speech of indigenous peoples, and means 'Big River' or 'Kind Peace'. Today a fitful sun has turned it blue: not the blue of cloudless sky, but an indigo looking glass in which the skyscrapers of Heihe shiver and reconvene. Its flow is urged by fading summer rains, yet the river here is a mere four hundred feet above sea level and in its long unravelling to the Pacific it will drop less than four inches to the mile.

Ships of deeper draught find their westward terminus at Blagoveshchensk, where in earlier years voyagers from Sretensk might exchange their boat for one more spacious. In 1900 a resilient Englishwoman, Annette Meakin – the first known European woman to travel the Amur – left her cramped barge on the Shilka river with profound relief. In its valley of riverine beauty she had been tormented by a plague of stinging, green-headed flies, and the torrid deck gave no breath of wind. But other craft were kinder. In 1914 an Australian traveller, Mary Gaunt, relished the velvet upholstery and mahogany panelling of the *John Cockerill*, with its lunches of sturgeon, chicken, and red caviar spread 'like marmalade on a British breakfast table'. A travelling British diplomat, who took in his stride the charcoal embers belching like fireworks from his ship's funnel, complained instead about the price of cigars, while the American cleric Francis Clark, travelling on the *Baron Korff*, wrote that a thousand miles upstream the Amur waters tasted 'sweet and wholesome', and were the colour of white wine.

But in all these ships the lower-class passengers thronged in suffocated crowds on the decks, and prison barges passed like floating cages on their way to the penal colonies of Sakhalin. Anton Chekhov, on his own way there to interview its convicts, noticed a condemned wife-murderer who was being transported with his daughter, a little girl of six. The child clung to her father's fettered legs whenever he moved, and slept at night among the heaps of soldiers and prisoners beside him.

The steamship companies lost their old control under the Soviets, of course, and their riverboats sailed under other flags and purposes: the Bolshevik flotillas of the Civil War, the Chinese Nationalists and the Japanese. But in time the floating cages of convicts returned, moving to destinations far crueller than those of the Czar.

On the wall of an old commercial building overlooking Victory Square, I find a bas-relief of Chekhov. It celebrates his stay here on 27 June 1890, and its brass lineaments have been smoothed by a wash of silver paint. Wing-collared and bespectacled, he stares out with a frown of judicious insight, one forefinger to his cheek, as if the prestige of later years had precociously aged him. It is a crude echo of a well-known portrait.

But his time in Blagoveshchensk was not spent meeting dignitaries. To his mother and sister he wrote describing incidents on the river, the deplorable state of his dress, the price of things and the quaint decorum of the Chinese. But to his old friend and mentor Suvorin he confided that he had spent the time with a Japanese prostitute. She was alluringly delicate and matter-of-fact, he wrote. Speaking little Russian, she touched and pointed to things instead, while all the time laughing and making little *tsu* noises. 'She is amazingly skilled at her job, so that you feel that you are not having intercourse, but taking part in a top-level equitation class.'

Such letters were never published in Soviet times, when private licence was cloaked by public prudishness. The fantasy of great men was inviolate. The silvered face of the writer, staring out at the war memorials in Victory Square, is a mask of wise concern. But the portrait from which it derives, painted in 1898 by Osip Braz, portrays someone subtler, sadder and less readable.

If you wander along the waterfront to the ferry terminal, where the passenger boats arrive from Heihe, you will scarcely glimpse a Chinese. It is Russians who toil ashore with huge, taped-up packs of merchandise from across the river. They are carrying all the domestic stuff at whose manufacture the Chinese excel, lugging it from Chinese dealers in Heihe to Chinese marketeers in the city. These hirelings look sturdy and patient. Many are middle-aged women. A customs officer threads a drug-sniffing Labrador among them, but if their packs are opened they spill out only piles of shirts, trainers and wedges of woollen socks, with maybe a kettle or a hairdryer.

This shuttle trade between the two cities burst into life in the early 1990s, with the break-up of the Soviet Union, and became so uncontrolled that the local authorities imposed fierce restrictions on incoming Chinese. It was easier and cheaper for Russians to negotiate the border, so the Chinese began employing them as porters. Now these cross-river *chelnoki*, first known sadly as 'bricks', then 'camels', arrive in organized groups after passing through border customs often bribed in advance. They earn less than ten dollars a trip. Meanwhile the Chinese brokers and wholesalers learn to manoeuvre, circumvent and diversify through a maze of tariffs, laws and backhanders. In 2006 their Russian camels were restricted to 35 kilograms of goods per voyage, and a few months later the Chinese were barred from owning or running market stalls at all.

The central bazaar looks like a vast building site at first, where a crane idles above a billboard announcing future office blocks. Beside it a rickety barbed-wire gate leads down a path into a labyrinthine inner city. Solid alleyways of open stalls ramify and diverge over unexpected acres, each aisle concentrated on its own product, like an Asian bazaar. Sometimes the alleys disappear into echoing halls.

The booths are narrow fronted, deep. Aisles of polyester bomber jackets, sweaters woven with acrylic reindeer, canvas shoes, jeans, kitchen and electrical goods, toys and mobile phones overlap the path, all cheap, all subject to dogged bargaining. And in this unruly maze of the cut-price, the counterfeit, the mass-produced, the Chinese are everywhere. They have evaded the ban on their owning stalls by engineering partnerships with Russians. Crew-cut, hard-faced young men, strapped about with money-belts and dangling keys, inseparable from their calculators and mobile phones, they work in the back of their shops – unpacking, stocktaking – while a lethargic Russian talks to customers in front.

A middle-aged Chinese, more genial than most, presides over a stall full of sequined handbags and rows of coarse blonde wigs. Alongside him an old Russian woman, cowled like a peasant, arranges boxes of cheap nail polish. Business has plummeted in the last year, he says. But he grins at his old partner. 'Of course I have to be with her, to make it legal.' He laughs and she cackles back, as if she'd understood.

The customers are few, and buying little. Whole lanes and alleyways are empty of passers-by. I encounter a few Central Asian vendors, some Kirghiz, even a man from Dagestan in the Caucasus. And a pretty Uzbek woman, who imports Chinese goods through Tashkent, says that yes, trade is very slow, but she is getting by. Because she speaks Russian, she feels no resentment around her. That is reserved for the Chinese.

'They're everywhere, the fuckers.' The young Russian is trying to sell their bicycles. 'Beyond my stall you'll see nothing but Chinese. It doesn't matter what Putin decrees, they get around the laws . . .' Another man joins in: 'They're even worse in Heihe. Nothing but fake leather, fake furs, fake logos, fake smiles. But yes, cheap.' He himself rents a jumbled store blazoned: 'Everything home produced!' In the clothes shops all around, the printed trademarks – Adidas, Reebok, Versace – are too common to qualify as counterfeit: just factory daydreaming. Even the traditional Slavic peasant skirts and dresses, along with the T-shirts labelled 'Russia', are probably made in China.

A grim-faced woman tells me: 'Nobody likes these people. They're quite ruthless. We only work with them because we must. It's grown very hard. We can't compete with them. My own wares come from Russia, China and even Kirghizia. But nothing sells. We're poor now.'

There is a sour repetitiveness to everything I hear. That the Chinese can't be trusted. They are aggressive and sly. They work hard, but they have closed hearts. Only Slava, weeks before, had sounded dissent: 'Let them come! Perhaps they'll teach us some business skills!' But the Chinese here belong to the poorer strata of their country, and they teach nothing.

The woman points to a nearby building, huge and newly built. 'That's where they work. I think they've got factories inside. But nobody can enter . . .'

This is the private heart of the market. Trucks are disgorging containers down chutes into its basement. They must have come by rail or truck. I lope inside and find myself walking down passageways stacked to their ceilings, up echoing stairs, storey after storey, where wiry Chinese are manhandling sacks in and out of storerooms and dormitories. There is an obsessed focus on what has to be done. In this sealed world, no Chinese will ever meet a Russian, unless a customer. Each will be insulated from the other's habits and taboos, their humour and camaraderie, all the challenges of incomprehension. I reach the fourth floor before a guard orders me away. For a while I get lost in the clothes alleys again. Then out of the market, I go past the stranded shipping containers that serve as offices and bedrooms, past the old storage cabins rusting in a deserted yard, and at last past outlying babushkas trying to sell a little fruit or pickles, and into the quiet streets of the city.

*

This evening I switched on my flickering bedroom television and lighted on a Moscow news programme. Its panellists spoke ponderously for five minutes at a time. They were discussing China. They repeated the regime mantra that relations were excellent, and beneficial for both economies. Somebody praised the joint military manoeuvres which I had escaped a month before. Then, to my surprise, one of the speakers complained vehemently: China is extracting precious Russian gold, timber and oil, he said, and giving nothing back. Siberia is being plundered. The invited studio audience answered with silence. Then the host deflected the intrusion into absurdity, into laughter. The audience clapped whenever he spoke. The exchange – a choreographed illusion of free debate – ended with a clip of Putin meeting Xi Jinping: twin inscrutabilities, the Russian president flintily cordial, the Chinese leader impassively smiling.

Perhaps it is only my imagination that discovers in Putin's stony stare a wan anxiety, and in Xi's smile the condescension of China's ancient centuries. But it was Putin, soon after his inauguration as president in 2000, who warned that within a few decades, if nothing was done, the Russian inhabitants of the country's Far East would be Asian-speaking. Realizing the vast disparity between Russia's regional populace and the burgeoning Chinese millions just south of the river, government officials, academics and army generals sounded spine-chilling warnings. China was moving to world dominance, wrote a leading economist, and would eventually seize Siberia's resources. And an oft-repeated warning by demographers stated that 'China has huge territorial claims against Russia and stimulates in every possible way the penetration of her citizens into Russian territory, building a basis for their legal presence.' A prominent Sinologist contended that China saw in Russia a weakened military adversary. Underground passages beneath the border could already channel millions of Chinese northward, ran the rumours, while a leading general feared that by the middle of the century all Siberia would be lost, and China would be facing Moscow over the Urals.

As early as the 1990s the governor of the Far East province took issue with the Kremlin for its negligence, and started to act unilaterally against Chinese immigrants. The governor of Khabarovsk, the Amur's largest city, asserted that narcotics and crime poured into the province in the wake of Chinese traders, and that the whole region might be overrun.

These fears have a troubled hinterland. For thirty years until 1987 the two powers lived in strident enmity, and even now the Chinese have not formally retracted their claim to the territory seized by imperial Russia north of the Amur. Meanwhile, the imbalance of population in the great river basin has only grown. The three Russian provinces along the Amur are home to a declining populace of barely 2 million. The three Chinese provinces opposite hold almost 110 million. The old phantom of a Yellow Peril has returned. Early estimates of Chinese infiltration maintained that as many as 2 million had crossed into the Russian Far East; an eminent economist even guessed that they outnumbered the Russians.

The wilder estimates have abated, but the fear has not gone. Illegal migrants evade any statistics, people say, while an old anxiety surfaces that Moscow is far away, and has abandoned them. A few years ago a Russian documentary, *China – A Deadly Friend*, went viral on the internet. Chinese tanks, it claimed, could reach the centre of Khabarovsk within half an hour. Every Chinese migrant might be a spy. A vendor in the market – a well-dressed woman trying to sell Siberian furs – murmurs to me that the Chinese are coming back, and are everywhere. She could not tell me exactly where, because they lived unseen, waiting.

Such rumours were stoked by alarmist local newspapers: that the Chinese lurked in the forests, in closed communities, where even the extortionate police did not venture. And always they are seen not as persons, but as a composite mass. Images of insects and pollutants abound – ants, locusts. 'Small groups of a hundred thousand people each,' ran the Soviet joke, until paranoid minds perceive in them the mindless agents of Chinese state control.

But no such forest villages have ever been located. Recent statistics for the number of Chinese living in Russia's Far East assess them at a modest 30,000. The Chinese themselves are reluctant to stay: the weather is bitter, they say, the police rapacious, the people hostile. Intermarriage is rare, although some Russian women declare a preference for Chinese men, more diligent and sober than their own. Above all, with the collapse of the rouble against the Chinese yuan, business opportunities have faded. In Blagoveshchensk I hardly saw a Chinese person. There are restaurants still, and group tourists who sometimes conform to the Russian stereotype of them ('shouting, spitting, queue-barging'). Even the lines of Chinese-made public bicycles stand unused.

There is no one left to remember the Chinese migrants who from 1858 infiltrated northward across the Amur, ironically, into the territory they had just lost to Russia. But soon, in the towns which their own skills largely built – Khabarovsk, Blagoveshchensk – they numbered one third of the populace. They flocked through the dirt streets of Sretensk, where the newly arrived Annette Meakin, marvelling at their smocks and pigtails, mistook them for girls. They surged back and forth across the Amur as seasonal labourers. They worked the wretched diggings of the Zeya goldfields, and built long sections of the Trans-Siberian Railway. Their junks sailed the river with vital grain and merchandise. The whole region became deeply dependent on them. Indolent Russian townsmen, it was said, lived in Chinese-built houses filled with Chinese servants, ate imported Chinese food and sipped Chinese tea, while their wives flaunted Chinese-tailored dresses.

The fear of these Chinese foreshadowed that of a later time, and there were similar attempts to curb their enterprise. They never assimilated as Korean migrants did. In some areas they became all but self-governing, with their own exclusive guilds, even law courts. A British traveller described them in the windswept streets of Khabarovsk as 'crowds of weak, withered-faced, slouching men, who shrank to one side' when a Russian approached. They were accused of sabotaging the region with their imports of opium and China-brewed vodka. The writer and explorer Vladimir Arseniev, among others, argued ardently for Russian protection against 'the yellow domination', whose usury was reducing indigenous peoples, and even Cossacks, to slavery.

Yet the Chinese were the lifeblood of the Amur, and more sophisticated Russians regarded them with bemused ambivalence. Their fracturing empire was seen as the ruin of a stagnant despotism, yet of a unique and timeless culture too. Karl Marx, the notional father of a future Chinese Communism, conceived the country as a hermetically sealed mummy, which would disintegrate with exposure to the fresh air.

Then in 1937–38 Stalin slaughtered or deported almost the whole Chinese population on suspicion of their being Japanese spies, and for half a century there set in a long, slow forgetting that they had ever existed.

Today's economic penetration arouses an old apprehension. The Chinese remain profoundly alien. Almost no local Russians learn their language or travel their hinterland. Yet the Chinese they see are no longer the flotsam of a failed empire, but the citizens of a formidable nation. The concentration of Russia's power in faraway Moscow underlines an unease that the country's East is drifting away. Although few people fear sudden invasion, an anxiety exists – a subdued fatalism – that in some unknown future Beijing will transform its economic ownership into political sovereignty, and that the Russian Far East will become a Chinese province.

The fear of this stealthy takeover may be rooted in an unspoken apprehension of how China works. Even in their languages the concept of a border subtly differs. The Russian *granitsa* describes a boundary as specific as any in the West, but the multiple Chinese characters for border can suggest a line more supple and open to change, as if remembering the imperium of an older China, radiating frontierless to a tributary world.

Gleb sits beside me in a Chinese restaurant. Its clientele and staff are all Russian, but the unseen owner, he says, is Chinese. Gleb has a scanty ginger beard and flint-grey eyes. We eat in near silence. But I feel his stare on me, probing above his spectacles, as if he were debating something. He can show me the sights of this district, he says, as our chopsticks idle: anywhere I want. I cannot tell if he is lonely.

His car is an old Suzuki, adapted in Japan for Russia's right-hand driving, and it was once expensive. Its windscreen is cracked. We drive down the wide streets, the town's early grid, where stucco façades mingle with grey-brick tenements. A wedding palace has spilt its party onto the pavements, the bride standing bare-shouldered in the cold beside her stolid groom, while passing cars hoot. Gleb is trying to reach Harbin on his mobile phone, hoping to close a business deal, he says. Harbin is barely three hundred miles away in China, but the connection keeps breaking. We go through suburbs of run-down factories and barracks. The sights that Gleb points out are those of commercial triumphs, his own. He works freelance as an agent, importing Chinese machinery. Twenty years ago he studied Mandarin at university, as if he knew the future.

'It's hard dealing with them at first. They always drive a tough deal. And no, they're not honest.' I sense he is smarting from some long-ago fraud. 'But the Chinese do business from a distance now. The only ones you'll see are in the markets.' His phone rings, then stops. 'It's Big Brother,' he jokes. 'Listening to us.' So Orwell's tyrant reaches even here. The phone rings again. It's Harbin. He talks in bursts which I rarely understand. Sometimes, after he finishes a call, he wants to share some concept that my Russian fails to grasp, and he hunts for an English translation via the app on his phone. His laughter is darkly ironic, often so slight that it hardly sounds. He says: 'Over the years I've made the right contacts. I know them all. In Heihe, Harbin, Khabarovsk.' It's hard to tell if he's applauding or steeling himself. 'Whatever people want, I can arrange. Everything can be done! Is there a word for such a person in English?'

'An entrepreneur, I think.'

'There are different sorts of intelligence, aren't there? Cleverness, wisdom . . .' A whisper of half-laughter. 'But what's the use of wisdom? It's know-how that counts. In Russia we have a word for someone like me. He is *smekalisty*, we say. It may be untranslatable. But it runs the world . . .'

I laugh back. 'And maybe it cheats you.'

'Yes, maybe.'

Above the Amur wharf he points to a rank of detached rotor blades for hovercraft travelling the winter ice. 'Those are my imports. Of course, from China.' They are obsolete now, beached above the port in a rusting line. 'But those were all mine. And first class!' Next we pass the city football stadium. 'Years ago, its pitch was bumpy, horrible,' he says. 'I got in Chinese equipment for flattening it out.'

The arena looks grim. 'Is it a great team?' I ask.

'No. Hopeless.'

Soon afterwards we have left Blagoveshchensk behind and are crossing an open country of swamp and untilled fields. He swerves down a track over a deserted railway line and I stare across at a pink-walled compound. 'That's a poultry farm,' he says. 'And my equipment, got in from China.' He tries to telephone a friend there to admit us, but nobody answers.

And all the time I am wondering why he is doing this. I have mentioned writing a book. Does he hope I will write about him? (And of course I am.) Or is he planning to involve me in a deal? But more likely, I think, this tour arises from simple pride. He is parading his achievements before a Westerner rare in this remote region, even one as bedraggled as me.

But my faint bewilderment continues. He must be about thirty years younger than me, I realize, yet I imagine him senior (and so, I think, does he). He looks at me from over his glasses with a kindly but unrelenting inquisition. He reminds me of someone. His hair recedes from his forehead in grizzled inlets. There are leather elbow-patches on his blue-grey jacket. Then I realize whom he resembles: a revered schoolteacher from my boyhood, perfectly named Toppin. Unconsciously I have transferred Mr Toppin's authority to Gleb. I am even in danger of calling him 'Sir'.

Gleb turns down a track that seems to lead nowhere. But after a minute he stops dead. A trio of enormous silver cylinders is looming in front of us, threaded by iron gangways. They ascend enigmatic in their emptiness, like an amassment of castle towers. 'It was built in 2007 by five hundred Chinese workmen,'

Gleb says. 'A factory for making vodka. I bought in all the equipment from China. They finished building it in just one-and-a-half years, faster than any Russians could dream of.'

He parks in the dust. I get out and stare up in amazement. Then I see that the cladding is falling from the cylinders. They are bleeding rust. One of the iron stairways is dangling loose, and buildings alongside have fallen in heaps of brick. The place is derelict.

'Yes, it's closed.' Gleb crosses his forearms. 'We did fine at first. Then an official from Moscow entered the local government. He wanted money, too much of it. Tax, he said. But of course it was bribery.' He looks resigned for a moment, then the swagger re-enters his voice. 'So I ripped out the machinery and sold it to a company in another town, outside this area. We made a fat profit!'

In a run-down arcade beneath, some leftover business is going on. A friend of Gleb's is extracting fertilizer from coal, and sacks of wood shavings surround a wonky machine where Gleb employs another man (who is not here) to compress sawdust into pellets for boiler fuel.

'What will you do with the vodka factory?' I ask. 'Will anyone buy it?' But he shrugs. It will join the ruins that litter the countryside. Sawdust pellets, coal fertilizer, these are the salvage of an audacious failure. I know I am seeing only the shadow play of Gleb's life, not the labyrinthine substance. Sometimes he answers my naivety with only an amused smile.

But he says: 'That man was in our local government only for a year, then he was gone. He demanded too many back-handers. Was he Mafia? Well, yes, everyone's Mafia. Only your friends are not Mafia.'

He grows more sombre as we drive away. Behind us his tarnished monster of a factory, imposing even in wreckage, disappears as abruptly as it arrived. This journey, I come to feel, resembles less a triumphal parade than a nostalgic farewell. Gleb's good fortune seems to belong in the farther past, before the collapse of the rouble and of oil prices. He wears the same jacket with its elbow patches every time I meet him later, and he has no thought of repairing the Suzuki's cracked windscreen. I come to like him. His disquieting resemblance to Toppin works its alchemy, and in the end I imagine him the essence of fairness and integrity.

The regional museum of Blagoveshchensk spreads through the halls of what was once the wealthiest trading emporium of czarist Siberia. Its rooms pursue a timeline of mammoth tusks and native peoples – birchbark canoes, wooden idols, shamans' coats dripping discs and cowrie shells – past a wooden replica of Albazin fort and artefacts from the Zeya goldmines, climbing upstairs to the turn of the nineteenth century. There the walls are hung with photos of everyday life: shopkeepers, fur trappers, prospectors. A school group is trailing listlessly about, and for the first time in over a month I glimpse a European tourist. A museum guide is describing Muraviev's seizure of the Amur as a move against Chinese invasion, as if the Treaty of Nerchinsk had never existed.

But here, in an ill-lit room above the stairway, I come to a halt. In photographs from 1900, when insurgents of the Boxer Chinese rebellion shelled the Russian shore, white-coated Cossacks are mustering for Blagoveshchensk's defence, with ranks of civilian militia. In a nearby picture two sun-blackened Chinese soldiers, wearing skirts and feathered hats, look pathetically redundant. Pride of place is taken by a big oil painting of the bombardment. The Chinese shore is plumed in cannon smoke and half in flames. Russian guns are returning fire across the water and the steamer *Selenga* is feinting down the Amur to distract attention from troops crossing upriver. In the foreground, in pinprick detail, the Cossacks and citizens of Blagoveshchensk mingle behind an earth redoubt. A semicircle of fragile-looking innocents, they point their spindly rifles across the river, while peasant women succour them with pails of water. This delusive canvas was presented to the mayor of Blagoveshchensk in 1902, and hung in his public office for twenty years.

As I stare at it, a Chinese tour group arrives, herded by an angry-looking guide. She sweeps them through the room without a word. Local administrators have forbidden Chinese guides from delivering their own version of those days. For beneath this quiet, conservative city yawns a well of forgetting.

In fact, with the threat of a Chinese assault, the people of the thinly defended city had panicked. Overnight their fear transformed the Chinese population, trusted and peaceful until now, into an imminent peril. Fatally, perhaps, the Chinese had never assimilated; in everyday life they were routinely abused. And now, in the besieged city, fearful suspicions surfaced. Orders went out from the military governor for the Chinese to be rounded up. Over four days, while the subjects of the quaintly incompetent oil painting were facing an attack that never came, a force of Cossacks and newly raised recruits marched some five thousand Chinese men, women and children to the village of Verkhne-Blagoveshchenskoe, where the Amur runs fast and narrow. Those who faltered on the way were axed to death. There were no boats to carry them to the farther shore. Shopkeepers, restaurateurs, domestic servants, they were ordered into the river, but they could not swim. The Cossacks flailed them on with whips, then shot them in hundreds on the bank. Before a fixed bayonet charge they plunged into the current and were swept away. Cossack citizens – even old men and boys – picked them off in the water. A horrified Russian officer imagined that he could have walked across the Amur to

China on their corpses. In surrounding villages some seven thousand more were killed. The governor and police chiefs urged on their end, and mass looting followed.

Then silence fell. The Chinese threat evaporated, and a Russian army burned to the ground their provincial capital of Aigun, along with sixty-eight rural villages, and thrust deep into Manchuria. For five years no official word of the massacre was published. People in the region went dumb, as if after momentary madness. Even the local *Amurskaya Gazeta*, which expressed initial horror, later imagined that 'the Chinese swam across the River Amur'.

But four days after the carnage a Russian colonel, Alexander Vereshchagin, sailing to Khabarovsk, found his steamship ploughing through Chinese corpses, all floating downstream. The whole width of the river, he wrote, was covered with bloated and decaying bodies. 'They float along the width of the Amur as if haunting us. The passengers came out of their cabins to see such a rare scene. It will stay in my memory for ever . . . "Breakfast is served" announces a waiter . . .'

If today you travel the eight miles upriver to Verkhne-Blagoveshchenskoe, you find no memorial. The border fence along the Amur reappears in serried watchtowers and a concrete bastion topped with razor wire. A monument to Count Muraviev once stood here, where he came ashore with the formidable Archbishop Innocent to christen the little outpost 'Blagoveshchensk', 'Annunciation', but floods have washed it away. The opposite bank is seven hundred yards distant, perhaps, and hangs in a dark wall of trees. The river runs fast and deep between. Of the five thousand Chinese herded here, a hundred may have reached the far shore. But in Blagoveshchensk all knowledge of this slaughter has thinned into oblivion.

*

Svetlana is sixty years old, perhaps, a child of the Soviet Union. Her dyed blonde hair laps about the face of an overgrown girl, a girl imbued with the certainties of another time. She has tracked me through my hotel, and wants me to address her students. Sitting in the strip-light glare of her classroom, I imagine them afraid of her. But they look comfortable in their jeans and woollen jumpers: early teenagers, with barely a hint of the crushed hopelessness of the Sretensk pupils. Gone are the girlish fringes, the topknots and butterfly hairclips of the village. These students even smile. But where the Sretensk teacher was pliable and a little sad, Svetlana harangues in a strident monotone. No pupil, I imagine, has dared question her.

This time, when I ask their ambitions, a sheaf of hands goes up. 'I want to go to Canada!' a girl announces. A plump boy adds: 'I like Los Angeles.' Another boy: 'I want to live in Paris!'

Svetlana turns furious. This is not going to plan. She shouts: 'You are not good patriots!' But they look unabashed. 'And why Paris?'

The boy says: 'Because it's beautiful. I want to live somewhere beautiful. Paris has the Eiffel Tower and Big Ben.'

'Big Ben is not in Paris,' says Svetlana triumphantly. 'It's in London.'

'I want to go to London on a language course,' another girl pipes up. She has light, restless eyes. 'To any university there. I don't know which yet.'

These are another race, I realize, with other parents: not rich, perhaps, but affluent enough for possibility, for dreaming. One boy has already been to Thailand and Singapore with his father on business; another to Germany and Spain. They want to start online businesses, design computer games, become commercial artists. Others don't know, of course. But the room rings with their future.

A gentler girl offers: 'Moscow. I'll go to Moscow.' She sounds hesitant. Moscow is abroad to her: four thousand miles away, farther than India or Japan.

Svetlana's voice calms. 'Yes, Moscow is the finest city.' She turns to me for confirmation. 'What do you think of our Moscow?'

But I imagine Moscow always under grey skies. My deepest memories there are of the Brezhnev years. Even remembered friendships are tinged with foreboding. I say lamely, predictably: 'I prefer St Petersburg.'

Svetlana bridles. 'Moscow is better! You get ill in St Petersburg. The days are all short. It's too damp. People get ill in their bones.'

'My bones are used to England,' I say, but nobody laughs.

They question me about Western salaries ('Are you rich?'), pop concerts, men's behaviour (this, from a sullen blonde), Hollywood. When I mention China, no one responds. It is the West that glitters: its music, movies, style, the throb of young life.

But Svetlana is fed up with all this. In a while she ignores the students altogether and launches into her statement of faith. She talks in a bullying flow. 'Everything is getting better. The Russian Far East is reviving. Moscow is helping us. The Chinese are buying from us now, when it used to be the other way round.' She does not mention the collapsed rouble. 'The Chinese love our gold and amber – and our oil.' She lifts a teacherly finger. 'They take our oil!'

For a second I think that she is complaining about the extraction of raw materials to China. But she goes on: 'Our oil has a special flavour.' She is talking about cooking oil from soya beans. 'I've seen Russian clothes on their way to China. Boxes and boxes of them – leather jackets with real fur. The Chinese are buying them all . . . boxes and boxes . . .'

I imagine Western students fidgeting by now, muttering, switching on their mobiles. But Svetlana's class goes on staring at her with dulled eyes. Her world is not theirs, and they have retreated inside their skulls.

Svetlana goes on oblivious, powered by the mandatory state optimism, or by self-delusion, her jaws quivering. After all, what could these children know? 'Our Russian Far East is rich! Our people are returning here. Even from Mexico and Brazil. Even the Old Believers, who went away years ago. They're coming back. I saw it on TV. They were still in their old clothes! They said how beautiful it was to hear our Russian language again. Our Far East is repopulating. President Putin . . .'

Why then, I ask irritably, did the census figures show a steep decline: about a quarter of the people gone in less than twenty-five years? The campaign to repopulate Siberia had yielded almost nothing.

But Svetlana brooks no intrusion. Her voice shakes. Her certainties echo in my head from forty years ago: the blindness of national desire, the dawn that the Soviet Union promised, with fading light. I cannot meet the students' eyes.

Svetlana closes down the class early and ushers me into her office. She says at once: 'They're stupid. They don't know anything. They just see things on the internet. When they grow up, they'll change. They'll want to stay in Russia, and live here in Blagoveshchensk.'

She slams the door on the roar of students in the passageway outside. Her office is cramped and seedy. But she offers me bread and jam, and the familiar papered sweets, apologizing for them, and for her language class. Sometimes a student pokes her head through the door, wanting to ask something, but Svetlana barks at them and they disappear.

Then she resumes her harangue. I am her class now. She wants me to keep silent. And along with my irritation I feel a strange sadness, whose origins I cannot locate: a condescension she would hate. She says: 'Under Putin our lives are getting better. Have you noticed? He is putting in gyms everywhere, and we are smoking less, much less. I know there are gyms in London. I've been there. And I've read what your papers say about us. I've read everything. And it's not true. Do you think we're stupid? Russian children coming back from university in the States know more than the American students about everything. History, geography . . . The American students aren't even sure where Moscow is!'

I say: 'The Americans question things. That's how the country works.'

I hear a second's silence. Then she concedes: 'Yes, they are better at critical thinking.' Such thinking sounds, in her mouth, like an obscure academic category, optional. She pushes the bowl of sweets towards me, and lets out a faint, enigmatic sigh.

A few minutes' walk from the river, the Cathedral of the Annunciation ascends in a surge of spires, gilded cupolas and tiered Orthodox crosses. Near the entrance, a double statue of Muraviev and Archbishop Innocent – one grasping his sword-hilt, the other's hand poised in blessing – sanctify the old collusion of Church and State. A Russian flag flutters behind.

I do not expect to hear anger in this sanctum, but an elderly man, seated in the cold sunlight beside me, is incensed by the Chinese tour group photographing themselves in the porch. 'Those people,' he says, 'they don't believe in anything. They're just here for business. Heihe is a city of two million now and we're still just three hundred thousand [both figures are fantasy]. They don't care about us. Why should they?' He barely focuses on me. He may be a little drunk. But he is dressed for church, in polished leather shoes. And then his anger switches elsewhere. He is suffering from some bureaucratic slight, and his voice fills with piqued dignity. 'The officials here are all corrupt. Everything takes for ever. There's nothing left for us. We have no work, no security.'

I ask: 'Where is better?'

He says more softly: 'Nowhere is good. Everyone's Mafia. Putin, Medvedev, all of them. They're all Mafia.'

Now he is anxious to leave me, as if he has said too much. He gets to his feet and looks up at the golden domes. 'This is what we have.'

I go inside the basilica. The mesmeric chanting is fading from the divine liturgy, the wine-soaked bread of the Eucharist has been consumed, and in the great screen of the iconostasis, limned with dark saints, the blue and gold doors are slowly closing. As the celebrant vanishes through them, it seems as if a great secret has been shared, then withdrawn, and that beyond the iconostasis there opens some mystery of which the congregation of old women and a few men has been granted a blessed intimation.

They disperse among the surrounding icons as though visiting old friends, kissing the hands and feet half-lit by votive candles. And here the icon of the Albazin Madonna has come to rest, after a spell in an atheist museum: the same relic that the rough Cossacks venerated before they fell one by one at the siege of Albazin, and which the survivors carried westward.

It hangs in a blue and gold kiosk above the glimmer of lamps. Rosaries and dedicatory crosses cascade beneath it. But the painting is so encrusted with costly metals that I can scarcely discern it. Only her darkened face escapes the overlay of beaten silver robes and precious stones. Even her shoulders are stamped with jewels, and gold cherubim hover at her cheeks. She presents the Christ Child standing upright in a mandorla at her breast. But his body is blackened to anonymity, and in the Holy Mother's face, circled by a gem-studded halo, I can make out only the trace of formulaic eyes and lips, as if worship and longing had emptied her.

* * *

Twenty years ago, when crossing the ragged pasturelands east of Lake Baikal, I would glimpse fields brimming with cabbages and watermelons. Among the tracts of ruined collective farms, Chinese and Korean migrants were cultivating these immaculate plots and living alongside under canvas shelters far into the autumn. Now it is Chinese companies that are rumoured to rent or own 20 per cent of the arable land north of the Amur. Their farms thrive even on mediocre soil and short summers. But their intensive use of chemicals arouses alarm – their farmed pigs, fed on chemical-soaked forage, are bloated monsters – and the sale of their crops in Russian markets has slumped with the fallen rouble.

Gleb, sitting in his garret office off Lenin Street, promises to take me to a Chinese-owned farm an hour's drive to the north. He works in a small room, presided over by a photograph not of Putin, but of Gleb's elder brother, prematurely dead. While he negotiates a transaction over the telephone, I wait in the passageway outside like a disgraced schoolboy (the shade of Mr Toppin surfaces), then we drive to where the first road bridge between Russia and China is nearing completion over the Amur. For years the Russians have delayed this, while the Chinese tried to push it forward. But now its converging spans – girders and bolts forged to resist cold of –70°F – are due to be united. We meet the new highway running over marshland to the crossing, with cranes and dump-trucks multiplying towards the still invisible river, grit being poured, tarmac laid.

Even Gleb cannot calculate what effect this artery may have. He is sceptical of any progress here. He has pinned his faith on Chinese business, and it is stagnating. For a long time, I sense, things have been growing harder for him. Perhaps his telephone has miscarried too, because his habitual ebullience has veered into churning irritation. 'There's no hope for us here in the Far East. No future! Even the Chinese who invested over here are starting to regret it.'

I say: 'They seem to be resented too.'

'Yes, they are. The Asia Hotel – it's the grandest in Blagoveshchensk – is owned by a Chinese man who drives a Bentley, and a Chinese businesswoman bought up our factory for brewing *kvass*. But things have got worse for them now.' He emits a glint of *schadenfreude*. 'Where is there any future? In western Russia, perhaps? In Moscow?' His fingers grind on the steering wheel. 'I don't think so. I'm a good Russian, but I don't want to live here. I don't want my children to live here. We live in a prison.'

He goes silent. For a while, in this featureless terrain, he does not recognize where we are. Then he says: 'I think the farm is here,' and we swerve onto an overgrown track. We see no signboard, and nobody is about. And suddenly we are moving down a corridor of ruin. On either side, aisles of skeletal wooden arches, framing nothing, disappear into wilderness. Where once their canopies sheltered ranks of vegetables or soya beans, we see only waist-high weeds.

Gleb breathes: 'It's given up. It's gone.'

At the end is a high gate and a derelict yard. Two Chinese watchmen, harsh-faced and unkempt, come to the barred gate and shout in answer to our questions, their faces a yard from ours. But they are grinning. 'The place is finishing,' they say. It's as if they have been abandoned here, or have forgotten to leave. 'When will anyone come back? We don't know. We think never.'

So we drive disconsolately away. Gleb does not know how typical this failed venture may be. He only says: 'The Chinese go where the money is.'

I've long ago lost trace of where we are. Amur tributaries are wandering over the swamplands in bright sunlight. The log villages seem asleep. But Gleb always has a destination in mind. We turn through a quiet hamlet where anglers sit at the confluence of two rivers. He says: 'This is my home.'

We come to a group of cottages behind a high, protective wall. They look commonplace, yet more pristine than most, their eaves and window-frames filigreed brilliant blue and white. At the touch of a button the walls part and we enter a precinct blazing with flowers. Beyond stretch beds of straw-berries, raspberry canes, marrows, pumpkins, leeks, lettuces, onions, vines. Gleb presses another button. More walls move. 'My garage!' It is huge. We get out and walk farther, down pens of chortling geese and turkeys, black chickens, coops of quail. He works these acres himself, he says. He makes wine, harvests honey. And in the centre a pair of painted cupids leads to a full-scale sauna. A stone-filled furnace bathes its platform in the Russian way, to induce a sweltering torpor. This, I imagine, is where he entertains his friends, lounging on sybaritic holiday, while the tensions of daytime ebb away, intimacies transpire, schemes are floated (and elicited) in a sweat-drenched euphoria.

Inside his house this celebratory tour continues. He stokes the boilers with his pellets manufactured in the ruined vodka factory, and his coal-based fertilizer is heaped nearby. Beneath a mat in his son's bedroom a trapdoor opens on a cellar packed with tomato and cucumber preserves.

His son, a gentle slip of a boy, fourteen years old, is sitting alone at a desk, doing his homework. His mother is absent, and perhaps the child wants to avoid us. I find him studying Chinese characters, in obedience to his father. 'How is it?' I ask.

'So-so,' he answers. 'Rather boring.'

'Boring!' Gleb has overheard us. 'Mandarin's the future! Get on with it!'

The boy smiles shyly at me. He seems younger than his age. His boon companion is a pet mouse – a tiny, auburn-striped creature that plays across his palm. I think he takes refuge in it. Once, in an act of silent trust, he transfers the mouse to my palm too, but in its nervousness it pees there, and he gentles it back to himself, almost tearful, as if it had disgraced him.

This home and its bird-filled garden might be a child's paradise. A ginger cat basks on a window-ledge, oblivious of the mouse, and Gleb's electronic gadgets coexist with walls and ceilings of polished pinewood, like those of *izba*s centuries old. Into his rooms, as if out of Russia's collective memory, this intimacy with wood instils a rustic mellowness. Pine, Gleb says, holds less resin than birch. It makes for smoother joinery, and he loves its smell. The walls are furnished only by his wife's framed embroideries – butterflies and Orthodox saints side by side – woven during the lonely winters.

I wonder again why he is showing me all this. Sometimes I catch him watching me, waiting for my praise. 'Do you in England have houses like this?' he asks, and when offering homemade carrot or pumpkin juice: 'Have you such drinks in England?' Then suddenly, sadly, he says: 'You know all those vegetables, this poultry, we can't sell them any more. No one has the money. Even this property is worth half of what it was.'

All day, as if to remedy this, he has been trying to telephone certain business contacts in Heihe. Their faces stare unreadably from a snapshot on his iPhone: a middle-aged Chinese businessman with his able-looking wife. They deal in Chinese antiques, he says, collected from around Harbin. The story goes that in 1945, under attack from Soviet bombers, the retreating Japanese abandoned the treasures they had rifled from old tombs, so that precious ceramics found their way into the homes of peasants scattered through the region. His partners are buying them for a song, he says, and can ship them out through Hong Kong. 'They just stamp them through' – he franks a phantom trophy – 'No problem.'

He asks if I am interested, or know of anybody in London . . . And it so happens that I do. This is how Gleb works, I imagine. He cultivates people. You never know who may come in useful.

He becomes more emphatic now. When I cross over to Heihe, as I plan, he says, I must meet his partners. He will arrange this. Then I will photograph the ceramics. I will show them to people in London. His partners are well known in their field. He hands me a heavy, 200-year-old crystal vase they have given him. Something about its standard painted cranes strikes me as fake.

But now Gleb is considering how I will survive in China. China can be cruel. He does not know the Amur country where I hope to go, it is too remote. Even if the police don't prevent me, a lone foreigner will be cheated or robbed. I should not go. But if I insist, he will find a Chinese man to accompany me along the river, at least for part of it. He knows people in Heihe. He is *smekalisty*, after all. I may have a chance. But the grey eyes that assess me over his spectacles are troubled. If something happens to me, I will not return to London with news of his ceramics. And in his gaze I find a softer, reticent concern. He may even like me a little, as I do him.

*

Next morning, the day before I cross to China, I lock myself in my hotel room and prepare to ease into the language that I learnt poorly more than thirty years ago, and have rarely spoken since. My Mandarin notes and textbooks, squashed into my rucksack, spill out like ancient scripts, still covered in my tutor's red biro, and stained with the rings of coffee cups. Beyond my window, through an opening in the shoreline flat-blocks, a section of the Amur gleams, with Heihe lying beyond under a clouded sky. A Russian patrol boat is crossing the gap.

The only sounds in the room are my own. I return to my makeshift table. It's a relief to leave behind the complexities of Russian grammar, the dual aspects of verbs, the exacting cases of nouns, the sheer length of words. Chinese, which lacks verbal tenses, genders, even the singular and plural, seems suddenly, radiantly simple. I shift my table to the light of the window and the glint of the Amur, and my exhilaration rises. The vocabulary flows back. Sometimes I have the illusion that I am not remembering, but learning anew. I anticipate the stark thrust of Mandarin replacing Russian wholesale. A change of language feels like a change of person. Sounds and structures dictate emotion. New concepts emerge, while others die. I have the illusion that I become more aggressive in Mandarin, and that my voice descends an octave. Perhaps I will need this. I have no idea what dialects may be coming my way. Yet for a long time I hear Mandarin returning, and imagine all will be well.

But as the hours go on, this happy remembrance stiffens. The unfamiliar structures start to weigh on me. There are words I have clean forgotten. Perhaps it is all too long ago. The blessed existence of Western borrowings (in Russian there are many) is all but absent. Mandarin is a tonal tongue – its words change meaning with their pitch – and the language turns, in my memory, to an echo of discordant gongs. I remember finding it easier to speak than to understand: the reverse of what I wish. Suddenly I miss the pliant beauty of Russian.

By evening a self-induced dementia has set in. When I go down to the hotel restaurant I mistakenly ask for the lavatory in Mandarin, then order a meal in Russian and chat to the bewildered waitress in a deranged mixture of both. Often my poor grasp of either leaves me suspended in mid-speech. I have no idea what is going to come out of my mouth.

Dusk is settling over the waterfront when I wander out. The air is cold. A troupe of women in peasant skirts is singing folk songs, accompanied on the accordion by an elderly Cossack covered in even more medals than Alexei. But in the half-darkness on the promenade, there is hardly a soul to listen. Across the water the lights and music are starting up in Heihe. I sense its pulsing life. Russians no longer talk of it as a theatre set rigged up to torment or dupe them, but as a city grown rich selling them shabby merchandise. I look across at it with a tingling curiosity at what I cannot predict. The whole Chinese Amur, it is said, bristles with defence like its Russian counterpart. But Heihe gives no sign of this. It is lit like a funfair, whose columns of reflected neon tremble across the water to my feet.

7

Black Dragon River

Somewhere in midstream, where the current deepens and grows dark, the river becomes Chinese. The Little Father Amur transforms into the Heilongjiang, the Black Dragon River, and suffers another change of sex. Flowing water, in China, is anciently female, just as mountains are male, and the great arteries of Central China, the Yangtze and the Yellow River, are conceived as a generative life-force. These rivers are imbued with timeless reverence. In Confucian and Daoist philosophy, water was an intrinsic moral good; its flow, however dangerous, embodied right living, and its management was crucial to national harmony. If the rivers ran riot, it was a sign that Heaven had withdrawn its mandate from the emperor, and his throne shook.

The Heilongjiang, like all the greatest waters of China, flows west–east, an axis still deep in Chinese thinking, and this geographical trajectory might suggest that the river belongs to China; for the mightiest waterways of Russia all flow northward. Yet the Heilongjiang lies far from the Chinese heartland. Its dragonish character erupted in periodic floods, but its anger raged through a distant wilderness, never touching the imperial centre. The sources of the Yangtze and Yellow rivers were debated as if they might reveal the secret wellspring of Chinese life; but that of the Heilongjiang, lost in Mongolian marshes, held no such promise. It was fraught with precariousness. It was the place from which invasion might come.

The towns along it are young. The precursor of Heihe, a fortified trading settlement, was levelled by Russian troops in 1900. Thirty years ago its successor was a mere village. But I step now onto a wharf where the Chinese are offloading their merchandise onto dejected Russian porters, and the Russians, herded together like cattle, are queuing in the customs house. The Chinese border officials take forty minutes to process my visa, passing it up a ladder of bemused authority until it is stamped with an unsettling frown. 'Only Russians come this way.'

My bus enters wide, clean boulevards among skyscrapers topped with working cranes. The waterfront bulks out in the same granite as that of Blagoveshchensk, but seems yet more immense, and plumed in young trees for miles. It is early October and the start of 'Golden Week', commemorating the foundation of the Chinese republic in 1949, and the avenues of eight-branched street lights flutter with scarlet flags. A giant globe, topped by a flying horse, proclaims Heihe's moment as China's top commercial city, and bursts of greenery are sculpted into Russian dolls and onion domes in a gesture of welcome – and hope of trade – to those across the river. These illusions of topiary are in fact bamboo frames holding miniature shrubs shaved smooth, with designs sprayed on in red paint. Everything is tended, immaculate. The domes and turrets that shone across the river like a mirage of Europe turn out to house civic amenities. The Gothic cathedral is the Citizens' Fitness Hall and the baroque palace, still building, will become a recreation centre for pensioners. Gone are the second-hand Japanese cars of Blagoveshchensk, with their awkward right-hand drive. Parked beneath the grander flat-blocks, where spruce young women are walking in platform boots, I see lines of brand-new Subaru, Lexus and Toyota saloons, and Land Rovers with tinted windows.

Towards the centre the streets turn dense with people and traffic, and I start to walk. Golden Week is in full swing. The Toyotas and Range Rovers jam and hoot among mechanized carts and trucks, and in pedestrian Wenhua Street, the city's main artery, the din of commerce rises to a furious cacophony. Behind their narrow fronts the shops recede in bright-lit palaces, trumpeted in front by a raucous crossfire of loudspeakers. Others spill out their wares onto the sidewalks in stalls heaped with cheap clothes, crockery, digital goods, even pet turtles and goldfish. Half the garments are labelled 'New York', 'Benetton', 'Yankee' or 'Gucci' (never 'Moscow'). There is even a packed Kentucky Fried Chicken. Vendors set up their own sound systems, and hustlers are everywhere, insisting on restaurants, thrusting out vouchers and pamphlets. They assume I am Russian. The clamour and tumult mount as night comes on. Neon signs, in the jagged maze of Chinese characters, flash into synthetic colours, and the lilting music so seductive from across the river ascends to a deafening uproar. It is holiday time for children. Strapped into harness, they bounce on street-side trampolines and drive plastic tanks and sports cars through the crowds.

Meanwhile, on overhead shop televisions, a state banquet is proceeding in Beijing, and a chilling parade in Tiananmen Square has gone by, with news shots of the military exercise that I had skirted a month before. And everywhere attempts to woo the Russians remain. Cyrillic is paired with Chinese on the road signs, survives misspelt in shop windows or runs in neon streams above them, and occasionally Russian still pours out of the sound systems. At street intersections stand pseudo-topiary *matrioshka* dolls and Orthodox church spires, complete with evergreen crosses.

Yet I see no Russians. Opposite a statue of Pushkin, the café where Russian traders used to congregate has been turned into a depot for cheap glass. I go up the stairs of the nearby Pushkin Bookshop, into sudden quiet. The stairway is lined with photographs of Russian writers and ballerinas, and abuts a stinking toilet. I can find no Russian books, and ask an assistant, in shaky Mandarin, where they are. She says there are none. It is years since there were any.

Back in the streets a funfair gaiety is starting up. Bands of drums, horns and cymbals are marching between troupes of sashed dancers in crimson and green, waving fans. Some wear dark glasses and pork-pie hats. In Brazil this outbreak might herald a carnival, in India a religious festival, but here in Heihe they are advertising 'China Gold'. One old man, grinning and out of step, wanders away altogether, flaunting Manchu dress embroidered with dragons and a little round cap, as if rejoicing in a past long denied him. The quietude of Blagoveshchensk is barely a memory. But out of the crowds two young Russian women – a shock of fair hair and blue eyes – approach me, laughing.

'We had a bet you're not Russian.'

'Why not?'

Their laughter peals in chorus. 'Because you look happy!'

In this harsh turmoil of commerce they seem to belong elsewhere, closer to a world I find familiar, the world I cannot shed. Now they say: 'Isn't all this horrible? We hate it. Just money-money-money. What do you think?'

I pull a face. 'But I'm fascinated.' I have a fleeting qualm that this energy they hate may one day subsume them, but I warm to their laughter, their blithe beauty, as we go our separate ways between the dancers.

*

Gleb is as good as his word. Through some Heihe business contact he has arranged for an unemployed Chinese man to accompany me, if I like him, for the first few hundred miles along the Amur-Heilongjiang. That way, he'd said, I wouldn't be duped or assaulted. I will pay the man the little he asks.

In my Heihe hotel, a rowdy pile in the town centre, I wait to meet Liang. I fear a verbose guide or even an intelligence agent. But when he arrives in the reception hall, dressed in faded jeans and a worn jerkin, he looks out of place. Beneath his flat cap I see an owlish face that returns my smile with a kind of melancholy calm. We are both embarrassed, unsure who is interviewing whom. He finds my journey strange, of course. Beyond Aihui, old Aigun, twenty miles away, he says, the river is unknown to him. His people came from Jilin province, far south of Heilongjiang, in the big migrations of the 1960s. They were a family of ten. He pulls off his cap from a balding head. Only a thinning dust descends from a forehead which a lone furrow crosses like a knife scar. He had worked in Heihe as a printer, then as a carpenter, and had even tried a stint as a city guide, but there was no longer money in that. Perhaps it was from those days that his talk fills with an outlandish Russian, while I reply in faulty Chinese. We must sound terrible. He has only been once in Russia, he says, on a group holiday to Novosibirsk with his wife. 'We were all mugged. A gang of Mafia. But we fought back.' He smiles in the hardy Chinese way, on an assembly of dented teeth. I instinctively like him, and I sense he is relieved by my appearance: a little down-at-heel, like him. We agree to start in two days' time.

The Heilongjiang runs clear and auburn beneath the city's esplanade. The offices and apartments nearby have gone quiet for Golden Week, and in the fringe of river parkland old men are playing cards under the trees. A scattering of art students above the wharf is painting the view in light oils, while passers-by cluster round their easels, commenting. The students have learnt to ignore them. 'These people aren't our sort,' one tells me. She is tall and thin and wears a T-shirt proclaiming 'We are all Stars'. 'Heihe is very small, you know. We all feel isolated here. There's no one to talk to. And we'll be at the college here four years.' She comes from the affluent city of Zhengzhou on the Yellow River. 'I want to go back.' She paints only a section of her view, just water and trees. She has eliminated all its buildings.

The people she disowns are strolling the promenade at noon. The women go in flowery dresses or trousers, the men in black anoraks and peaked caps. It is easy to assign their short, compact bodies to rural ancestry, only a generation from poverty, the fruit of immigration from more populous provinces to the south: Shandong, Jilin, Liaoning. And in this young city an older generation is taking the air, hobbling on the arm of a son or daughter. Their clenched faces seem imprinted by more bitter times, so that even now, perhaps, the glistening promenades, with their statuary and pleasure boats, remain a little wondrous.

All that they see is younger than they are. Thirty years ago this was a shingled beach. Now, on a towering plinth, the figure of a giant mother holds aloft a winged baby, and the occasional tour guide declares her the symbol of a united Heilongjiang-Amur. As you wander downstream, the promenade thickens with trees, and with a folklore statuary of bears and cats and allegorical conceits. On a sculpted see-saw labelled 'Knowledge is Power', a smug child with a pile of books outweighs an obese oaf with a packet of cigarettes.

Beyond a watchtower, where soldiers are observing through binoculars their Russian counterparts across the river, the island of Da-Heihe comes snaking into the current. Da-Heihe belongs to China, and two airy bridges leapfrog the water to claim it. Along its northern bank the promenade emerges again, advancing for a mile under a palisade of trees to the island's tip. In the early 1990s, China declared Da-Heihe a free trade zone, where Russians could barter without visas, and from Blagoveshchensk I had glimpsed the buildings of its International Market City crowding the horizon.

But as you head for it, the esplanade becomes deserted. The only sound is muted birdsong. Across the river, the silhouette of Blagoveshchensk lies low and broken. I pass my old hotel rising faint across the water, and tramp on by parterres fringed with hornbeam, willow and oak trees. Then, at the island's end, comes a huge, vacant car park, and beyond it a deserted funfair with its ferris wheel idle in the air. The great steel curves of the market building spread abandoned. I peer through padlocked doors into gutted arcades.

Once, when the rouble rode high, the Russians swarmed here in their thousands. Ten years later the free trade zone was extended to Heihe itself. The Chinese endeavoured to accommodate Russian tastes, with locally made vodka, clothes fashionable in Moscow, more generous sizes in skirts, belts, bras. The dogged 'camels' came and went. Even the municipal waste bins, in misguided welcome, were shaped as *matrioshka* dolls, causing Russian outrage that these talismanic babushkas should be receptacles for rubbish.

Now, in a new, smaller complex, a few disconsolate storekeepers inhabit the site of International Market City. 'It's lousy business,' a salesman says. He is young, restless. 'This place was built brand new, but nobody comes.' His stall is piled with the nested dolls. 'Actually these are turned out cheap by a Chinese factory. People don't tell the Russians, of course . . .' He motions carelessly at his ranks of souvenirs. 'I miss the Russians, those guys who bought in bulk . . . especially the women.'

'They bought more than the men?'

'No, it's their long legs.' He gives a lascivious grin. 'That's the best thing about the Russians. The women's legs go on and on . . .'

He's heard that in Russia, unlike China, the women outnumber the men. He knows of interracial marriages. He thinks the Russian women once had money. But his face clouds as he talks of them. 'The Russians can't stop drinking . . .' He turns to scanning his assets on an old laptop computer. He does not know how long he can survive this business. The promised future, with its Siberian wealth and marvellous legs, is fading away in his distracted voice.

The Russians never reciprocated Heihe's welcome. In Blagoveshchensk, I recall no Chinese street or shop sign. Even the Chinese restaurants announce themselves in Cyrillic. But a Russian statue honouring the work of the Amur 'camels' shows a young hero striding forward with the immense, rectangular cases of their traffic. In Heihe the Chinese responded with a similar statue, but their camel is sitting on a suitcase, holding a mobile phone, and he is very tired.

It is evening now. The sky is deepening to violet. In central Heihe a few lights are coming on in Russia Street, beyond a wide arch blazoned 'Welcome'. The shops are selling Russian amber reworked in China, jewellery at competitive prices, vodka and Russian chocolate. But there are no Russian customers; and the so-called Russian restaurants revert to Chinese dishes after a course of *zakuski*.

Beyond the arch, Russia Street slides into red-light anonymity. But the Russian sex tourists that used to come, stirred by the strangeness of Chinese bodies, are nowhere in sight, and the sex shops might have shut long ago. Only once, some pink bead curtains part on a lamp-lit room, where a bleak woman calls out to me, '*Anmo, anmo*', not a plea to the Amur, but the Mandarin for 'massage'.

Beyond this again, the street turns very quiet, and it is here, in a big, dark-wood mansion, that Gleb's antique dealers operate. If I bring back photographs of their ceramics to London, the outcome will be important to Gleb – perhaps the reason for his friendship – and one of his agent's brothers is at home now, with some sleek male assistants. I climb a massive wooden staircase into a panelled passageway. Everything is darkly lustrous and heavy. The rooms that give onto the corridor are all closed, but I am ushered into a chamber like a deserted boardroom. The whole building gives the feel of huge, immured strength. I sit at a polished table while the dapper young men come and go with ceramics for me to photograph: creations, they say, of the Northern Song dynasty a millennium ago. They lay them in my hands like babies. They are all but priceless. A vase, a plate, an incense-burner. Their glaze is beautiful. It shifts and glows in my camera lens. Their colour lies somewhere of their own, between opal and turquoise blue.

I wonder, in passing, how photographs can convey the sense of these objects, let alone their value. But an expert eye, it seems, can sometimes tell.

Months later, when I submit them to a London expert, he pronounces them fakes.

* * *

The small town of Aihui, old Aigun, twenty miles south on the banks of the Heilongjiang-Amur, is the site of the infamous treaty signed in 1858, by which Russia absorbed all Chinese lands north of the river. By all accounts Aigun – a place of bitter national memory – is forbidden to foreigners, but I am sunk beside Liang on a provincial bus. I remember such buses thirty years ago, crammed with peasant farmers beside aisles of spittle and cigarette ash. Now, among village families with bright-dressed children, only the old, in their frayed jackets and caps askew, are recognizable from a generation ago.

We move through a new country. The straggling homesteads and vegetable patches of the Russian shore have given way to fields of maize that reach unbroken to the horizon. Liang says he remembers forests as a boy, where the land is bare now. Cottages of plastered brick stand among immaculate ranks of plastic-shrouded vegetables. Everywhere is occupied, cultivated. Only to our east, every few miles, the river is signalled by a pale watchtower in concrete seven storeys high.

It is years since Liang was in Aigun, he says, but he remembers no police checkpoints. He has never travelled beyond, but we blithely plan to continue five hundred miles along the river to Tongjiang, where I will go on alone. He carries nothing but a little brown washbag, and he looks content. It is Golden Week, after all, and holiday time.

In the main street of Aigun there are no buildings over two storeys high. It is lit by quaint hanging lanterns, and a small market has overflowed the pavements. From somewhere a lilting music sounds. In the side streets geese are spilling out between wrought-iron gates and fences, and along the river a pathway of flower-filled baskets is awaiting a wedding party. The river flows very full and calm. The immense Zeya tributary, muddy in times of flood, has joined it just upstream, but it keeps its khaki-green darkness, and nothing sails on it.

Only the museum that rises in the town's heart – huge, modern, disproportionate – suggests some unreconciled past. It appears beyond a wide pathway, suddenly crowded with visitors. On one side a steep bastion is crowned by a vermilion temple. On the other rises a curtain of hanging bells – over a thousand of them – that tinkle in the faint wind, as if with some memory of their own. Foreigners are doubly prohibited here, I've heard, but the ticket-seller stares at my passport, which she cannot read, and asks only if I am Russian.

The exhibition halls are spacious and soft-lit. I walk them with growing astonishment. This is less a display of early artefacts than a didactic history lesson – a 'patriotic education base', built in 2002 – and its visitors are trooping through in rapt silence. Above showcases of rusted bridles and swords, its notices reclaim the Heilongjiang-Amur for China. Far to the north of the river, it confirms, the native peoples were tributary to the emperor in Peking, and hanging maps show China's borders deep inside today's Russia, embracing mountains far beyond the Amur. Even at the northernmost limit of the river, a Ming dynasty temple, high on a bluff, once celebrated a Chinese naval expedition in 1413.

This northern frontier, in Chinese eyes, was confirmed by the Treaty of Nerchinsk, sealed with pedantic parity in 1689. And now I arrive at a tableau of life-size waxworks depicting its conclusion. They exude benign concord. The Manchu envoy, it is true, stands taller and more stately than his Russian counterpart, but the portly Count Feodor Golovin, in a flowing black wig, stares pleasantly back, and the two men tender each end of the document in their fingertips, in delicate amity.

You cannot tell, of course, that the country they debated was the wilderness home of early native peoples. Hanging texts proclaim that it flourished under the Manchu Qing regime, and a model of Aigun shows a spacious town ringed by a double stockade with ramped gateways, moats and clustering temples.

But by the mid-nineteenth century, with the Qing decline, the fateful Treaty of Aigun ceded all these lands to Russia, and

I find Liang staring miserably at their captions on which the words 'invasion' and 'forced' recur. Together with the Treaty of Peking two years later – by which China relinquished its dominion east of the Ussuri river – more than 1 million square kilometres of territory, a notice laments, were lost to Russia. The written outrage of both Marx and Engels at this seizure is blazoned across the walls.

The waxwork tableau that follows is grimly eloquent. Count Muraviev, a blond bully sashed and dripping gold epaulettes, looms above his greying opponent, the wretched Prince Yishan, whose head droops in resignation. The Treaty of Nerchinsk is reversed at a blow. Muraviev becomes a national hero; Yishan returns to disgrace in Peking. This happens at the height of what China now calls its 'century of humiliation', in which Britain, France, the United States, and soon Germany and Japan, wrenched concessions from a dynasty in sickly decline. China has since labelled these late treaties 'unequal', extorted under threat, and the old imperial predators, of course, have surrendered their dominion now. Only Russia has never contemplated returning the enormous territories it usurped. The changed border was painfully reaffirmed in a series of agreements between 1991 and 2004, and inscribed boulders maintain it along either shore. But the wound lingers. During the Cultural Revolution, when the loudspeakers of Red Guards bombarded the Russian bank with propaganda, a sleeping hatred resurrected. Even now, with the border officially settled, the Chinese hold to their 'unequal' definition of the Aigun treaty.

The museum itinerary moves into mounting grievance. Liang walks beside me, cradling his camera. As China's Boxer Rebellion spilled over against Blagoveshchensk, the year 1900 darkens. The Russians reacted by invading Manchuria and razing Aigun to the ground. Photographs show nothing left but its gutted clay battlements. Its heroic but incompetent soldiers and citizens often died where they stood, and the museum halls transform into a recreated townscape of wreckage and flames. Its inhabitants are waxworks who die in melodramatic defiance among the corpse-littered ruins. An old woman clutches her husband's memorial tablet; soldiers brandish outmoded halberds and broadswords.

As for the mass drowning of Chinese townspeople in Blagoveshchensk – a horror that the Russian museum had suppressed – I momentarily imagine that here too it has been withheld or even forgotten. But instead, towards the museum's end, there opens up an immense, accusing cyclorama. The crowd around me gazes at it as if stunned. The tableau of Aigun's sack had depicted victims whose killers were merely silhouettes at the far end of streets; but here – as if painted in frenzied outrage – the Cossacks go heartlessly to work. The carefully moulded foreground, littered with corpses and cast-off clothing, blends into a vast canvas where struggling figures, as far as the eye can see, are being shot, clubbed or hacked to death. In isolated incidents the women, men and children cringe and plead or battle vainly back, but they merge at last into a crowd of despairing bodies as they are pressed towards the river. The Amur itself, awash with their heads and arms, blurs from coldly articulated waves to a horizon where the Chinese shore lies hopelessly out of reach. And as we watch, a son et lumière begins. The scene turns dark, then a wan spotlight illumines lone atrocities. There are disembodied screams and the neighs of rearing horses, while a sombre voice intones its narrative. The number of dead has risen to six thousand.

As we leave the museum, among silent visitors, nobody meets my eye.

*

Liang tells me that from a young age he was taught that the Treaty of Aigun was imposed under threat, and was as invalid as those that installed British Hong Kong or Japanese Taiwan. Only the 1689 Treaty of Nerchinsk was authentic, by which the whole Amur basin passed to China. And this schooling continues today. It is as if China officially pursues conciliation, while educating its youth in another possibility. Back in Russia a row is growing on the internet, where a Blagoveshchensk citizen is complaining about an outdated Russian schoolbook which states that the Amur was grabbed by force. I didn't know I was living on Chinese soil, he fumes. Russia did not strong-arm China, but had merely 'taken advantage' – and the Amur had returned to its rightful owner.

These sensitivities can mount to paranoia. The Russian border still emanates fear. It even occurs to me that Moscow's joint military exercise, with its 300,000 Russian troops and meagre Chinese contingent, was less a signal to the West than a veiled warning to China of the power that could be marshalled on its doorstep.

Liang has friends in Aigun, but he cannot remember precisely where the Wangs live. We tramp down streets where children and wary dogs run, and come on their cottage by chance. Aigun began to revive a century ago, but the elderly couple do not know when their people arrived here from the south. Their laps and knees are thronged with grandchildren for Golden Week. The old lady sits in a spangled blouse and indulges them with sweets. She is buoyant and watchful, her husband fading. Liang and I perch on their *kang*, the traditional brick platform heated from inside, while relatives come and go in gales of laughter. They ply us with cherries, strawberries and watermelon. Life here is better than in the cities, they say, where work is scarce now. The mud floors are spread with new linoleum, where the children play, and on a painted cabinet sits a big television. Their yard is heaped with maize and its eaves dangle red peppers.

It seems no trouble that I come from the West. I am an exotic adjunct to their celebrations (I am trying to speak Mandarin) and a subject of genial banter. A plump daughter with 'Infinite' on her T-shirt asks me the whereabouts of London, while her husband calls up their own eight-year-old daughter on his phone screen, and the child asks my age and bursts out laughing, and I tell her she's pretty, and she vanishes from view. The grandparents, meanwhile, are joking about their age too, how many teeth they have left (not many) and what they cannot eat. The old lady donates me a comb because my hair is sticking up, and I give her a key-ring attached to a miniature bus, and she says she'll ride it to meet me in London.

By the time Liang finds a bus going east, it is almost night. But the air is still warm, and beyond our window the wayside homes are softly lit. The river road is unknown even to Liang, and I have never heard of anyone travelling here. I've read that the border is bristling with arms, like the Russian shore, and I anticipate being turned back, or arrested. I do not confide this to Liang, in case he loses heart. But as our bus winds through the dark, we encounter no police post or roadblock, and scarcely any vehicle at all, and after an hour we reach the small town of Dawujiazi, and disembark tired for the night.

Dawujiazi, I've heard, is a last haven of Manchu, once the official language of an empire embracing almost one third of the world's people. In the brief minutes of our walking, I imagine changed faces, different pasts. For the Manchu origins lie with the semi-nomadic Jurchen tribes, whose northern limit, home to the so-called Wild Jurchens, was the Amur. In 1644 the Jurchens stormed the Great Wall, ousted the decayed Ming dynasty, and created a dominion larger than any Chinese empire before it, ruling as the imperial Qing. Even after they moved their seat of government south to Peking, the Manchu kept a fierce nostalgia for their homeland, cherishing it – even as they abandoned it – as a land of near-sacred purity, and a country of precious ginseng, furs and gold. By stretching their thousand-mile Willow Palisade of earthworks and linked trees across much of north-east China, they tried to insulate this ancestral heartland from southern immigration, so that for decades Manchuria (the term is Western) lay neglected, while the garrisons along the Amur became stranded outposts. Through the eighteenth century the region turned into China's contradictory Siberia, where criminals and disgraced officials were exiled. But by the time the Manchu dynasty ended in 1911, ethnic Chinese migrants had long ago infiltrated these fertile lowlands, and had so subsumed the Manchu population that travellers could identify no difference.

In Dawujiazi, where Liang and I hunt for a hotel in the dark, the high-rise flat-blocks seem as anonymous as those of suburban Heihe. Liang admires their one-child apartments – they are warmer than the old cottage compounds, he says – while I wonder at the displacement, all over China, of that old, communal life. By the time we find a hotel immured in a tenement block, Liang has told people brazenly that his foreign friend, Mr Too-be-long, wants to hear Manchu spoken, and he assures me that word will get out. 'Don't worry. By morning everyone will know you are here.' Meanwhile he never contemplates single rooms, but opens his little washbag in a twin-bed chamber overlooking the town square, and sleeps in his underpants, nursing his phone like a baby, while Mr Toobelong lies awake in the silence of a town that has turned dark hours before.

*

This is an older town than most along the river. Few settlements, I've heard, trace any Manchu heritage. But in the morning, as Liang and I stroll after a sparse breakfast, there seems nothing to distinguish it. A few women on motor scooters are paying early visits, and small trucks are on the move, laden with soya beans. Then we cross a canal winding between stone balustrades carved lightly with a crouching bird, which Liang imagines an imperial symbol. And when we return to the hotel our door bursts open on a small, swarthy man who bounces down on Liang's bed and announces that he is Manchu. In fact one quarter of the people here are Manchu, Yun says – two thousand townsfolk – but almost no one can speak a word.

No widespread language can have vanished more swiftly. The Japanese occupation of Manchuria between 1931 and 1945, setting up a puppet Manchu emperor, followed years later by a Cultural Revolution that persecuted all difference, had converted Manchu pride into shame and self-condemnation.

The little peoples were all persecuted at that time, Yun says. 'My parents were almost broken in the Revolution. They were accused of shamanism. That was in our Manchu heritage, of course, but they never practised anything . . . They died too young, younger than I am now.' He runs his fingers over a stubble of greying hair. 'People tried to hide their Manchu identity in those years, and this was very hard.'

I wonder aloud how he retained the language.

'My parents spoke Manchu together in the home. I picked it up from them as a child. They even looked like Manchu, my father very tall. We resembled Mongolians, I think. Small eyes, big cheeks.' He draws his hand down his own face, as if he had inherited this. But he conforms to no ethnic stereotype. Beside the amber oval of Liang's face, Yun's is wide and rosy, and his eyes black crescents that glitter with happiness at this sudden interest in his life. His eyebrows are curiously broken, as if by some accident, and his mouth, which rarely smiles, hangs thick and loose. He can remember his family genealogy, he says, for five generations back, and they were pure Manchu, and spent all their lives on the Heilongjiang.

And what was the river to them, I wonder.

'It wasn't exactly holy. But we still call it our Mother River. My ancestors were all soldiers on these shores. We belonged to the White Banner.' He is glowing now. The eight Manchu banners had supplied the military elite of their dynasty. 'My son is a soldier too. And tall, like you.' He calls up a photo on his phone of a strong young man, swimming somewhere in the Yellow Sea.

Liang breaks in: 'Does he speak Manchu too? Mr Toobelong likes languages.'

'No. Only a few old people ever spoke Manchu here, and they've died. Except me. People aren't afraid to say they're Manchu any more, but they only know Chinese. Even my older brother – he's dead now – never spoke Manchu. For some reason I was the only one. I think as a boy I was always listening . . .'

Only when I ask him if he's proud of his heritage does a moment's confusion surface. Perhaps in obedience to the Party line, or in deference to Liang smiling beside him, he says: 'No, not proud, we're all the same now.' He makes a levelling motion with his hand. 'We are all Chinese.' After a silence he adds: 'All the same, I'm sorry my son doesn't speak . . .'

It was in the distant Amur outposts that the language had held out longest. There are still speakers of a related tongue two thousand miles to the west, where Manchu soldiers had once guarded the frontier against czarist Russia. But the number who know true Manchu nationwide is unknown, veering between twenty and a mere three, with a few academics studying early Qing documents. The language itself belongs to the obscure Tungusic branch of the Altaic family, shared by Turkic peoples, Hungarians, Finns and Mongolians. Even the last Manchu emperor, it is said, spoke it only haltingly.

Yun too, when he starts to speak, looks stolidly puzzled. It is as if the words occupy a basement in his memory, and have to be pulled up one by one. But slowly they start to loosen and flow, and finally become a whispering stream, full of short vowels and blurred gutturals. Occasionally the gong-like tone of a Mandarin loan-word sounds, but even in Yun's voice, in which every word blends into the next, Manchu emerges softly staccato, seeming closer to Japanese.

Yun looks happy now, in his far ancestral tongue. I wonder what he is saying. It sounds somehow important. This, after all, was the language of a dynasty that had ruled the fifth-largest empire ever known, extending deep into Inner Asia and far north of the Heilongjiang. I imagine a vocabulary adapted to verbose edicts or shouted battle orders. But when Yun ends, and I ask him, he says he knows too little of history or politics to voice them. Sealed in a language that nobody else understands, he has been talking about his domestic troubles.

As the Heilongjiang curves eastward, littered with sandbanks, tracts of reclaimed marshland lie in the autumnal quiet of harvested maize, soya and wheat. They spread sepia and dull yellow under a stormy sky. Here and there a canal or a farm track runs in between, and villages cluster under roofs of blue or cement-coloured tiles. They look poor, but Liang says the farmers here are better off than people in the towns. He means himself, of course, and his wife too, who worked in a shop that has just closed. The fields around us may no longer belong to collective farms, he says, but to company-run ventures that buy up and amalgamate family plots, 'which makes for all sorts of trouble and corruption'.

Sometimes our bus mounts into hills thronged with deciduous trees – its engine panting and whining – then we emerge to see the river far beyond, more than half a mile wide now, winding pale through the distance. There is no sign of the barbed-wire bulwarks that curtain the Russian shore: only a white watchtower here and there, or nothing at all. As we travel farther, deeper, my anxiety that we will be turned back begins, perhaps dangerously, to fade.

A relay of buses takes us east along the river for three days, and we start to feel on holiday. An obscure disappointment is lifting from Liang, as if somebody else had been waiting behind his faintly crestfallen figure and is now set free. We eat breakfasts of steamed buns or *kasha* in bare restaurants, where rough-hewn workmen and farmers set up a jovial clamour. The young men are hefty boys with hedgehog hair, often a foot taller than their elders, and sometimes an ancient couple, tiny and wizened, occupies a corner to share a bowl of dumplings.

Liang loves these restaurants. In the evenings, in the towns where we sleep, he hunts them down in a bustle of excitement and indecision. They mostly look the same to me: eating houses unimaginable in provincial towns thirty years ago. Laminated menus spread across their walls, illustrating as many as eighty dishes, and when Liang and I finally settle in, each course arrives so huge – suited to whole families – that even he can barely dent it, and he piles whatever he can into a doggy bag. But these suppers are the high point of his day. His chopsticks fly between stir-fry and chow mein, orange chicken and sesame beef, black fungus, ginger shrimp (if we strike lucky), tofu and a medley of dishes whose Mandarin names and tastes I cannot decipher. We talk still in the mélange of my erratic Chinese and the mangled Russian that Liang insists on trying. My Mandarin sends me on tortuous detours to explain simple things, while Liang often replaces the clustered consonants and fricatives of Russian with a despairing mew. Between us there emerges a hybrid of grotesque disharmony. I also become an object of covert attention in these remote haunts, where people have scarcely seen even a Russian, and Liang likes to discuss me with any interested customer, as if I will understand nothing. 'Mr Toobelong is a writer from England . . . He fell off a horse in Mongolia . . . Yes, his eyes are deep-set and his hair sticks up [despite Mrs Wang's comb] . . . He is very old, but he can use chopsticks . . .'

But when the hubbub dies down, and our food has exhausted us, he goes outside and lights up his Hongtashan cigarette – he is a chain-smoker – and we return at last to our cheap hotel – they cost less than ten dollars a night – through darkened streets. Our room always has a television, even if nothing else works, but we ignore the patriotic newsclips that are playing in the slipstream of Golden Week. In the face of their saccharine optimism, I start to miss Russia's violent thrillers, and even its monitored political debates. Liang, in any case, generally opts for a period soap opera whose soulful melodrama is broken every few minutes by advertisements for Tsingtao beer and Ambrosial Greek yoghurt.

The towns where we pass the nights have sprung up yesterday. Their long, six-storey flat blocks, serried shop signs and broad streets where cheap Chinese cars go, look coeval with one another. At Xunke we walk in harsh wind along the river, whose esplanade stretches and bulges out as if for some grand future. Waves are slapping at its foot, seagulls crying, and two men bathe in the freezing shallows. Near the promenade's end an inscribed boulder, which Liang peruses in silence, confirms this as the border with Russia.

Next day we follow a thin, concrete road to Jiayin. Harvested maize rustles to either side, with purple fields of soya, and often reaches from one horizon to the next. Our bus is almost empty, and hardly stops. Shelves of sand bank up along the way, like terraces carved from the earth. And once the Heilongjiang emerges startlingly close below us, split into channels, sky-blue among their islands, while to the north hang the silhouettes of Russian hills.

The festive flags and lanterns of Jiayin dangle along near-deserted streets, as if the event they honour has been forgotten. But then, where they end above the river, our bus releases us onto a teeming waterfront. The whole populace seems to be strolling its grey-stoned promenade. Vendors have wheeled out stalls of cheap jewellery and souvenirs where the badinage and laughter reach a raucous crescendo. Fake trademarks are running amok, with poor townsfolk bartering for Givenchy handbags and Reebok trainers. They march along a riverine walkway fluttering with red pennants and posters, where the engulfing smile of Xi Jinping enforces happiness. In this cold, brilliant sunlight everyone is photographing everyone else, including me.

The river has transformed to porcelain blue. Its pleasure boats cruise the shore on half-hour excursions, the passengers sheltering on deck under little pagoda roofs, while graver craft are moored nearby: a police sloop, a boat for taking soundings of the river, an External Affairs ministry vessel from Heihe. And once a larger launch churns by, crammed with holidaymakers, its prow ascending into a towering plaster brontosaurus.

For Jiayin is 'Dinosaur Town'. More than a century ago fragmentary skeletons were eased out of its eroded riverbanks and the first duck-billed dinosaurs were identified. Since then, the whole region has become a palaeontologist's dreamland, and a flamboyant museum has sprung up. Statues of duck-billed dinosaurs scatter the town in commemoration, emerging as babies from giant eggs or sitting cross-legged on park benches. And now, in Golden Week, a fresh menagerie has broken out. No vista escapes the thorny backbone of a stegosaurus or a Tyrannosaurus rex, and thirty-foot-high sauropods browse every municipal garden. Moulded in plaster or silicon rubber, they lumber along the verges and erupt from rooftops in the town square. They decorate dustbins and crane from office balconies. Children are riding mechanical ones. And Liang wants to photograph them all.

We arrive exhausted at evening in a restaurant filled with shouting banqueters. Its centrepiece is the plaster skull of a grossly horned triceratops, which everyone ignores. Liang orders a miscellany of dishes, then scrolls past his dinosaur photos and arrives at the snapshot of a young woman which he turns towards me. She is sitting in a café, a cup lifted half to her lips. Her sunglasses are tilted back over free-flying hair. She does not smile.

I ask: 'Who is this?'

'This is my daughter.'

I mumble a compliment, but she seems to carry her father's sadness. He says: 'She lives in Qingdao.'

I cannot read his expression, and he scrolls on past her. Qingdao is over a thousand miles to the south. 'What does she do?'

'She teaches at a dance school.' As if to explain her absence, he says: 'She makes 400,000 yuan a year in Qingdao. You can buy an apartment for that.' His forehead has wrinkled. 'It would be hard for her to come back to Heihe. There's no work and the young people are leaving. Those who go away to university never come back. Even the public baths are emptying. Things may be going well in Shenzhen and Shanghai, but here in the north we are very poor.'

Shyly he calls up earlier photos on his phone. I see a younger man and his wife, in better times, with their little daughter on tiptoe between them. The child's ribboned hair is bunched on either side of her head like outsize ears, and her grinning face tucked into the red scarf of the Young Pioneers. Liang stands proudly alongside, in jacket and tie, and his wife behind him, dressed in the uniform of some earlier profession. She has an open, vivid face. 'Life was better in Heihe then.' But in a later snapshot she has grown anxious, narrow-eyed, and the teenage daughter touches her own cheeks with long fingertips, uncertain how she looks.

Liang says: 'She is twenty-five and still not married. She will never come home.' Perhaps it is easier to confide in a foreigner, in a garbled tongue. Perhaps it somehow does not count. But the long oval of his face becomes a mask of sadness. His daughter is the offspring of the one-child policy, he says. She is all they have. Such children carry the burden of their ageing parents alone. I sense she is self-absorbed, perhaps spoilt, but cherishing her independence. He is afraid for their old age.

This reverie is disrupted by a beggar who has inveigled himself into the restaurant and now hovers over our food. Liang snaps: 'We all need help, but we have to earn it!' and the man starts in surprise, then retreats, crestfallen.

Liang goes on unperturbed: 'Things are still hard with us, harder than with you. Even my own father lost his job in the end. And he came through bitter times.'

'You had to care for him?'

But he says simply: 'I loved him,' and I remember Batmonkh.

'You have brothers, sisters?'

'I have an elder sister, but she's a witch.'

The Confucian duty towards parents has never died. Liang's earliest memories are of his father's devotion and suffering. 'His generation was consumed by the Cultural Revolution. He was just a small-time cadre at the time, secretary to a People's commune. But he was arraigned by Red Guards. They put him in a dunce's hat, then yelled criticism at him for five hours. I was just a child of six, but I was forced to watch. I had to watch while he was beaten and humiliated. I didn't understand. I just saw his bowed head . . .

'People still don't speak about the Cultural Revolution. It's not done to criticize it.' He glances round him, but we are safe in our hybrid tongue. 'Our family was disgraced, of course, and we were expelled to the countryside. We lived in a peasant village. We were rationed to ten white noodles each a month, with two *jin* of rice and sixty-two soya beans.' He laughs sourly. His chopsticks idle by a bowl of shredded duck. 'The young have no idea what people went through in those times. My daughter says she can't even imagine it.'

Sometimes, he says, when he and his wife visit her in Qingdao, he bathes for hours in the ocean. Years ago they even went to Hainan island in the South China Sea. Something about the regularity of the waves, he says, sets him at peace. But his daughter chooses to stay indoors, afraid that the sun will darken her white skin.

Little more than a century ago, travellers described the Chinese frontier along the Amur as devoid of life. While the Russian shore was punctuated by Cossack forts and settlements, the Chinese side, for hundreds of miles, showed little but steppe-land and pine-blackened hills. The Manchu bannermen on guard here were stranded in poverty. Towns like Jiayin and Xunke, if they existed at all, were squalid villages standing in fields of mosquito-plagued millet, or clusters of native tents.

Yet for almost two centuries Chinese farmers and traders had been infiltrating the Willow Palisade. At first they settled in lands far south of the Amur, but then their migration became a steady flow. Typically they were leaving the provinces of Shandong and Hebei close to Peking, whose crowded fields could no longer support them, to farm the rich-soiled emptiness that stretched beyond the Great Wall. The Manchurian climate was harsh, and the growing season short, but these migrants planned to move for a few years only, to support their families back home, and expected one day to return. Unlike Russian settlers in Siberia, who cast off ties to their past and created a Siberian identity, the Chinese communities reproduced themselves in the image of their origin, and at first advanced northward only in cautious stages. Above all, they feared dying in an alien land. 'The falling leaf', it was said, 'returns to the root of the tree'; but many came home only in their coffins. Into the last century these could be seen at the crossing-point of the Great Wall, strapped five abreast on carts, their great planks sealed and laquered. On top of each coffin perched a caged cockerel, whose crowing would remind any wandering spirit of where its body lay, as they crossed the border home. The sure sign that a Manchurian village was becoming permanent was the possession of its own graveyard.

But in the early twentieth century, as in Russia, the migrant flow quickened to a flood. The region's turbulent politics – even Mao Zedong's mass social and economic disruptions – only exacerbated migration into what they called the Great Northern Wasteland. During Mao's years Manchuria became China's industrial powerhouse, a zone of steel and oil, and the plains of the Heilongjiang transformed into a vast network of supportive state farms. The migration only reversed towards the century's end, after factories fell obsolete, villages emptied into cities, and the old collectives began to streamline into company ventures.

The 200-mile road from Jiayin to Suibin, tracking the Heilongjiang south, eases out of these old turmoils into mountain quiet. Here the last reach of the Khingan massif shoulders eastward to the river, and the southernmost drift of

Siberia's Bureinsky range descends to face it on the far shore. The road makes a concrete sliver through the blaze of autumn forest. To either side the bloom of birch, oak and maple undulates across the hills in bursts of red and gold. For miles our bus winds upward through corridors of burnished undergrowth, then levels at last into plateaus where distance dims the forest to purple-grey, as if a great fire were burning out on the farther mountains.

Once, where a Manchu fort had overlooked the river, everybody disembarks to smoke, and I clamber down an overgrown path to the waterside. Gliding through its mountain defile, the Heilongjiang has deepened and darkened. Its water comes cold to my touch. Although its surface is barely broken, I sense the body of the river moving with a new, constricted power. The Russian shore ascends in a rampart of shrouding trees beyond, with no man-made barrier in sight. Perhaps this forest wall is judged steep and dense enough to repel intrusion. But to my surprise a watchtower is tucked into a fold of the Chinese bank, and a young soldier comes down the path. He just wants to smoke. Yes, he says, the far shore belongs to those Russians, the Hairy Ones, but he has never seen any. It's very boring here.

By early afternoon the mountains have shrunk and scattered, and our bus is crossing a plain where the wheat fields radiate for miles, and the Khingan massif is an ashen memory in the sky. Egrets stand along the canals, but they are the only life. Often the villages look derelict, their homes abandoned or in ruins, and strewn with rubbish, and this desolation follows us over the floodplains of the Songhua, the Heilongjiang's greatest tributary, to the town of Suibin, which even Liang has never heard of.

The mountain freshness of the air has gone. We enter suburbs of scrap-iron yards, coal heaps, rundown workshops, stranded farm machinery. At nightfall we check in to a big, dim-lit hotel, and go down to the Songhua over torn-up pavements. Everything here looks rougher, poorer. Stallholders and passers-by stare and cry 'Foreigner!' and children detach themselves from their parents to follow us. But we reach the river alone along unlit banks. It flows here as wide as the Amur; but when I thrust my hand into the current, it disappears beneath my wrist into water thick with silt and pollution. Harbin, Jiamusi, Jilin, Changchun: a string of industrial cities thread its banks upriver, pouring in factory effluent and sewage. In 2005 a chemical plant exploded and sent down a fifty-mile-long slick of toxic benzene that panicked cities as far away as Khabarovsk. Beneath our feet the stone-littered banks have been shored up with wire mesh, and are seamed with bedraggled weeds and trash, and the close, fetid smell of the water brings dismay.

Perhaps I have dreamed the river pure until now, while knowing it is not. Out of Mongolia the Onon flows clear and soft-watered, but where the Shilka meets the Amur, it is already contaminated by mercury from antiquated goldmines, and its salmon depleted. As for the Songhua, it has become so crowded by industry that it is the Amur's prime contaminant. On the Russian shore downriver they say the fish taste of chemicals.

As Liang and I climb back into the streets above, I feel a rankling sadness, as if the river were in some way mine. Liang's cure for this is to seek out the best local restaurant. He has already had bouts of taking me under his wing, then relentlessly pursuing any casual wish that I express, and now he blocks up a whole road demanding of passers-by where sweet-and-sour pork may be found, because Mr Toobelong is an author who will write it up.

We settle over a dish of fiery boiled mutton and some cans of Harbin beer. Half a can raises a pink glow to his cheeks.

Every twenty minutes he goes outside to smoke. He is feeling maudlin because tomorrow he will be returning to unemployment in Heihe, but soon we are laughing together at misfortune: how I have fallen off a horse, of course, and how he goes everywhere on foot since driving his motorbike into a tractor. Often, it seems, he conforms to Chinese cliché, with his passion for food, his care with money, his obsessive photography. But for Liang old duties have deepened into domestic tragedy. Perhaps it is the Harbin beer that loosens us into intimacy, into talking about the complicated past. His mother, he says, was paralysed young after a stroke, and lingered many years, until she was no longer speaking. But it is his father who remains his exemplar.

'I obeyed him all my childhood. He was like justice to me. Only once we argued, when I failed my school exams and didn't really mind. Then my father wept. Not because I'd failed, but because I didn't care.' He strikes his heart. 'I never forgot it. I only realized then how much he loved me.' And still Liang cannot erase from childhood memory his father's head bowed in the dunce's hat, and the gale of incomprehensible insults. 'In the end he got Alzheimer's and for three years he just lay about, not recognizing anyone. I was the favourite son. I stopped work to look after him.' He is staring at me blankly. Half his life he has been surrounded by these demanding ghosts. Since then, his work prospects have faded away. But he only repeats like a mantra: 'I loved him.'

So we return, a little drunk, to our hotel, and we are brought up short to see our scant baggage waiting in the reception hall. The hotel proprietor has called in the police. Neither he nor they are in sight, but a nervous cleaner tells us we must wait. The owner has panicked at the thought of a foreigner. Foreigners don't come here. A few hotels in remoter cities, I hear, have notices behind their reception desks telling staff what to do if foreigners appear. Most are not allowed to receive them, and only the small ones don't care.

Then two burly, unsmiling men in battledress barge into the foyer. They are border police, although we are now far from any border. One of them says: 'Foreigners are forbidden here. Are you Russian?'

'No, I'm English.' The word suddenly sounds hostile.

The senior officer amends: 'Foreigners never come to this town. Who do you know here?'

They pass my documents between them. The questions come formal, chilly, familiar: When was I last in China? Why am I in Suibin? Which is my company?

I feel at once rancorous and unnerved. This is close to an older, xenophobic China, where guesthouses turned away foreigners as if in ancestral fear. Now the officers commandeer the hotel computer, call up my passport and data, make abrupt telephone calls. It takes a long time. Liang is standing beside me, looking unperturbed. Perhaps he is drunk. The police are rifling through my rucksack. At last they line me up to be photographed beside the senior officer – I am wearing a resentful scowl by now – and then they photograph Liang beside me. I cannot tell what this may mean for him. But he stares back expressionless, as if this is the standard way of things. The officers consult dourly together, out of earshot, then ask more questions: Who sent me here? Where is the rest of my luggage? Then they duplicate my visa, and at last leave, still grim with bafflement.

We are allowed into a big, gloomy bedroom. Liang says the police are only covering themselves, and he falls into innocent sleep, still cradling his phone, while I lie awake for another hour, listening for the return of footsteps.

*

A narrow road moves up the left bank of the Songhua, then cuts across marshlands to where a ferry is moored among the reeds. It carries our bus across the clouded waters. The current is heavy with silt, and spumes of bubbles float downriver. For a while we are coasting along swamplands; then the city of Tongjiang emerges to our north in a spectral line of cranes and islands.

You might imagine it a metropolis of warehouses, oil refineries and offshore barracks. But as we draw closer the islands appear unnaturally tall and steep. With the sun in my eyes I even imagine them banded in promenades or houses. Then I realize they are not islands at all, but barges stacked mountainously with Siberian timber. Six or seven of them are trailing upriver towards some landfall deeper into China.

This is the export that infuriates and embitters so many Russians: the felling – much of it illegal – of their native taiga. To them the forest elicits not economic greed but a glow of national identity. It harbours their myths and earliest beliefs. Yet Russian logging companies, in league with Chinese sawmills and entrepreneurs, lay waste to swathes of pristine forest and protected species, and the timber passes through middlemen and corrupt officials until its origin cannot be traced. Estimates claim that every year sees the devastation of an area the size of Belgium. In the end, without regeneration, all that is left is erosion and stripped grasslands that often rage with carbon-reeking fires.

As our ferry curls into dock, these sad, moving islands are gliding out of sight. They are on their way to paper mills and furniture factories, probing far upriver, and the centre of Tongjiang sees nothing of them. With its wide streets and blazoned ground-floor shops and six-storey tenements above, it might be a blueprint for any of these towns along the Heilongjiang. Its closeness to Russia – the Songhua joins the

Amur just to the north – is echoed in a scattering of shop-signs; and a leftover notice – inexplicably in English – points to an underground complex tunnelled in the time of Mao Zedong, in fear of nuclear war with the Soviet Union. Liang says that Beijing and Harbin are still full of such labyrinths. In Tongjiang the subterranean city has been sealed up or converted to shopping centres whose abundance and variety would have astounded Mao. In these fierce-lit emporia crowds of young women are sampling scents and queuing up for manicures. Even Liang is momentarily transfixed by a hoyden in a T-shirt printed 'Bad Girl', trying on a raft of gaudy lipsticks. Others buy jewellery worked from Russian gold; and a notice to tourists, who no longer exist, still invites them to attend a traditional tea ceremony.

We wander the streets at random. In the Sino-Russian Culture Park, where we are the sole visitors, we enter an avenue of sculpted Greek deities, outsize Chinese urns and spear-wielding Hellenic horsemen all leading to a cast-iron steeple topped by an Orthodox cross. In this hybrid wonder-land Liang, staring up at a fleshly Aphrodite or Apollo, feels vaguely affronted. 'They aren't Chinese. They're not even Russian, are they? Why are they here?'

I can't answer. Somewhere in the Chinese imagination (but not in Liang's) Russia belongs with classical antiquity. Beyond us the pantheon descends to replicas of Donald Duck and Mickey Mouse, jostling among *matrioshka* dolls, some still used as rubbish bins. The whole complex, built at a time of promised Russian–Chinese commerce, has shrunk to an empty embrace, an invitation to people who have left, or never came. The venues nearby that still flaunt their Cyrillic welcome – the Playboy Club, the Slow Cat Café – appear foolishly rejected too. Then 'Look!' Liang exclaims. 'Is that a Russian thing?'

Beside us a five-spired church confronts the street with a flagrant golden cross. We make our way inside beneath a Chinese inscription, 'God is with us', and find ourselves in an immense prayer hall whose wide dais and lectern trumpet Protestant evangelism. Liang, who has never entered a church before, looks nonplussed. And he's longing for a cigarette.

But a sweet-faced warden finds us, and answers questions piecemeal before his replies trail into pieties. In the Cultural Revolution, he says, no such building was allowed, of course, and people kept their faith alone. 'Then in the early days, when there was another church here, the Russians used to visit from the Culture Park. We couldn't understand each other, but it didn't matter. God knows all languages. And music united us . . . Then three years ago this church was raised by the sub-scriptions of the faithful.'

I say: 'How could they? This place is enormous.'

'The message spread by word of mouth. Now we number a thousand. It's true that many of our people are old. But the old are nearer to God, after all, nearer to judgment and salvation. And we are all sinners . . .'

Perhaps I am still haunted by the Cultural Revolution and by the persecuted Christians I had encountered years ago, but I hear myself say: 'You aren't afraid?'

'There are millions and millions of us Christians now, you know. More than sixty million, they say.'

'Yes, I know.' Yet they are a drop in an atheist sea.

'Twenty years ago we would have been afraid. But not now. Not in today's China. And our priest is a woman.' Perhaps he thinks this protection. 'Only God sees the future . . .'

The golden cross that shines above us as we leave seems to illumine the street with an evangelism that is forbidden. Liang says he cannot understand Christianity at all, nor the Buddhist monastery that is building opposite, as if in competition. We enter its gates in puzzlement. It is vast. Arcades of cells are awaiting future monks, and a hostel for pilgrims is nearly complete. All is new, gleaming, empty: a maze of marble and plated gold. Some benefactor of monstrous wealth must be creating this, but there is no one to ask, not a builder or monk in sight. Only a low, continuous chant, throbbing like an unearthly heartbeat, sounds from somewhere we cannot locate.

The main temple rears before us in a stack of curved roofs and polychrome eaves, while inside, from among crimson-laquered columns twined with imperial dragons, a twenty-foot Buddha monopolizes the altar, flanked by goddesses. The traditional elements are all in place. They await only age to confer the patina of holiness. The Goddess of Mercy floats behind the Buddha's altar, backed by a panoply of sages and worshippers, adrift on blue clouds. Tiered shelves of tiny, near identical Buddhas – some ten thousand of them, I calculate – are banked up gleaming through the dimness, as in some divine supermarket.

In a separate temple dedicated to the Maitreya, the Buddha of the Future is no longer the clairvoyant titan whom I had witnessed in Tsugol monastery, but has transformed to a golden pudding of a half-god, the 'Laughing Buddha', his belly spread before him like a patient's tea tray, lolling among a swarm of children. More than a thousand years ago the Future Buddha, feared by nervous emperors, had been converted from an apocalyptic threat to this figure of passive merriment, patron of joy and success, and even now a family of three – the only worshippers we see – is kneeling before him and murmuring a petition that Liang cannot distinguish.

He doesn't trust such hopes, he says, nor any worldly utopia. Beijing's promise of a revived north-east, like Moscow's for a prosperous Siberia, reminds him of a moment in childhood, in a temple somewhere he cannot recall, where he asked the

Buddha for a future that never came. He settles suddenly on a dusty balustrade. 'When I was on holiday in Russia,' he says, 'the maid who cleaned my room told me she'd been brought up believing in the Communist utopia. But she'd lost her only son and was looking after her parents without state help. She said the whole country was a fraud.'

Perhaps because we are about to part, Liang is releasing long-suppressed thoughts. He knows I am researching a book, and he wants me to write this: 'I think we should never have agreed to sign that treaty with Putin validating Russia's land-grab. Many of us resent it. We are strong now, so why did we do that? Frankly, I hate the Russians.' Like other Chinese, he calls them 'Hairy Ones', with a linguistic intimation of savagery. 'They used to come to my wife's shop in the old days, and I laughed when they lifted their big arms and our cheap Chinese shirts split under their shoulders. But we hate them most because they took our land.'

We roam the porticoes for a while, searching for the praying monks, whose chant has quickened and deepened, like a swarm of angry bees. Then we discover them. They are singing disembodied from a cassette recorder which someone has left in an empty cell. So we leave the monastery for a farewell meal. Liang mentions a Korean dog restaurant, but I veto this, and soon we are sitting over bowls of ox tendon and bass brain instead. Liang has gone quiet. He pulls a pedometer from his pocket – he has kept this secret until now – and he is pleased to have taken nine thousand steps so far today. 'My blood pressure is high,' he says. 'That's why I worry about my snoring. A blocked nose puts pressure on your heart.'

'You don't snore.'

He imagines, I think, that he may end up paralysed, like his mother. That is why he never cared when he and Mr Toobelong became lost returning to their hotel at night, a little drunk. It put up his step count. He looks suddenly mournful, and older.

'The government doesn't give much for poor health.' He is little more than fifty, I think, but envisaging old age. And his only child is far away in Qingdao, living her own life.

We say goodbye in an empty street, hugging self-consciously. I feel a lurch of sadness and wonder at this affection across the borders of space and years and broken language. He drops his cigarette to hold me, then walks away without looking behind again. Back in Heihe, snow is falling.

For a hundred miles over farmland and watered plains a deserted road shadows the Heilongjiang north-east. The bus costs three dollars. Without Liang beside me, the passengers show open curiosity. Mothers manoeuvre children onto their laps to view the foreigner – perhaps the first one they have seen – and he is discussed in the Mandarin that he should not understand. His eyes are weirdly deep, of course, and something has pulled his nose forward, and he must be poor to travel like this. Somebody takes a furtive photograph. From time to time someone else lifts the open map from his hands to scrutinize it. A pair of old men trail their fingers over its hills and rivers. They recognize its cities by Chinese names familiar from the Qing dynasty. Blagoveshchensk becomes Hailanpao, Khabarovsk turns to Boli.

In the map's west, where a speckled line delineates a railway snaking up from China to Russian Birobidzhan, Stalin once inducted Jewish settlers, whose descendants barely survive there. A thin fracture in mid-river betrays that the railway is incomplete. The two-kilometre Chinese section of the bridge, built to bring Russian iron ore and timber south, was finished more than two years ago. It leans far across the Heilongjiang to meet its Russian counterpart: a mere three hundred metres which hangs unjoined above the water, in old distrust.

For a long time a violent sunset gashes the sky, then the dark comes down and our headlamps shed a yellow mist in front of us until the lights of Fuyuan glitter above the river. Here is my Chinese journey's end. A few miles to our east the Heilongjiang turns back into Russia, becoming the Amur again, and starts its long way north to the Pacific. Sometimes, I've heard, ferries cross the river from Fuyuan, reaching the Russian shore thirty miles downriver at Khabarovsk. I hope to cross here too, but tonight I am glad to find a hotel small enough to evade the police, and I wake in a quiet room at dawn to the glistening closeness of the river.

In these days of late October the Amur is already fringed with ice, and the air tingles. You walk the streets to the cry of seagulls. Around you the crowding hills, glazed with weak sunlight, nudge the town towards the river in streets more diverse than others, touched here and there by the grace of rooflines floating domes and turrets. Instead of grimy suburbs, every other vista ends in a curtain of trees or a gleam of water.

From the town's edge you may climb up among ancient oaks and lindens along brick paths to a steep lookout. The tree branches are knotted with the ribbons of brides, who come on their wedding day. From a small pavilion near the summit, littered with Harbin beer cans and empty Panda cigarette packets, you can glimpse the town descending from its wooded valleys to the quayside, and beyond it to where the Heilongjiang fades to an isle-strewn lake.

While I wait here, surprised by how small Fuyuan looks below me, panting groups arrive on holiday: sightseers, photographers, lovers. Once an old man wheezes up the pavilion stair and slumps complaining beside me. What has happened to his legs? he wonders. Why do they feel like someone else's? He is dressed in an old-fashioned, high-collared jacket. His eyes are failing, but they glimpse the collegial comfort of my white hair.

These young people, he says, he doesn't understand China any longer. His voice rasps and whispers. 'If an old man falls down he'll have to pay one of them to help him up. They just think of money, the young.' He is rubbing a grazed knee. 'Mao Zedong said we should care for one another, love one another. But I've heard that on the internet they say Mao was mad.'

A long while later a quiet couple lingers in the pavilion, eyeing me curiously, and we fall into halting conversation. They run a local kindergarten, and are bright in each other's eyes. From here the Heilongjiang flows to China's farthest frontier, they say, where it meets the Ussuri tributary, and they offer suddenly to drive me there. So the afternoon passes in the dream of a happier China. They seem innocent of politics or history. Those matters are managed elsewhere. If their internet is sanitized, they do not know or will not speak of it. Fuyuan is looking up, they say. The railway reached it several years ago, and it has a small airport now. They drive a Chinese Jiangnan car, which works, and she is pregnant with their second child. Sometimes they touch hands.

We reach a point where the Ussuri – very pure and fast – marks the eastern limit of China. Here, where the Heilongjiang engulfs it in a mud-coloured continent of water, a windswept viewing platform spreads, ringed by marble balustrades and spiked with winged columns. On the Ussuri's distant bank, near the rivers' confluence, we can make out a Russian village and a lonely watchtower. Beyond them, cutting China off from the Pacific, a long range of mountains ascends, black with larch trees.

Tentatively I mention the Treaty of Peking, by which Russia seized these lands. The kindergarten teachers remember it dimly from their schooldays. There is nothing in those mountains, they say, and when I murmur that Chinese poachers penetrate them, they lift their hands in horror. 'No! Nobody goes there!' But they still call them by their Chinese name: Zhuajishan.

We walk together for a long time along the platform's perimeter. Nearby, in the last Chinese guard-post, the soldiers are airing mattresses in their courtyard. People often come here to view the dawn, the teachers say, the first sunrise in their world. The shining platform, thrust out into space, defies mundane geography: we are at the same longitude as New Guinea and central Australia. We gaze over at the stolen hills in silence. All is at peace now, they say, all settled, and it is easy to believe them as we look down on those stilled plains, in the waning sunlight.

China ebbs away. The sky hangs huge above the flattening hills. Fuyuan fades behind the slipstream of the hydrofoil as it makes downriver for Russia and Khabarovsk, and passengers are confined below deck. The shoreline gleams with ice.

Around me the cabin is crammed with Russian 'camels', whom I never glimpsed in Fuyuan. Their bundles of massed clothes and footwear had sped through Chinese customs and are now heaped on the deck above us. The camels are middle-aged women, poorly dressed. They look sleepy and contented. Their blonde supervisor, who has marshalled them in Khabarovsk, is tutoring them about awkward Russian customs officials. Beside me, under long coats, the arms of two younger women, travelling to buy jewellery, are bangled to the elbow with watches and bracelets.

For a long time, beyond clouded windows, the river is so broken and confused by sandbanks that I cannot tell if we are sailing past an international frontier or an intervening island. Then, as our channel clears, the Amur's immensity breaks in. Swollen by the great tributaries of China, it stretches over a mile across. Beneath the Russian shore its waters glide in a dark band of their own, while the mud that has poured in from China radiates across more than half its surface. I imagine this pollution-stained advance through Russians' eyes. Their industrial poverty has kept the Amur purer, while the resurgence of China is defiling it. I stare out on a leaden sea, remembering others of the earth's great rivers that carry no such tensions: the Nile, the Yangtse, the Ganges, the Amazon, the Indus. However threatened, they flow like lifeblood through their nation's heart. Only the Amur divides.

8

Khabarovsk

I step ashore with a fleeting illusion of return to Europe, and climb the quayside alley on patterned pavements over a drift of birch leaves. Buildings of mingled brick and stone fluctuate overhead. A green-tiled turret appears, and classical columns hold up someone's balcony. But a glacial wind is blowing from the north, and the city above me barely makes a sound.

Twenty years ago, at the millennium's end, I had passed through Khabarovsk while crossing Siberia, and now the place awakens piecemeal in my memory. With half a million inhabitants, it is the largest city on the Amur, founded little more than a century and a half ago. Yet compared with the Heilongjiang shore it seems old and touched with melancholy. The brittle Chinese energy has gone.

As the Amur freezes, locking itself away for six months, I know I must leave, to return in the spring. I find my last room in a hulking hotel on Lenin Square. Chinese businessmen used to patronize it, but no longer. Lenin's statue stands nearby: I glimpse his trouser-leg from my bathroom. His arm is not lifted to hail the promised future; one hand fingers his lapel, the other is stuffed into his pocket, while on his plinth the inscribed words exalt a Communist vision shattered thirty years ago.

The square is immense and charmless, the hotel moribund. But for a day I walk the streets in a long recollection. After the towns of Heilongjiang, the buildings that move down Muraviev-Amursky Street, the city's main avenue, seem insanely playful and divergent, sprouting domes like vegetables or Tartar helmets, with brick gables and dormer windows that quaintly mimic the women's *kokoshnik* headdress of tradition. To either side the streets dip into parallel valleys stretched through autumn parklands. For a few hours I share the Chinese surprise at the diversity of passers-by, at the yellow hair and ginger beards, the multiform noses and cavernous eye sockets with the varicolour eyes inside them, at the outlandishly ugly or beautiful. Even in this cold the young women walk in the high-heeled boots and black tights of universal fashion. And in place of the firecracker sharpness of provincial Mandarin, the language around me has softened into clustered Russian consonants and half-swallowed vowels.

Now an icy rain is falling. I follow the ridge of Muraviev Street to its end above the river. Years ago, when I reached this square, I found a lonely archway and gaping emptiness where the city's cathedral had stood until destroyed after the Revolution. In old photographs this sanctuary appears spacious and earthbound. Now it has been rebuilt. In its place looms a sacred skyscraper, crowned by a quintet of spires and golden orbs. The 200-foot uprush of pink and white stuccoed concrete almost vanishes into the thickening hail. It is as if the earlier church had been squeezed upward into this neurotic colossus: less a haven of worship than a histrionic showpiece.

I shelter inside. The liturgy is over, and a chill pervades the half-lit saints. The ceilings rise too narrow for a dome, or for the frescoed Christ who ritually occupies it. Instead, a golden chandelier hangs from a blank tower. When I open a door to leave, I find the sleet quickened to a blizzard and the city whitened away, as if to put a full stop to the river somewhere below me, and to the fading year.

* * *

The dream of Russian power entering the Pacific was pursued only sporadically until Nikolai Muraviev, already a hardened soldier, was appointed governor-general of East Siberia at the precocious age of thirty-eight. From then on this relentless and irascible visionary drove forward his mission of annexing the Amur, routinely flouting orders in the face of jealousy and distrust among bureaucrats in St Petersburg. The Czar quipped that in his obsession over the Amur, Muraviev would go insane. But with the Treaty of Aigun in 1858 Muraviev, soon to be ennobled as Count Muraviev-Amursky, realized for czarist Russia a riverine highway from inner Siberia to the Pacific Ocean.

This paradoxically liberal firebrand – he proposed the abolition of serfdom long before its day – ended up living disillusioned in Paris, his career prematurely finished by his own intemperance, and died of gangrene there in 1881. Buried in Montmartre cemetery, he was for decades dismissed or forgotten in the country he had enlarged by almost 400,000 square miles. In 1891 a statue was raised to him on the headland of Khabarovsk, the city he founded – passing Russians used to doff their hats to it – then in 1929 it was toppled and replaced by one of Lenin. But by chance a cast of the original bronze survived, and sixty years later Lenin was evicted and the bellicose governor rose again on his plinth. A hundred and ten years after his death, he was disinterred and entombed with pomp in Vladivostok. Reproduced now on the 5,000-rouble banknote, Muraviev's statue towers on the clifftop above the

Amur, a telescope clenched in his folded arms, gazing towards the Pacific.

The river here is in turmoil. A braid of the Ussuri joins it as it bends stupendously north-east, and low islands complicate its flow. Close to shore the current corrugates and darkens, tightened by its surge north, but levels out midstream to steel-blue calm and a shadow-line of mountains. From here, for six hundred miles, the river-sea flows through regions where I hope still to follow it, past the once-secret arms manufactory of Komsomolsk-na-Amure to villages where its earliest native peoples remain. Northward again, at Nikolaevsk-na-Amure, Muraviev's chosen springboard at the river's mouth, it floods out at last into the Okhotsk Sea, an expanse as unfamiliar as itself, and into the Pacific.

By May the last ice-floes have drifted downriver with unearthly groaning and cracking, and Khabarovsk has woken from winter sleep. The pleasure boats are plying the river again, and people lounging on its beaches. Walking down Muraviev-Amursky Street in the sun, with my body healed, it is easy to feel this an old, almost cosmopolitan city. Yet Muraviev founded it a mere 160 years ago, naming it after the buccaneer Yerofei Khabarov: another rehabilitated prodigy, whose statue confronts passengers emerging from the railway station. The diversity of buildings, a legacy of pre-Revolutionary commerce, reflects a time when Khabarovsk flourished as a centre of foreign enterprise and government administration. A traveller in 1900 wrote that half its inhabitants were in uniform, and there was scarcely a woman to be seen.

Now the only uniforms that pass me are the pseudo-battledress bought by men from cheap department stores. The days are already long, the alleys flowering with crab-apple trees. I eat in bars that fill with revelry by early evening, their decor interspersed with photos of Russian cathedrals and Western pop groups.

It is night when I climb to the high bluff of Glory Square. The memorial to Khabarovsk's war dead spreads newly built here beneath the Cathedral of the Transfiguration. In avenues of black marble slabs twenty-five feet high, more than thirty thousand inscribed dead are ordered in their zone of conflict. From the monstrous casualties of the Second World War, they sink to more private conflicts: Angola, Armenia, Tajikistan. The skirmishes with China on Ussuri's Damansky island claim three, Afghanistan more than sixty. Those in the North Caucasus hang vacant, since 'our people', an old caretaker tells me, 'are still dying there', and deaths in Syria stand at four. I wonder bleakly if these scrupulous slabs will one day confess to casualties in Ukraine.

Above them the white body of the new cathedral lifts its gold domes into the night sky. Inside, among the tiered saints dimmed in candlelight, even the murdered imperial family hangs canonized: the short-sighted Czar and his unpopular German wife and sad children, all with golden haloes. The caretaker imagines that this cathedral, like a beacon gleaming on its heights from far away, was raised above the river as a warning to China: *Here is Russia, for ever.*

Beneath every Siberian region lies a bitter shadowland. The generations are passing away that inhabited those darker times, but sometimes the scene of this affliction survives, like a troubling palimpsest. In Khabarovsk the grand, cream-coloured complex of the Federal Security Service, successor to the KGB, supplants an inner yard where tractors were once revved to drown the fire of execution squads. Opposite, in 1937, during Stalin's paranoid purge of his security service, the workrooms of the secret police – now a range of

rose-coloured showrooms, travel agencies and hairdressers
– fell silent as its hundred officers were executed.

In a parallel road, still named Dzerzhinsky Street after the
architect of Lenin's Red Terror, the apartments of a vast,
faceless edifice once housed the families of police officers who
were either tortured before being deported to Kolyma, Stalin's
deadliest gulag, or summarily shot. Its faded yellow bulk still
seems to repel intrusion, although ordinary families inhabit it,
and a sleepy youth unlocks its gate. I find myself walking down
long passageways stinking of cats' urine. I wonder who can
bear to live here now. Iron doors lead to clusters of three or
four flats together, but each group is sealed off from the next,
until the whole building becomes a toxic honeycomb.

'My great-grandfather lived here in 1943,' the youth says.
'He'd been working in military telecommunications. He was
lucky to escape the purge. He said a secret passage runs
between its walls. Everything was secret. Everything could be
overheard . . .'

In a forested cemetery miles beyond the town, the victims
of the police lie buried. Beside a chapel at the gates, dedicated
'To the eternal memory of the slain innocents', the same marble
slabs as those that commemorate the war dead stand upright
like the leaves of a tragic book. They are inscribed with the
names of the 4,302 shot in Khabarovsk alone. I walk round
them numbly. Dead carnations lie strewn at their feet. Nobody
else is here, only my own face reflected in the black marble.
Nearby an engraved stone rises above the mass grave of 12,000
'killed in the years of Stalin's anarchy', and claims their
memory recovered, so that they rest in peace.

The House of Life is a tiny evangelical fellowship whose home
is an apartment near the top of a Khabarovsk flat-block. Their
group was born nearly thirty years ago, after the break-up of

the Soviet Union, when the Holy Spirit, says Sasha, shone again on Russia. Her face is warm with certainty, and rather beautiful. Every Sunday they hold a little service, she says, but they have no pastor yet – 'We hope to call one, please pray for us' – and in the congregation of sixty, perhaps ten come from those indigenous peoples who survive in regions sprawling north along the Amur.

A chart of these small, once-persecuted nations – the Nanai, Ulchi, Nivkhi, Evenk, some thirty more across Siberia – hangs on the apartment wall, and it is these threatened cultures that Sasha and her friends seek to unearth from forgetfulness and Soviet atheism, and animate into Christian faith. They travel to remote villages, preaching, hoping to form Christian cells. The greatest sorrow, they say, lies with the old 'Internat' system, which carries children hundreds of miles from their homes to Russian boarding school, then returns them to their families in mutual estrangement.

'Sometimes those children are nine months away from their parents. They come home speaking Russian, thinking Russian, to families who are reindeer-herders or fishing people.' Sasha's talk is punctured by 'Let us pray for them' or 'Pray for me', and her face loosens into fervent sadness. 'We've known times when the parents have gone away and just abandoned their children to the school. They must have hearts of stone. Then you want to gather those children to yourself but you cannot, and in the end they can probably find no work and they take to drink . . .'

There are others in the room: a young man who never speaks, and a Yupik woman, an Eskimo, baptized Christine and more hardy, I think, than Sasha. She has a tight, smiling face.

She says: 'I was lucky. I lived in the same village as the district Internat school, and my mother didn't mind my speaking Russian. But other pupils came from far away. They came from places where there was only shamanism, which is like living under a curse. It does not offer love.'

Christine pulls from her bag what appears to be a minute lyre, touches its iron stem between her teeth, and plays. It is a Jew's harp. 'This makes people friendly to me. I play their native themes, Nanai and Yupik. It makes them less afraid.' Her lips are pursed around it, while one finger seems to pluck at her lips with a low, twanging vibration. This, and Sasha's gentleness, are the weapons of Christ.

Sasha says: 'We draw people to God through their own singing and dancing.' She switches on her iPhone – 'here is a sister in Christ' – and I see a handsome woman in a Nanai headband, beating her shaman's tambour against a backdrop of flaming torches. 'This is our Christianity too . . .'

I ask in wonderment: 'Who is she?'

'She was once a shamaness, but she slowly converted. It took ten years.'

'How did her people receive that?'

'The shamans from nearby villages arrived to get her back. But God protected her.'

I hear this with mute unease. I wonder about a vulnerable people being drawn to a faith that is not theirs, or if instead Sasha and her friends are not bringing some sweetness and hope where there is none.

Christine is still playing her harp. Sometimes its reverberations sound as if a crowd of tiny people were crying to leave her mouth.

Sasha says: 'The hardest thing is when people have no earlier faith at all, and we are talking to atheists. The Evenk were once shamanistic, but now have no religion. It was frightened out of them in Stalin's time. But last year we went to a village beyond Nikolaevsk-na-Amure – a place of reindeer-herders – and I believe we started what may become a church.'

I ask in astonishment: 'How do you choose where to go?' Nikolaevsk is six hundred miles to the north, beside a hinterland scattered with desolate villages. I am hoping to reach there.

She says: 'We pray to God. God tells us where to go.'

God had chosen a place which they had to approach by helicopter, with an Evenk female guide. Then the three women had taken a reindeer sledge into the blue, and conceived this seedling church.

As I prepare to leave, Christine asks me: 'Do you have shamans in England? Do you have Internat boarding schools?'

'Not like that.' I remember my schoolboy tears, and they are suddenly trivial.

Sasha asks: 'Now may we pray for you?'

I hear my own 'Yes' come hesitant and somehow ashamed.

So they pray for my journey and my book, and give me chocolate cake and postcards illustrating native legends of the Amur, while I feel a confused warmth for them, and a sadness I cannot explain.

At the southernmost limit of Khabarovsk, where the Ussuri reaches the Amur through a maze of islands, a long wall encloses rambling parklands. Down its paths you come upon closed cafés and a small hotel, a bar advertising karaoke and billiards, a children's playground. The verges are scattered with plaster kangaroos and monkeys. The whole complex, you imagine, is the inheritor of those workers' holiday camps that scattered the old Soviet Union. But at its centre, where the pines drop to the river, a two-storeyed villa rises in an airy confection of pink and blue, wrapped round by summer balconies and columns. It was in this toy palace that the last emperor of China, the vicious and pathetic Pu Yi, was kept prisoner by the Russians for five years.

In his frail figure, the great Manchu-Qing, who had expanded their frontiers wider than any Chinese dynasty before them, reached their ignoble end. Pu Yi had become emperor in 1908, lifted crying onto the Dragon Throne at the age of two, and abdicated three years afterwards as a wave of republicanism splintered his country. Thirteen years later, ejected without title from his shrunken quarters in the Forbidden City, he took refuge in the misnamed Garden of Serenity in the Japanese concession in Tianjin. In this cosmopolitan city, rife with intrigue, he adopted Western habits while still dreaming of imperial return: a dandified and petulant autocrat, living in illusory eminence. Here, by his own account, he sported a silk cravat and diamond tiepin, went for walks in a haze of eau de cologne with his abject wife and concubine, and attended grand balls where he never danced.

But in 1931 the Japanese enticed him to Manchuria, which they soon annexed to their empire. They named this puppet state Manchukuo, and installed Pu Yi as its emperor. There, splashed with medals but bereft of power, he remained in mock state, a virtual prisoner. It was not until 1945, with the sudden invasion of Soviet armies, that his sham court dissolved. He attempted flight to Japan, almost alone, while Manchukuo was overrun by Russian tanks and Chinese guerrillas. On the tarmac of Mukden airport, while he waited for transport to Tokyo, Soviet aircraft arrived instead, and he was abducted north to Chita. Meanwhile his deserted empress died from opium addiction, insane, on a Chinese prison floor, and he was escorted at last to the dishevelled parklands in Khabarovsk, where I found his villa-prison.

A disgruntled caretaker shows me inside, but little is left in these depleted rooms to evoke Pu Yi. The place has become a wedding palace for local couples. In one room, where (says the caretaker) Pu Yi was interrogated, some pieces of his furniture survive, gifts from his Manchukuo palace: a few chairs, and small tables inlaid with mother-of-pearl. From a screen on one wall a video highlights his gratitude to the Soviet Union for rescuing him, followed by a patriotic song trumpeting the love between Russia and China, with photos of beaming crowds and hand-clasping politicians.

Pu Yi lived here in terror that he would be returned to execution in China. He wrote fawning letters to Stalin begging to stay for ever. He received no reply. But he lived comfortably alongside relatives and leftover Manchukuo officials, with some Japanese generals upstairs. His sacred person had always been preserved from everyday tasks. He couldn't tie his shoelaces or brush his teeth. Even now it was Chinese orderlies and dutiful relatives who brought him his meals, washed his clothes and tidied his room. He remained obsessed with slights and privileges, but could no longer beat his servants as he once beat his wives and eunuchs, only slap their faces. In obligatory studies of *The History of the Communist Party of the Soviet Union* and *Problems of Leninism*, which his relatives had to read aloud in Chinese translation, everyone froze into bored incomprehension, and Pu Yi's attempts to learn Russian never went beyond memorizing a couple of folk songs. In the evenings his followers indulged in spirit-writing on little planchettes to know their future, while the Japanese played opera on a gramophone upstairs. Then Pu Yi would retire to his room to recite the *Diamond Sutra*, probe his fate with a coin oracle, obsess over his health, or worry about his jewels hidden in a false-bottomed suitcase.

From this barren regime he was extracted only once, in 1946, when he travelled under escort to Tokyo as a prosecution witness at the Tokyo War Crimes Tribunal. There he perjured himself, transferring the blame for his collaboration wholesale onto the Japanese.

It was not until 1950 that Pu Yi was forcibly repatriated by Stalin to China. He was sure he was going to his death. But instead he underwent nine years of 'thought reform', in the gruelling marathon of confession and repentance by which a prisoner becomes his own judge and accuser. He entered the process with grovelling humility and perhaps with old acumen, until he transformed himself into what the regime desired: a model exhibit of Communist superiority over the old order. In the end he received his pardon; and the ex-emperor, ex-god, dressed in a blue serge Mao suit, became a part-time worker in the Beijing botanical gardens. Between cleaning greenhouses and watering seedlings, he wrote an autobiography imbued with the stilted language of a remoulded man, in whom China's rulers, and perhaps even he, had come to believe.

Meanwhile, in Manchuria, abandoned by their retreating armies, some 300,000 Japanese settlers were left to Russian and Chinese mercy. Many committed suicide. The atrocities of the Japanese occupation began to be avenged. By the end of summer 1945, in the dense Gulag of Siberia and the Russian Far East, a maze of new concentration camps contained some 600,000 surrendered Japanese soldiers and civilians. They laboured to rebuild Siberia's towns, railways, docks and mines, and within ten years 62,000 had perished.

In the forest cemetery far outside Khabarovsk, where the chapel to Stalin's victims stands, hundreds of acres of the city's dead lie under the Red Star or the Christian cross, their photographed faces laser-etched onto their headstones. It is as if a vast, diffused multitude were watching among the trees. The Japanese compound is small and railed off. A memorial stela stands eloquently blank. The granite outline of a few graves is traced in the grass. The birch leaves have almost drowned the names of the dead, on thin plaques that have to be brushed clear.

Almost all the Japanese who died in labour colonies lie elsewhere, unknown. In a remote suburb, on the site of a vanished camp and a mass grave, lies a monument to absence. Those who remember are few now, and far away. Beyond trim paths a lime avenue leads to a cenotaph traced in plain brick. A blank oval and a central cylinder lead to a pure circle, where you seem to be stepping into the sky.

While one dynasty was dying in the helpless figure of Pu Yi, another was being obscurely born. The Changbai mountains along the Chinese–Korean border were the legendary birthplace of Pu Yi's dynasty, the Manchu-Qing, in the region of their Jurchen tribal ancestors. But here too, in 1942, North Korea's Dear Leader Kim Jong-il, the father of today's dictator, was born on the volcanic slopes of Mount Baekdu, where his own father was fighting the Japanese from a guerrilla hideout. Kim Jong-il arrived with glorious portents. The ice-bound lake beneath the mountain cracked open to announce his greatness; a new star appeared above and a double rainbow forked skyward while a swallow descended from heaven. In his precocious babyhood the Dear Leader could walk within three weeks and talk fluently two weeks later. And in later years he became a prodigy of intellect and sport, writing 1,500 books within three years, and able to control the weather by his moods.

In fact Kim Jong-il was born in the nondescript village of Vyatskoye, north of Khabarovsk. His father had fled from the Changbai mountains over the Amur, and was commanding a battalion of Brigade 88, a force of fugitive fighters against the Japanese, when his son was born here in 1941 (a year less auspicious than 1942, so it was changed). The Dear Leader shared with his father and son, the present Dear Respected, the smooth, androgynous plumpness that suggested a nurturing deity to his people.

Despite his propaganda, he was mundanely earthbound, and frightened of flying. He travelled only in a luxury carriage of his own armoured train. On a secret journey to Moscow, his Soviet escort described him eating fresh lobsters airlifted in every day, with roast donkey and champagne, while his people starved.

Today in Vyatskoye there is no memorial to his birth, although it was Soviet records that betrayed it. Only a new monument to the international Brigade 88 – a sheaf of gilded rifles – has been raised by the Chinese outside the village.

In the Khabarovsk regional museum, close against the headland where Muraviev-Amursky stands, the cabinets of darkly iridescent butterflies and golden-winged dragonflies, of quartz, crystal and grains of moon rock, lead to mammoth skeletons and the sleek boats and fish-skin shirts of native people. All the creatures you might never glimpse in months of Siberian trekking have escaped the usual dilapidation of taxidermy and become glossily life-like. You see the dainty-footed Siberian musk-deer with its quaintly curved teeth, and the little snow-white ermine. A superb Amur tiger lounges on a rock. Here too you stare into the pinprick eyes and shovel mouth of the giant kaluga sturgeon, the ancient prince of Amur fish, whose flanks are ridged with vertebrae like an external backbone.

But the saddest creature is a blunted stone monster, squatting outside the entrance, which can barely be identified as a tortoise. You can dimly discern the bloated legs and a blank, upraised head. On its back it carries a broken stela whose inscription, if it still exists, has been plastered over. The reptile's mass looks all but unbreakable, yet it has been split in two, then crudely cemented together. A granite monkey attendant sits on either side.

A notice documents this as the 1193 monument to a Jurchen chief, discovered in an area north of Vladivostok. Such stelas were an ancient Chinese concept – the tortoise was a symbol of endurance – and the Jurchen people, progenitors of the Qing dynasty, adopted it along with Chinese script. During the Soviet Union's rancorous alienation from Mao Zedong's imperium in the 1960s, the great Chinese creature had been smashed, and only years later returned to its old place.

The presence of Chinese artefacts inside Russia's borders still stirs profound unease. A century ago Russian scholars and archaeologists, the so-called 'trans-Amurians', readily acknowledged Chinese settlements and influence beyond the Amur and Ussuri rivers, uncovering the remains of forts and temples far within Russian borders, and regretting the destruction of Chinese statues by Russian settlers.

But by the mid-twentieth century, in deepening mutual distrust, the notion that China had penetrated Siberia long before the Russians arrived was routinely denied. Under KGB directive, a host of place names were shorn of their Chinese identity, and inconvenient histories were retired to footnotes. Vladimir Arseniev, the most celebrated of the trans-Amurian explorers, died in 1930, but was posthumously condemned for conspiracy, and his wife shot. It was he who erected the tortoise-borne stela before the Khabarovsk museum, flanked by tablets blazoned in Chinese characters, now gone. Arseniev's old house, from which his native guide Dersu Uzala departed to die in the taiga, has vanished beneath the Intourist Hotel, but on Muraviev-Amursky Street the transient tribute of a tree has been planted in his honour.

I find myself wondering if the absence of any signs in Chinese along the Russian Amur derives less from apathy than from the subconscious fear of a Chinese claim to the land. Yet the Chinese presence in Khabarovsk is as elusive as in Blagoveshchensk. There are those who come seasonally and work in closed communities; but the building sites they once thronged now stand idle, or are worked by Central Asians. It is in the markets that the Chinese surface, to Russian disquiet. In the overflowing central bazaar, where contraband caviar shines in unlettered tubs and Siberian mink is promised, the Chinese are selling clothes and even flowers.

'Those yellow guys are prohibited,' Russians tell me. 'We don't know how they get in.'

But they get in, of course, in semi-legal partnership with Russians. Five miles outside the city, where I dismount from a bus full of women with big shopping bags, I hardly recognize the market I wandered twenty years ago. Then it was a ramshackle village of stalls under tin canopies manned by aggressive Chinese traders. Now it has been rebuilt in terraced avenues of mock Swiss chalets. Desperate reductions are advertised for everything from vinyl jackets to Arctic fox fur: 1,000 roubles dropping to 500, to 100 (less than $2). Ranks of plastic mannequins in sunglasses and big bras and nightdresses stand along the avenues – sometimes only disembodied legs in jeans – awaiting the Russians who can no longer afford to buy. And I hear the old resentment from Russian salesmen close by: 'The Chinese are coming back, you can't trust them, there are more of them than you think . . .'

Even in the dimness of the church Tamara wears dark glasses. With her black beret clamped low over her hair and a black anorak hunching her shoulders, she seems to be occluding herself. She is curious enough to speak with the foreigner beside her, but later, in a Ukrainian café, she does not remove her beret or glasses, as if poised for flight.

She asks in a half-whisper: 'Why are you here?'

'I'm following the Amur.'

'Yes.' She seems to find this natural. People love the river, the Little Father, she says, in spite of everything.

'In spite of what?'

The question provokes some memory; but over the café's hubbub I can barely hear her voice. 'The floods. Six years ago half our lower city went underwater. Now they've built a breakwater down there. China was flooded too. Many people died. Thousands of our houses went under.'

These summer floods are the bane and terror of the river. Climate change has not abated them. 'What happened to you?'

'My family had a cottage, a dacha, on an island opposite here. We used to plant vegetables in the summer – the silt is very fertile – but our dacha was built too near the water. Soon after the flood we went there and we couldn't find it. I began to cry. Then my daughter saw its roof just above the water. Ours was the only one left. The others had been swept away.'

The dacha had been her escape, she murmurs, but escape from what she doesn't say. She lifts the dark glasses from slanted, hazel eyes. She lets out her life piecemeal: she has two grown-up girls, and her husband has gone. Their cottage, she says, was always a shell. In winter it vanished under snow. She is sometimes afraid of bears there.

'They swim over?'

'Yes, they can. Sometimes they cross the Amur to escape forest fires. One walked into a supermarket a while ago, eating things.'

'I hoped it checked out.'

'Yes. They shot it.'

Her laugh comes late, but she removes her beret from a shower of auburn hair. She suddenly looks younger, starker, more troubled. I wonder why she was in church.

In Soviet times, she says, it was the only church kept open. 'I was baptized there. My father was a Party member, so my baptism was secret. But every winter after that, on a special day, my mother would queue up with me in the cold to receive the baptismal water that the priests offered. The queues were hundreds long. It was Amur water, of course, and muddy, but the priests dipped it with silver, so it was purified. You could feel it.' She touches her heart. 'When we came home my mother would sprinkle it over our rooms, every corner, as if baptizing them, and we'd keep some water through the year as a cure for illness.' Her voice has turned dreamy. 'A lot was kept secret in those days. At Easter we'd bake special cakes, very sweet, with raisins. But they were always baked at home. Nobody sold them openly.'

I murmur something about the resilience of believers.

She suddenly brightens: 'Oh! We weren't believers! My father was a Communist and my mother was an atheist! We were all atheists!' She is laughing at my perplexity. 'We used to buy sticks of dye to decorate Easter eggs too, in secret. But nobody believed in the Resurrection!' She adds, as if informing me: 'There is no God.'

She had walked into the church from habit, not from piety. She frowns now. 'I think it's tradition that people live by, not belief. We do what our parents did. That's what makes a people, isn't it? Habit and custom. In those years they became sacred. That statue in Lenin Square,' she goes on, 'they've pushed them down everywhere in western Russia, but we're slower to change things here. And I think it's right to keep him. He's part of our history now, he's part of who we are.'

She looks back in nostalgia at the Soviet years, I sense, even in their poverty and secrecy, because they embraced her childhood, and her childhood was happy.

'On Parents Day,' she says, 'nine days after Easter, we would walk to the cemetery beyond the city. In those days no one had a car. That graveyard visit was a custom that the Party didn't dare abolish. It would have been too dangerous. We would clean my grandparents' grave, and lay flowers, and pour them something to drink.' She smiles faintly. 'And now my parents are there, and I'm afraid to go alone.'

'Why?'

'Because of the dead.'

'But they are yours.'

'Some of them.' She looks confused. 'The graveyard is a place where homeless people go. I never feel it's safe.'

'I've been there,' I say. 'I didn't see anyone.'

'Well perhaps they're gone. But the dead are changing too. In the past the gravestones were very simple, because people were equal. Not all of them, I know. There were always the children of those in power. But the graveyard didn't show it.' Her anger comes muffled, sad. 'But nowadays families build these enormous memorials to people who were nobody. You've seen the Novodevichi cemetery in Moscow? It's full of famous people. But our cemetery is stuffed with nonentities and charlatans, and they build these great sepulchres, as if it will change their dying.' She replaces her sunglasses, as though to stop tears. 'Nothing changes dying.' Her coffee is finished. She clamps on her beret again, retreating to anonymity, and gets up to go. She says: 'The church I really liked was not for worship at all. It was turned into a planetarium. That thrilled me as a girl. You could see all the stars and planets. But it's gone now, and they've never built another.'

A faint mist has settled over the river and has dulled it far away to a plain of unreflecting glass. Soon a light rain starts to fall. My boat is almost empty except for some women cradling pots of vegetable seedlings and tomato vines to be planted at their dachas on the far shore. The growing season is short, they say, but they need the food. Yet the land ahead of us looks uninhabited. The islands are streaks of darkness above the water. The mountains beyond have faded to airy stencils.

Behind us, high on its bank, the domes of the Transfiguration Cathedral leave a gold florescence in the sky. Standing beside me, a cheery youth claims to hear a roar from the Lenin Stadium downriver, where Khabarovsk is playing Volgograd. He guesses Khabarovsk has scored. I gaze to where he points and only see, emerging from mist, the long, disconcerting barges like whole villages on the move, stacked with timber bound for China.

Ahead of us now the island of Bolshoi Ussuriisk fills the rain-soaked horizon with a blackness of trees. The river is churning greenish-brown. These islands are a source of old contention. The Sino–Russian border runs along the Amur's navigable channel, but every year the river changes. Islands rise and sink with drought and monsoon flood, some disappearing for ever. The channel alters course, complicated by emerging shoals and underwater sediment. Long before border tensions on the Ussuri exploded in 1969, China and Russia had been pulling apart, and with the start of Mao's Cultural Revolution in 1966, Red Guards would regularly bombard the Russian shore with loudspeaker propaganda, and sometimes cross the ice. Scuffles broke out with Soviet border guards, the Chinese wielding clubs and halberds, the Russians resorting to fists and rifle butts. In March 1969, on the Ussuri island that the Russians called Damansky, the Chinese Zhenbao, a Russian patrol was ambushed by the Chinese army. During the next two weeks a wave of counter-attacks failed to dislodge the entrenched Chinese forces, until the Russians called up rocket-launchers and cleared the island with a massive bombardment.

On this razor's edge, when the two Communist giants seemed poised for nuclear war, the Chinese clamoured for the return of their stolen lands north of the Amur. The Treaties of Aigun and Peking, they claimed, were exacted during their century of weakness, and were invalid. The Russians countered that the 1689 Treaty of Nerchinsk, in turn, had been extorted under threat. They feared that even a nuclear strike would not deter millions of Chinese from pouring over the Amur.

In easier times, more than twenty years later, as part of wider border settlements, the disputed island was quietly ceded to China, embittering local Russians. It was no more than a low-lying crescent of sand and willow tress, uninhabited, but it was soaked with Russian blood.

A larger question plagued the island now spreading in front of me. We are entering a strait, suddenly calm, between Bolshoi Ussuriisk – the Chinese call it Black Bear Island – and a narrow shoal. The Russians overran it in 1929, yet if the international principle of navigation were observed, Bolshoi Ussuriisk belonged to China.

But through the mist behind me lay Khabarovsk. The Russians were nervous of China's closeness to the city, and it was not until 2004 that this last piece of frontier jigsaw was resolved, and Bolshoi Ussuriisk was divided in two. On both sides public opinion was stormy. Russians felt they had surrendered too much; Chinese feared that they were relinquishing any claim to their stolen lands. But officials trumpeted a fraternal future. 'The island has become synonymous with "good neighbour",' beamed the Chinese: it augurs commercial links with Khabarovsk. It will become a visa-free zone for tourists, announced the Russians: it will be a place of human interchange, where the cultures of China and Russia meet.

As my boat glides to its muddy landfall, the island banks show only a procession of ruins. Houses of blistered plaster stand roofless, their doors and windows gaping sockets. The 2013 floods that submerged Tamara's dacha have inundated everything here. I wander under poplar trees down a track through a ghost village. Some ruins are stamped with signs warning of surveillance cameras, but the cameras have themselves been pilfered. A market colonnade has crashed inwards. Wooden slats hang like vines from the breached ceiling, and cellulose insulation gushes from its walls. The print of a Japanese garden still hangs here, its cherry blossom and hump-backed bridge severed horizontally by the flood-line, and everything rotted below. And all the time the spectral theatre set of Khabarovsk glimmers across the water with an illusion of well-being.

A woman emerges from a range of decaying houses. One of them is hers, she says. 'After the flood we were offered places in Khabarovsk, but I already had a flat there so I was given nothing. Most people left, of course.' She has a broad, stubborn face which moves from suspicion to bitter smiling. 'Why should I lose my home here? I refused to have it demolished, even when the Mafia got in with bulldozers. Then the looters came, unemployed youths from the village. They got to work with nobody to stop them, the place was half deserted. In the autumn gangs arrived from over the river, but they fought pitched battles with those already here, and ran away.' She has picked up a low-paid job guarding the track from intruders, she says, but she allows me to walk on.

I reach a long, pale building that looks intact, once a school for infants. Its basketball hoops and swings are still gaily painted, but shrubs have pushed up between its paving stones and choke the paths. Farther on, a line of cargo boats waits in the shallows of a deserted repair yard, and beyond these again the mud tracks of the village are lined with battered fences, and heaped with rubbish. A family is picking apart the wrecked half of their still-standing house. The water had reached to its eaves, the wife says. But she is smiling. This is her home, and she isn't going anywhere. Her vegetable patches are hoed and waiting for their seedlings.

A gross, squat figure, lugging two carrier bags from the boat, cajoles me into visiting his parents-in-law, beleaguered here. Vladimir wants to show off a Westerner. His black jerkin presses apart on a flaccid, hair-lined belly above black pants and shapeless legs. I sit in the restored home of a dignified old couple, while Vladimir pulls the vodka bottles from his bags and starts to drink. He fills my glass with every toast, while his mother-in-law, who wears an expression of salty humour, prepares *zakuski* snacks and tolerates him in knowing silence. I wonder where his wife is. Soon the kitchen table is spread with black bread and red caviar, gherkins, wild garlic stalks, and some wandering ants.

Vladimir clashes my glass and assures me he does not live here. 'No! I live in Khabarovsk. A big house, big! I don't live like this.' He gestures at the worn-out kitchen. 'I'm a millionaire!' He plucks his Stetson from a bald head and a fleshy face where the features appear to be sketched in as afterthoughts. Perhaps it is the vodka that drops him into an old Russian chauvinism. The Chinese are afraid of Russia, he declares, the Russian war machine is far ahead. The Soviets had even made the chassis of the American jets in the Great Patriotic War, and the Boeing 747 itself was mostly Russian made.

His father-in-law, who has worked in civil aviation for forty-three years, quietly refutes him. The old man carries a gentle authority. But Vladimir steams on oblivious. 'The Chinese are afraid of us invading their land' – he still calls it Manchuria – 'and they know we could crush them outright.'

His mother-in-law, cooking blinis on the stove, suddenly laughs. 'Why should we want their land? We've got enough as it is! We've got too much land.' She is filling the blinis with caviar and sweetened milk. 'Land is the only thing we've got too much of!' Soon she and her husband are debunking Vladimir in a murmuring undertone, not for his good – that seems hopeless – but for their own well-being.

He usually ignores them. Yet in his face a pair of tiny, watchful eyes is wandering the room until something alerts him, and they fix on me. He has experienced the world, he tells me *sotto voce*. He has had military training. He served in Lithuania until 1993, and did horrible things – 'Those bastards wanted independence' – then worked for the police, then in Japan at something criminal. He smiles secretly when I press him. He pretends to a glamorous corruption. And I find it easy to imagine his jovial mask transforming into something else. Only later do I realize why his black jerkin and thick, naked arms jar my memory: the flashback of a hirsute thug who trod silently in and out of my Damascus cell, where I had been detained by secret police the year before.

I wonder how the old couple had come to be marooned here. Outside the refuge of their cottage, among rusted outbuildings, their garden is littered with chair-frames and bedsteads from which the fabric has rotted away. 'We couldn't save things,' the old man says. 'We only saved our stove and fridge by piling them on tables.' He levels his hand close to the ceiling. 'The water came up to there. Fish were swimming through the window.'

His wife gives her defiant laugh. 'The whole island went under!'

Now I ask: 'How can I reach the Chinese border here?' I have heard of a lone church built on the frontier, near the island's centre.

But the woman says: 'Nobody goes there. There's no point. That church is just a symbol. If you want to approach the frontier at all you have to have a permit.'

'It was meant to be a meeting point.'

'It's a wasteland.'

Vladimir barges in. 'The Chinese side is wrecked too.'

'It's not,' I say. 'They've restored it.' I had passed nearby with the Chinese schoolteachers from Fuyuan last autumn. The site had become a wetlands nature reserve, its wooden boardwalks all rebuilt. It was attracting 60,000 visitors a year. But the border was deserted.

Vladimir sighs. 'The Chinese get things done.' Then he announces: 'I'm due to meet a Chinese delegation tomorrow. I'm promoting a Chinese magazine, as their agent. Did I tell you I'm a millionaire? Come back tomorrow and meet them. We'll celebrate!'

I half believe him. I try to imagine him entertaining a deputation in this ruined community, where the Chinese are surely hated. This, I thought, might be the way some business-men manoeuvred, in league with low-level Mafia, to bypass customs laws and taxes. Perhaps tomorrow Vladimir would be dressed differently, speak differently, before a mission of trim-suited Chinese. Perhaps he was not a foolish poseur at all, but the cunning player he enacted.

So I returned next day on the off-chance that the Chinese had found their way to his parents-in-law's poor home. But of course there was nobody: only Vladimir, rather drunk, stumbling in dark glasses. He would be going to Harbin instead now, he said, or perhaps to Vladivostok.

'And where are you going?' he asked. 'Ah, along the Amur to Komsomolsk. That's not safe.' He slumped brooding into a chair. 'That's dangerous.' Perhaps a true spark of concern had arisen. 'I could drive you there if I had a car . . .'

9

City of the Dawn

Seven hundred miles of jungled mountains lift a dense barrier before the Pacific, and here the Amur makes a sudden and tremendous turn north-east. The watershed of the Ussuri pours into it as it curls around Khabarovsk, then, along a bed often immeasurably wide, its augmented waters flow through a maze of islets and sand-bars on its last six hundred miles to the ocean.

In the east the summer warmth of the Pacific blows in on the forests of these Sikhote-Alin mountains, and the larches and firs of the northern taiga mingle with the subtropical flora of Manchurian walnut, maple, cork and linden. Giant lianas, grapevines and lemon-scented magnolias writhe up from a forest floor where jasmine and barberry grow, and the autumn-flowering ginseng draws poachers trading in Chinese medicine. Nordic animals intrude on southern ones. Elk, wolves, lynx and wolverine encounter Asian black bears and the beautiful, near-extinct Amur leopard. Wild boar feed where the soaring Korean pine drops its nuts, and the Amur tiger feeds on the wild boar. This superb creature, *Panthera tigris altaica*, the most formidable on earth, still ranges its territory half-protected: there are perhaps 450 left, where there were once 10,000. Weighing up to 600 pounds, it prowls the transitional forest on giant pads, moving by night along its own paths. It can charge at 50 miles per hour. It preys on sika deer, goral and elk, with the occasional bear or lynx, and a rare human. Sometimes it even goes fishing.

But I was leaving behind this distant littoral, from which the Amur turns away. The mountain ranges dwindle as they narrow northward, hemmed between the river and the Sea of Japan. The Amur enters a colder, harsher clime. Its banks are sparsely dotted with fishing and native peoples: the Nanai, Ulchi and Nivkhi, rumoured to worship bears. In autumn the water sees the inrush of salmon from the Pacific, and giant sturgeon. I am unsure how I will reach this country. The river is treacherous to navigate, its shoals constantly shifting. Sailors fear and hate it. In its solitary flow to the Pacific, it once carried Russia's dreams of ocean trade and power, but at its mouth the town of Nikolaevsk-na-Amure, founded in the nineteenth century as a springboard to conquest, is only a speck on my map, as if all human life dwindled away at its colossal estuary.

Nobody knows whether Sikhache-Alyan was once a shrine, a cemetery or perhaps a town. The path underfoot is orange earth and black rock, the Amur faint in mist alongside. Several million years ago a wall of lava, spewed out by a volcano now extinct, congealed for miles along the shore and was at last shattered by the fracturing ice of the river. These basaltic boulders, you might think, were once a rampart or a breakwater – their first explorers imagined them a broken city – but they are tumbled in glistening incoherence.

A small village, half Russian, half indigenous Nanai, is scattered in the birch forest above, and from its unvisited museum a torpid guide joins me clambering among the rocks. Every few yards, across some random surface, a blackly gleaming carving appears. Some of them are so faint that they seem no more than wrinkles in the rock: the hint of a spiral or of serried lines. Early investigators could sometimes identify their presence only by touch. But other carvings stare out with the shock of animated stone: crude faces, a crouching bird, the ribbed and antlered image of an elk, the outline of a man. Once I ease through a gap between boulders and am confronted by a glaring mask with bared teeth.

These figures are, literally, incalculably old. They belong to some distant Neolithic antiquity, perhaps six millennia ago, before the boulders were battered askew by floating ice in spring. The guide identifies a mystic boat – a slanted and corrugated line – which she tells me carried dead souls into the sky. And once I come upon a carving from some later age, where two lumbering beasts with bovine heads – maybe a creature now extinct – are cantering together across an igneous boulder, their legs and tails miraculously intact.

But the most common subject, recurring at random, is a mask-like face with hollowed eyes and simian jaw, ringed by a sunburst of spokes. Sometimes these visages gaze whole from the rock; sometimes only a pair of eyes is left, or the vestige of a grin, as if the figure had been ingested back into the stone. But these are not eyes that see, mouths that speak. They are more like inscribed ideas. Yet of what, or whom, is unknown. Their purpose and primaeval impact are pure conjecture.

A few of these petroglyphs, stranded in the riverbed, are seasonally submerged, and disappear. The greatest portrays a brooding monster from whose sloping eyes and brows there radiates, in concentric lines, an expression of depthless melancholy. When the river subsides in winter, this demiurge emerges from the water like its embodied spirit.

Perhaps the descendants of those who created these images are today's Nanai people, speaking a tongue close to Manchu.

Motifs that proliferate among the rocks of Sikhache-Alyan are conceived to reappear in the Nanai's decorative art, even in the wooden lineaments of their discarded idols. The divine serpent of their folklore – a reptile of benign wisdom – is rediscovered in the shadowy snakes incised on the boulders, and the boulders' carved birds are linked to a Nanai notion that the souls of the unborn are nestlings in the trees. But none of this convinces. The people who chipped their beliefs so painstakingly on the rocks – stone hammer on stone blade – perhaps preceded the Nanai altogether, and died or were absorbed to the puzzlement of ethnographers, and I climb away from the site in elated perplexity, a soft rain falling.

There is nowhere to sleep in the village. Almost half its people have left, seeking work elsewhere. But a man with an old Lada drives me to a half-closed holiday camp a few miles away, where a kindly Nanai woman finds me a cabin with a duvet, then goes away. There is nothing here to eat, and my iron rations are gone. All around, at nightfall, the forest echoes with the drilling of woodpeckers. A tiny tributary of the Amur, newly excited by rain, rustles in the darkness, and at dawn I glimpse between trees, down steeply falling hillsides, the grey-green flood of the river, seamed with white waves.

A cab driver takes me on eighty miles north to Troitskoye. We go through half-lit forests where the silver birch trees are massed down a road splintered by melted ice and patched-up potholes. To our west the Amur splays among sandbars. Sometimes its valley stretches five miles across. Often it lies out of sight. The cabby is small, shaven-headed, bright. He is happy to have work. 'This job was hopeless all winter. The snow stopped everything.' We eat in a cavernous roadside café: borscht, sausage, *pelmeni*. 'But why the hell do you want to go to Troitskoye?'

'It's the Nanai capital.'

'What's with the Nanai?' The town, he remembers, has a dwindling population of 15,000. Barely a third of them are indigenous. 'They're all mixed in with us Russians now.'

Of course this must be true. Of the so-called 'small peoples' who scatter Siberia and the Russian Far East, the Nanai are the most numerous in the Amur valley. Yet they number scarcely 12,000 here. In the nineteenth century, as the Russians and Chinese pressed in from north and south, the native peoples lost their prime fishing and hunting terrain and were often reduced to menial labour and debt slavery. Smallpox, alcohol and opium ravaged them. In Soviet times the formal creation of their own district, with Troitskoye as its capital, became a testing ground on which these impoverished people, deemed 'without culture', might leapfrog over history into the pure Communism of *Homo Sovieticus*. Now for them, as for the Russians, this inflicted identity has been discredited, and the Nanai culture that it oppressed – even the Nanai language – is fading away.

As we near Troitskoye, the forests give way to wetlands, where thin tributaries slide through swamps, and egrets fly. The town is as cheerless as the cabby warned: a conurbation of flat blocks, cottages and shacks, some decaying, some spruce under garish plastic roofs around roads too spacious for their people. Silver-lagged pipes, impractical to lay in the frost-hardened ground, meander between houses and loop over the streets. A war memorial and a gold-painted Lenin stand in an empty square.

The only sign of the Nanai is a small museum where a reticent caretaker, with the oblique eyes and lifted cheekbones of her people, hands me, for a few roubles, a ticket to her past. Perhaps it is her speechless shyness, or the predictability of the exhibits – the embroidered dresses, the fragile-looking bows and harpoons, the shaman's horned headdress – that leaves me with the sense of a culture less preserved than imprisoned. The Soviets installed many such museums, as though to define and terminate a society by consigning it beneath glass: *This will not return, this we have superseded.*

But the Nanai, before their subjugation, were reported a gentle people, liberal to their wives and reverent to the old. They lived communally, often forty to each big, windowed house, and followed the seasonal flow of fish in slender boats with corked nets. Their embroidery and carved designs were beautiful. In summer they wore tunics of watertight fish skin which hang in the museum cabinets, with a grinder for scraping off the scales exhibited below. In winter they went in dog or reindeer skin, in birchbark leggings and deerskin shoes stuffed with grasses. Their world was full of deities – the Amur was itself a spirit – embodied in toy-like wooden idols that now stand labelled and disenchanted, and they kept a special reverence for bears. In their myths, and sometimes in belief, their women had sex with bears, and children were born from them.

I go down to where the river spreads a mile across between pebbled beaches left by the receding water. It will not be here, I think, but farther north, on remoter shores and tributaries, that native vestiges truly remain. On a gutted blockhouse the old, delusive Soviet slogan 'Peace to the World' shows in the patterned brickwork under a sprayed graffito, 'Tolya loves Tatiana'. Close by, an Orthodox cross, flashed with spread wings, was raised twenty years ago 'To the Victims of Political Repression'. It stands in a chained and overgrown enclosure, inscribed with the verse of Anna Akhmatova, lamenting the nameless dead.

The only hotel has no rooms, but my cab driver has lingered, hoping vainly for a fare back to Khabarovsk, and drives me up the Manoma tributary to an empty guesthouse.

He secures me a key from a neighbour, who tells me the absent owner lives here too, and to leave some money on the kitchen hob before I go. So I am alone for an idle interval in someone else's home. It is a restless creation of woodwork and filigree, from the spindly outside stairway that climbs to my bedroom to the gang of carved dwarfs below. In the fly-blown kitchen a medley of stews and *piroshki* is smelling strange, but there is black bread, and eggs from the scavenging chickens. Outside, swallowtail butterflies fidget among beds of irises, and two plaster pelicans nestle aslant in a pond.

I walk at evening along the Manoma river, followed by a cat with shredded ears. I remember the encephalitic ticks that infest the forest in spring, but feel too carefree to turn back. The Manoma makes a long, silvery tumult between banks of drowned willows, turning on itself in strange eddies, before smoothing again, very full and swift, to the invisible Amur. The birch and maple buds are just unfolding, and wood anemones massing under the trees.

I return to sleep in a huge bed. The walls around me are made from sheets of compacted wood-shavings nailed together and stamped 'Exempt from Formaldehyde Regulations'. The torn-eared cat lies outside my door. I try to remember what formaldehyde is. Perhaps it will extinguish the encephalitic ticks. In the night outside I hear only the lisp of the Manoma.

After travelling the last hundred miles to Komsomolsk-na-Amure, a once-secret city of arms factories, you may emerge from flooded forests and move across a mile-long bridge to stand at last on the Amur banks at nightfall. Behind you rises the sound of thousands of frogs croaking from their swamp-land park near the Great Patriotic War memorial. Old people tell you that these are the voices of the dead, for Komsomolsk was built over a welter of mass graves. A warm wind is blowing in from the river. The promenade is deserted. But people are walking their dogs through the barely lit parkland – big, simmering mastiffs – and old men are smoking on the pathside benches.

Morning reveals a river esplanade stalled between re-building and decay. Twenty years ago I had come here on my way to Magadan, and nothing has changed. Placards show lavishly planned development: museums, sports centres, even a replica of the native village that Komsomolsk replaced. But instead you walk across an incoherent plaza over splintering pavements. Bulldozers stand idle round a derelict ferry terminal, where I had hoped to board a hydrofoil north. Dark hills roll over the far shore, and the distant skeleton of the cantilever bridge hangs in the sky.

Walled off above the river, a huge boulder commemorates Komsomolsk's founding hour in 1932, when a contingent of pioneers from the Komsomol, the Soviet youth organization, stepped ashore to build a city in the wilderness. Statued high on a plinth, twice life size, they advance inland with pickaxe and theodolite, led by a poetic youth and a handsome land-girl. It was a potent moment in Soviet propaganda. Soon the legend flowered of a metropolis built by sheer willpower, from Socialist fervour and sacrifice. But the pioneers had few skills and poor support. They spent the first winter in huts built of twigs and clay, in extreme cold, cut off by river ice and impassable forest. They suffered scurvy and night blindness, and in spring a plague of vipers. But in the city museum, where twenty years before I had seen the mess tins, paraffin lamps and graphic letters of these revered 'first builders', their memory has shrunk to a single reconstructed room, furnished with a samovar and a wind-up gramophone. In the echoing halls, where attendants bustle forward to help, there is more space allotted to the visits of Khrushchev and Gorbachev, even to the Afghan war, than to the founders of the so-called City of the Dawn.

Beyond their statue the First Builders Avenue starts as a path through blossoming trees, then runs over a vanished labour camp and becomes a boulevard through multi-storeyed tenements two miles to the railway station. Photos of the pioneers' early buildings show ranges of ill-fitting logs and lopsided windows. Each barracks had its Red Corner, with a bust of Lenin. But within two years these settlers were subsumed by a flood of political prisoners, increasing as Stalin's paranoia and the years continued, until a million convicts had passed through the streets. Their camps and mass graves lie beneath the city in a map of shadows. Such sites have now been overbuilt by a sewing-machine factory, a maternity hospital, a metallurgical works. Even in the museum their history has been airbrushed out. The past is changing. The only memorial I find in this notoriously suspicious backwater is obscured behind a bus stop on Lenin Street: a fractured monolith, circled in barbed wire and inscribed with the familiar formula: 'To the Memory of the Politically Repressed'. Someone has hung scarlet carnations there.

In 1945 some 50,000 Japanese prisoners-of-war augmented the failing numbers, and were retained so long and harshly that almost half of them died. Their monument is ironic. They beautified the city that destroyed them. As I go up the boulevards of the old centre, its tenements ascend from arched doors and windows to balustraded balconies and moulded cornices, all built by Japanese. Their stone façades shine through the city's heart in a tissue of stuccoed beauty: salmon pink, champagne, celadon, pigeon blue. Beside their Amur Hotel, a modest memorial stands in a copse of pines.

But any architectural grace dissipates as I walk on. A familiar drabness sets in. A few listless men troop the pavements, and heavy, durable women with peroxide hair. There are almost no cars. It seems like a city in abeyance, waiting for something to happen. Here and there a municipal skyline banner proclaims 'I love you, Komsomolsk', as if to recreate a waning loyalty. The population is in steep decline. On the charmless main square a big screen projects a future Komsomolsk of sweeping walkways and lamp-lit river esplanades. It hangs like dreamland over the people wandering below.

I am reminded of an older Russia, forty years ago. There are no window displays. Cashiers and shop assistants glower and bark. In a region below freezing half the year, I enter cafés through muffling iron doors, and often find nothing but chair-stacked tables, or a locked inner gate. Every office is immured in a warren of others, reached down unlit passages where the doors are mostly shut. I try to find a chaplain I had known twenty years before – a KGB officer turned Baptist minister – but his old flat door is opened by an angry stranger in a frayed pullover, woken mid-afternoon from drink or sleep, who has never heard of him.

I have taken a risk on Alexander. In my eagerness to reach distant villages, I have found him online offering fishing trips to remote Amur tributaries. This may not work at all, and I await his arrival with unease in my dingy hotel. Its hall fills successively with a shifty-looking youth, an old woman selling cigarettes, and a jaunty drunk. I silently rehearse excuses for refusing Alexander. At last comes a powerfully built man in army fatigues, strapped with a hunting knife and sprouting a chestnut beard. He looks like the kind of Siberian whom schoolboys dream of, the backwoods pioneer supposedly extinct.

But this, to my relief, is Alexander. He stares at me in frank appraisal. I am not sure what he sees. But I see a giant in his mid-thirties, exuding a robust, even defiant self-assurance.

Outside in the streets he is animated, walks fast. He speaks fluent American-English. 'I learnt on the job. I worked on Sakhalin island for a US gas company, then in Arctic Chukotka for Canadian gold miners. Good pay, but shitty job. The guys up there just thought about fucking the girls, Russian kids, who were in it for the cash or the chance to get to the US. In the end I'd had enough. I wanted independence. My wife said just do what makes you happy. So I started again, like this.'

For all his size, Alexander is somebody whom others approach in the street for a cigarette or a match. He has a kind of innocence. My last qualm about him disappears with our first beer in a rowdy bar. He looks me in the eye and says: 'Here's how we go. I've got this guy Igor. He drives a Land Cruiser. He does some business with sable pelts, but he knows fishermen up north who'll take us in their boats. They do poaching too, but that's how they live. Igor will arrive here after tomorrow.' He sees my grimace. 'It's OK. I know him. He'll come.'

In the next three days Alexander finds bars and bistros I could not have known existed. He eats and drinks tremendously. I find myself sinking into beery indolence, downing mugs of Harbin ale, Holsten 'World of Real Men' and a local brew on whose label Muraviev-Amursky is clutching a tankard along with a Nanai woman, a hockey champion and Khabarov. Between every other beer Alexander lumbers outside to smoke, so that I fleetingly think of Liang.

But Alexander has no urban worries – or if he has, he loses them in the wild. He has a wife and two small children in town, but he aches to be travelling in wilderness. The forest offers visceral excitement, and a paradoxical peace.

'Twenty minutes' drive from here you can be somewhere utterly wild,' he says. 'There will be deer grazing in solitude. On the road to Sovetskaya Gavan you reach a pass and suddenly you see a valley below you, and nobody there, only the taiga. You're among mountains in tropical forest with moss hanging from the trees. To the south it's so dense you can hardly hack your way through it. I hope I can make my children see that. And then there's the fishing . . .'

This is a passion he wants me to feel. In a sleepy bar his beer mug stays untouched. His voice is tinged with wonder. On the quiet island where he often fishes, the shores are patterned with the hoof-prints of deer and the rooting of wild boar, and skeins of duck are flying. He loves to identify the choice stretches of a river, study the pools and shallows where fish shelter, then feel the sudden quiver of the rod, the tug on the fingers: pike, crucian carp, snakehead . . .

He asks: 'Have you ever fished?'

'Only as a boy.' The memory rises of trolling a Canadian river, my father's hand steadying mine.

'Canada,' says Alexander. 'Bears.'

'I never saw one.'

'Well, if you see a bear here, just stand up tall. Make yourself big.'

'That's OK for you. You'd scare the life out of a bear. I'd climb a tree.'

'Bears climb trees.'

I am hoping, of course, to see a bear. Sometimes Alexander has glimpsed their tracks, and once the footprints of a tiger. 'You never see tigers or wolves.' He laughs. 'But they see you.'

I remember the howl of the wolves in Mongolia, summoned by the horseman Mongo in the dusk, then their drifting away unseen. Alexander relishes such things. Sometimes, as the evening and the drinks go on, he becomes dishevelled and his talk faster, more distracted. He propounds myths that must have entered local folk belief: how in the Civil War the White armies disappeared through tunnels beneath Khabarovsk, how the last Czar had escaped to his cousin George V in England and lain low, how the Russian army had bombarded the Ussuri island lost to the Chinese and sunk it. But he'd always add in his jovial growl: 'I expect it's all bullshit.' And then: 'You'll have to get used to me. I use this bad language. It just comes out . . .'

It is impossible not to like him. We clash beer tankards and hope for the future. But he says: 'I can be foul to have around. Sometimes I think there's two of me. There's an OK Alexander – he's here now – but then there's Lousy Alexander. The lousy one gets in a filthy mood, especially after drinking. Just ignore him. He'll change back.'

The old graveyard of Komsomolsk lies far from the city among wooded hills. Stairways of beaten earth climb up and down the slopes of silver birch trees, among black headstones and the blaze of artificial flowers. We are alone here, in clouded sunlight. The hills are fluting with cuckoos. The density of graves under the birch and lime trees, the illusion of living flowers and the stare of engraved faces from black stone evoke the feeling of some private community on which we have trespassed. Many graves are flanked by metal chairs and tables, so mourners may converse there with one another or with the dead.

Then we reach an area grander than others. Platforms of shining marble bulk out into the glades under towering tombstones etched with life-size figures. They are all of young men, casually loutish. Their stelae are inscribed with angels. Their lives are very short. These are the graves of the Mafia chiefs who flourished in the chaotic Yeltsin 1990s, when mobsters became the shadow rulers of the Russian Far East. Komsomolsk, in particular, was their domain. Here was the tomb of Alexander Volkov, assassinated, and of Sergei Lepeshkin, who hanged himself by his shoelaces in prison at the age of twenty-nine. They stand in baggy trousers and leather jackets, hands thrust into their pockets, as if those hands had committed nothing. Triple-barred Orthodox crosses, engraved sunrises and kneeling angels attend them, and iron roses. Someone has left a few sweets for them.

Alexander reads their dates without emotion. 'In my schooldays they controlled everything. We students all had the chance to join some gang, and plenty of us did. Those kids were doing minor jobs, running small errands, but not for long.' He laughs sourly. 'Only one of my mates seriously tried for it. He and another guy beat up some drunk, thinking it would get them kudos. He wanted to be a Mafia big shot, but they didn't accept him. He lives with his mum now, and wears pink shirts.'

We are passing the graves of others, mostly murdered in turf wars in their late thirties, one as young as twenty. The faces that gaze out never smile. Their epitaphs pretend to no repentance, only regret. 'Brothers! How sad to bury your friends. Better to sit around and talk . . .' They ask that their sins be forgiven and that they enter heaven.

'In the end those gangs turned on one another,' Alexander says. 'The Khabarovsk Mafia broke from the Komsomolsk Mafia, and they shot each other up, and got weaker. I remember as a boy I was watching a cartoon on a restaurant television when there were shots a block away. Two masked guys with AK-47s got out of a van and blasted a criminal boss and his bodyguard. Nobody ever arrested them, of course. But all this stuff was damaging foreign investment, and Putin sent in the FSB and suppressed them.'

The most powerful and notorious of these gangsters, the godfather of the whole Russian Far East, was Yevgeny Vasin, nicknamed Dzhem, whose empire of extortion and protectionism embraced every enterprise from casinos to shipping. In the years of post-Soviet anarchy, his rule in Komsomolsk carried the illusion of benign patronage, and the city appeared safe and well ordered. Yet Dzhem spent half his adult life in prison camps, and extended their criminal subculture into the outside world. In 2001 he died of an apparent heart attack in jail aged forty-nine, and rumours of darker causes proliferated. More than two thousand people thronged to his funeral, with the elite of the ex-Soviet underworld, and he took his place with their remembered aristocracy: the Moscow overlord 'Yaponchik' Ivankov (assassinated in his seventieth year); Grandpa Hassan (killed by a sniper in 2013); 'Sylvester' Trofimov (blown to bits in his Mercedes in 1994); the hitman and escapist Alexander Solonik (strangled in 1997); the Georgian ex-wrestler Otari Kvantrishvili (shot dead in 1994).

Dzhem's grave is the most lavish in the cemetery. A laser-etched Virgin Mary grieves beneath his memorial cross, and a sentimental epitaph pours out loss and sorrow under extravagantly winged angels. Yet on his engraved headstone we stare at an overgrown boy in a creased waistcoat and a loose-knotted tie. He looks lumpish and simple: the playground bully.

Three years after Dzhem's death this cemetery was still watched by his henchmen. There was said to be gold buried with him. But we go back alone down the glimmering aisles of silver birch, where last year's leaves and polyester flowers lie crushed underfoot, and hear nothing but the harsh cries of crows. 'Even now,' Alexander says, 'if you own your own flat or car, older people think you must belong to some Mafia.'

We find a taxi back to town. The driver has a gaunt, worn-out face. A tattooed cobweb covers one hand. 'That means he's robbed apartments,' Alexander murmurs. The cabby looks old enough to have worked for Dzhem. 'Those tattoos are like badges of honour, and a warning against anyone messing with you. It's a whole language. Tattoos on the shoulders mean a big boss, and you get a cathedral dome tattooed on your back for every prison sentence.'

The cabby weaves between ruts and potholes. He complains that the country is run by fools and criminals.

Close to the river, beside its marshland park, spreads the Great Patriotic War memorial. Cut from granite slabs, seven giant faces rest on the paved square as if they had just emerged from below. The sculptor took his cue from the diary of a Wehrmacht officer who marvelled at the rock-like Russian resistance to the German advance, and the set mouths and unyielding eyes, segmented in huge blocks, share the naked obduracy of stone.

Their plaza is a favourite of skateboarding teenagers sporting T-shirts printed with 'Misfit' and 'I love NY'. They twirl and crash across its paving. But the stone visages seem embedded in their own time, staring in massed alienation. They lie beyond the age even of the teenagers' grandparents.

'The old veterans must hate this,' I say.

Alexander mutters: 'There are hardly any left.' The earlier Soviet trumpeting of the war has slowly declined, he says. The tank museum nearby has been turned into a football pitch. 'We were taught it all at school, of course, but nothing was taught to help us live today. Everything was out of date, with some bullshit history. I want my kids to grow up better equipped for modern life, and independent.'

I say, not quite knowing: 'That may be easier than it was.' We hear the yell and clack of the skateboarders.

'But it's getting worse. Half the time you don't notice, and the propaganda seeps into you. When I was working for the Canadians in Chukotka, I realized that I was starting to resent them and getting angry, and I wondered why. I never watch our television – it's too boring – but up in Chukotka there was nothing else to do, and I realized that I was being brainwashed by watching, and starting to dislike Westerners.' He grins at me, as if I wasn't one. 'So I checked myself and went back to normal.'

That evening, in another bar, over a table shiny with spilt beer, his buoyancy dims with thoughts of the future. He goes out for a smoke, returns. There is a lot he hates. He hates the local government, the moribund school system, the threat to wildlife, Communism, feminism, and, of course, the Chinese. But Moscow, above all.

'We all voted for Putin to start with,' he says. 'But now people see what's happening. We're reverting to being the Soviet Union. Everything's owned and run by a few bosses. That's the trouble with our country. The wrong people are always ruling it. Even in the Revolution, a lot of weirdos and crooks got in. As for the government now, sometimes I think those motherfuckers just want to take what they can until we're ruined, then they get out.'

As it grows late, and our drinks multiply, his baseball cap slips into reverse, and the eyes that wander over mine are losing focus. His talk ranges over the world's foolishness, and I hear myself joining in, adding to it, until we start back at last to my hotel.

'As for those fucking Chinese, they're like cockroaches. They get in everywhere, eat anything.' Alexander's bulk, marching beside me, starts to look threatening. 'Every deal they do, they pretend weakness, but then they screw you. I think they mean to take us over. I'd just clear the bastards out.'

But I'd scarcely seen a Chinese in Komsomolsk, I say, only a few Uzbeks, still wearing their *tubeteika* caps, and some Tajik builders.

'You don't see them.' Alexander is adamant. 'But they're cutting down our trees in swathes. Some of our forests have been rented to them for *fifty years*. Hundreds of square miles around Chita and Khabarovsk.' He too had seen the great, timber-stacked barges moving upriver to China, and felt sick.

Back in the hotel, Igor has still not come.

The site of Komsomolsk was chosen because of its remoteness from any threat of invasion or espionage. The uncertain Chinese frontier lies two hundred miles away, along with the Trans-Siberian Railway and its occasional prying foreigner. But the lonely river gives the city access to the Pacific, and the Baikal-Amur Railway, built to shadow the Trans-Siberian far to the north, crosses here on its safe and half-deserted way to the interior. For eighty years Komsomolsk's lifeblood has been the manufacture of arms. Its aircraft and shipbuilding factories engulf much of the working population, sealing the city into a self-contained fortress.

Twenty years ago, in heavy snowfall, I had tramped its industrial suburbs with a part-airbrushed map, when half its arms industry was adapting to the construction of trawlers and yachts. Now, when I take a bus to the Gagarin Aviation Plant, the largest in Russia, I enter a micro-region whose streets teem with men and women in uniform. Beyond a statue of the astronaut-hero Gagarin reading the 'Book of Cosmic Law' (to the mockery of locals), I am stopped by guarded turnstiles and a high iron fence. I gaze beyond Stalinist offices to ranges of hangar-like buildings that stretch for half a mile into the forbidden distance. The park-like quietude reveals nothing that happens inside.

Over the years this powerhouse has turned out thousands of military aircraft. After the collapse of the Soviet Union and a decade of precipitous decline, a tentative recovery began at the turn of the millennium. One of the first acts of Putin in 1999 was to assure the factory that it would remain state-owned. The Sukhoi series of jet fighters was created here, breaking a virtual US monopoly – the SU-27 took its maiden flight from the factory in 2010 – and they have sold heavily to China and India ever since. Decades ago the Soviet Union had modernized China's forces. Now, with the reversal of economic power, the sale of fighter jets to China brings Moscow precious cash, together with a nervous realization of Beijing's advancing technology.

I wait in the Sukhoi security office on the hopeless quest for permission to enter. The FSB officer sinks my heart the moment I look at him. His fallen jowls and hooded eyes seem locked in congenital suspicion.

'A foreigner must apply forty-five days in advance.' He barely lifts his gaze to me. 'Even then permission will not be granted.'

Close to the river, where its slipways drop into a secluded inlet, the Amur Shipbuilding Plant is forbidden too. Once the Soviet Union's foremost builder of nuclear submarines, it has been racked by problems for thirty years. But just as I am leaving, after another stone-faced refusal, an elderly man emerges from nowhere. 'Come to the museum.' He looks sorry for me. 'But don't tell anyone I let you in.'

It is a dusty, harmless collection of documents, old photographs, inscribed awards and miniature models. He enumerates them with paternal affection. His favourite is the replica of a seismic survey ship built for India, then sold at a pitiful loss to South Korea. This oddity amuses him. 'But it's a beautiful model, isn't it?' The factory is converting to civil craft now, he says: passenger ships, cargo boats, pleasure yachts. The military engine that once furnished the Soviet Pacific Fleet with 270 vessels was moving to a site near Vladivostok, accessible to the ocean, far away from the difficult Amur.

All at once he looks infinitely sad: sad, I think, not only for his ailing factory and for the museum that is his pride, but for a lost Russian greatness which still throbs in the national psyche with something like homesickness.

Igor arrives next day in a mud-battered Toyota Land Cruiser packed with fishing tackle, crates of beer and Georgian water. He talks a growling Russian in one of those half-swallowed basses beloved of opera houses and the cantors of the Orthodox Church. He is almost as big as Alexander, with an impassive, hirsute body, heavy-shouldered and enduring. His Toyota, adapted with a left-hand steering wheel, will get us wherever we want, he says.

So we leave Komsomolsk for the north in high spirits. Our road is a long, gravel track over the hills. We follow green passageways through the birch trees – the dark cherry and the silver intermingled – and on through sombre swathes of spruce and larch, bearded in lichen. Once or twice a village opens on the river. It is vast and cold now: a level plain of moving water under low-hanging clouds, its surface lashed with foam, running between dark hills.

We plan to follow it for over three hundred miles, almost touching the Pacific where the river weaves into shallow lakes. Beyond there, Igor says, he befriended fishermen years ago. Here the Amur grows more desolate beside the villages of native Ulchi and Nanai. For another hundred miles we could sail on whatever boat we find to the last Russian outpost at Nikolaevsk.

We stop by an auburn stream and picnic on *kasha* and a cold cooked duck, which Igor shot somewhere. We fall into easy camaraderie, exhilarated by the road ahead. Alexander and Igor feel at home here. Igor lives on the Amgun, the last great tributary of the Amur, where the sea mists roll in. In winter he hunts moose and traps the glossy sable tree marten, whose precious pelt first drew the Cossacks eastward four hundred years ago. Crossing from the Urals to the Pacific within sixty years, they hunted out the sable as they went, imposing a tribute of furs on the cowed tribespeople, until this 'soft gold' was all but extinct. Even now in Igor's village each hunter was restricted to trapping ten sable a year. He lays his snares by snowmobile tracks, he says, where the creatures like to travel, and when they escape his dogs up the trees he can shoot them in the underbelly, without damaging their pelts.

'The finest hunters are still the Nanai and Ulchi,' he concedes, 'the old fellows especially.' Every year he drives his village's three hundred sable furs to sell to Turkish and Greek entrepreneurs in St Petersburg. For a moment his hands leave the steering wheel to scroll down a snapshot of the sable market. There I see Igor standing with a rare smile before a brimming showcase. The massed pelts mount upward from the grey-blue beauties at the stall's foot, through standard specimens, to the near-rejects at the top, riddled by mice or half eaten by other sables, for they are cannibals. Just as centuries ago a prize fleece might make a trapper's fortune, so now two or three animals in every hundred have silken, smoke-blue coats which fetch the monthly wage of an office worker.

These are the hunter's passions that Igor shares with Alexander. Every few miles we cross a peat-brown tributary rushing to the Amur, and their eyes sharpen with possibility, noting the way the river runs, while they debate if it's good for banded catfish or Chinese sleeper. Their heads crane and hobnob above the Land Cruiser seats in front of me: Alexander's swathed in russet bristles, Igor's shaded under a prized cap with a seagull printed over one ear, Peter the Great over the other. They rock to the same radio music – 1990s Russian punk – laugh at the same jokes, are attracted to the same remembered women. But Igor is paler than Alexander, more patient, with quiet, creamy blue eyes; Alexander is vivid, warmer, more mercurial. He explodes at injustice; Igor laughs at it. Alexander seems innately young; Igor is an age I cannot guess.

So we drive onward to the throb and snarl of Sektor Gaza's 'Hit the Gas!' (although we crawl between potholes at thirty miles per hour) and 'Make Merry, Man!' The far hills are splashed with light, but I cannot tell if this is a broadleaf forest shining among conifers, or the inroad of sunbeams. Here and there a stream beside us is still edged with ice, its water angled into dark channels through frozen blocks and ledges, where stranded willows rise. Yet it is already early June. Sometimes, where a forest fire has raged, the taiga breaks apart on a plain of blackened stakes, where the young growth is returning in an underbreath of green.

At the village of Bystrinsk, where our road cuts east to the Pacific, Igor has friends. Three generations are crowded into one wooden cottage. The old couple has diverged in a now familiar way: he heavy and worn, perhaps by drink, while she stays stoutly jovial, her hair still stubbornly dyed fair. Lemony skin and blue eyes run through her family. Her daughter is her younger self, but withdrawn, almost absent, alongside a dark, assertive husband. Their children are beautiful. Their eight-year-old daughter, dangling drop-earrings, fixes me with piercing sapphire eyes, and a tiny, tallow-haired boy shelters in his father's arms. They are poor now, they say. But their home – ramshackle with sheds and outbuildings – opens onto sudden warmth inside, where every rug and cushion is a farrago of bright colours, and every surface heaped with toys, ornaments, medicines. And soon, in long tradition, their table is spread with moose meatballs, salads and sweets, and the vodka toasts are going round, while the children migrate from lap to lap. Only their mother is clouded in some unreachable melancholy, her wide-set eyes straying to the blurred rain in the window, before returning to me in unfocused wonder.

My arrival is an event in this remote place, her husband says, and he lifts the little boy's face to mine and tells him to remember he met a man from England, and the child stares at me quizzically, then laughs. Nothing happens here, the man says. 'Our village is dying. Nobody has children now. They can't afford it. In our school there are fewer than thirty pupils, with eight ageing teachers. Anyone young gets out. As for our own children, we'd like them living nearby' – he fondles his son's head – 'but they should go away if they want a future. We are fishing people, but the government curbs us, gives us quotas.' His sudden guffaw signals that he ignores this. 'Five years ago, officials even laid nets across the whole Amur mouth, starving everyone upriver. It was madness. The spawning salmon haven't recovered even now. That year we just grew vegetables, and got by. Things are not much better now. Even bears are coming into the village.'

Everyone has a bear story. These are the formidable brown bears of Eurasia, whose males weigh up to a thousand pounds and stand over eight feet tall. Igor has encountered roving males in the spring melt season, he says, when the females with cubs become dangerous. Sometimes a rogue male kills the cubs of her previous partner to mate with her. I remember Mongo and Ganpurev's talk of Mongolian bears raiding ants' nests in the spring and running amok, soft-headed with formic acid. The fishermen in Bystrinsk, the man says, keep their hooked sturgeon fresh by tethering them to the shore on spikes, but recently the bears have been hauling them in at night and eating their spines.

'A great delicacy for them!' The old woman laughs. She remembers worse times than this. When she was a child, she says, every village between Komsomolsk and Nikolaevsk had its labour camp, whose prisoners were worked to death building a useless railway to Lazarev. Her mother and other village women would take out food and tea to them because the convicts were weak and starving.

Our toasts fade, but our glasses are instantly refilled. The children are growing bored. The small girl tugs at her mother's hair, to no avail. The boy is running his model car back and forth over the hairs of his father's forearm. But the feisty matriarch is getting into her stride. Even tigers are returning now, she says, because they're protected. 'One of them comes too close to our village for my liking. We're almost on its path.'

These tales no longer surprise me. The great tigers, as their prey dwindles, may range over a thousand miles, padding by night along their secret territorial paths. For the first time the pale mother reaches out and takes her little girl's hand.

Years ago a tiger had killed a man in a neighbouring village, the old woman says, where her own mother had lived. 'He'd gone out for a pee in the night, and it broke his back. Crack! My mum went off to alert my brother, who was in the local baths, lazy bugger, and the tiger leapt at her. But in her surprise she fell flat on her face. Plop. The tiger missed, and she survived, because a tiger won't leap a second time. Later they shot that tiger and had it stuffed and put in the local museum, where somebody stole it . . .'

It is evening before we start on the seventy-mile road to the little port of De Castries on the ocean. Igor, who has refrained from drink, is quiet at the wheel. As night falls a mist thickens over the road, and two hours later I wake to see the lights of De Castries glinting through fog. We search out the only hotel left in town. Now we hear the sound of waves, and the wind smells of the sea.

*

Even before the Treaty of Aigun declared that this coast no longer belonged to China, the Russians had built a military outpost on the bay of De Castries. The harbour had been named years before by a French naval commander to flatter the minister who had sponsored his voyage. Its bleak site, in a region held only precariously by the Czar, became the scene of peripheral, now half-forgotten conflicts. So little charted were these waters that during the Crimean War a French and British squadron, pursuing a Russian fleet, believed that the strait between the mainland and Sakhalin island was an immense lagoon, and lay fruitlessly in wait for a prey that had already sailed through to the other side.

Chekhov, visiting the port long after, wrote that it consisted merely of a few houses and a church, and that its bay was treacherously shallow. Thirty years later, at the end of Russia's Civil War, a White Army garrison took refuge here, holding out for seven weeks in the vain hope of relief. Even now, long after the Japanese abandoned Sakhalin in the Second World War, the town retains a wartime bleakness. Beyond its scattered houses, in the overcast morning, we see a deserted harbour banked with felled trees in their hundreds of thousands – larch, spruce, oak, elm – waiting for shipment south, of which there is no sign.

The rain has turned most tracks to the sea impassable, but Alexander and Igor ache to go fishing, and we circle down to a black-rocked shore where a gutted blockhouse is tilted in the water. They cast their lines into pools choked with ruined machinery and cables. To our east, a steely skyline underlines Sakhalin island, while to the north we glimpse the lighthouse, marooned in a thrashing sea, where the White commander was executed by the Reds.

For over an hour Alexander and Igor catch nothing; but I start to share their quiet obsession. I cast a line from Igor into the shallows, and agitate its spinner as he does. He guides my arm with an odd gentleness. His hunted sables, often hanging alive in his traps, would die in the winter cold, to his indifference. But to me he shows this mute solicitude, steadying my line in the great paw of one hand. I feel touched, but disconcerted. Over the past weeks, in a hotel mirror, I have seen with surprise an old man in his eightieth year, then forgotten him. Now I realize what Igor sees: a stubborn pensioner, frailer than him, trying to cast a line into a stagnant pool. Then I remember Batmonkh's and Slava's intermittent concern for me, and Liang's quaint caring. Suddenly I wonder: what did they see or think? How great account must they have taken of my age? I feel a spasm of bewilderment. Did even Medusa take pity on me?

A stony track goes through mist and deep forest to Lazarev, our last destination on this solitary coast. With the poor fishing, and our emptying beer bottles, the Lousy Alexander rears his head. In his intolerance of stupidity he had snapped at the hotel manager before we left. Igor grumbles: 'We might need that man some time.'

Alexander barks: 'I don't see guys that way! "Using" and "not using"! I either like them or I don't.' He glowers into the mist. 'Why is everyone so fucking stupid?' He turns on a cassette of Korol i Shut's 'Vampire's Confessions'. Then: 'Where the hell are the fish round here?' But within an hour his shadows lift. He announces formally: 'The OK Alexander is back!' and when we halt for a while he embarks on survival techniques for the taiga. He sinks his hunting knife into a silver birch, just budding, and siphons off its sweet liquid into a bottle. Meanwhile Igor is stabbing a stick into an ants' nest until the insects attack it and leave the acid from their rumps for us to suck.

So we come with a bitter-sweet aftertaste to Lazarev. The town is yet more derelict than De Castries, half its houses gaping and empty. But to the east the 600-mile-long island of

Sakhalin lunges barely four miles away across the Tartar strait. From a gap in the forest road we go down an overgrown footpath, and suddenly we are out above the Okhotsk Sea. We are standing at the waist between two great waters. Grey waves fall on rocks far beneath us, and to the south shines the Sea of Japan.

We walk between copses of alder trees, and over a wasteland of grass and gravel. Then, turning inland, we stop dead. At our feet yawns a vertical shaft. It descends in a funnel of segmented steel: twenty-five ribs that drop past twisted girders more than two hundred feet into darkness. I step back from its brink. It measures over thirty feet across. At the bottom glimmers a circle of long-sheltered snow. It looks like some archaic, stricken stairway, but you would go down at your peril. Withered grasses cascade from its upper tier. No sign or barrier stops you plunging down a vortex of naked iron.

This chasm was in fact the labour of 5,700 prisoners in the last years of Stalin's Terror. They were saved by its closure at his death in 1953. The vertical shaft marked the start of a secret, six-mile-long railway tunnel beneath the sea, planned to unite Sakhalin with the mainland. But I stare across the strait in astonishment. Sakhalin has vanished in mist. It is impossible to imagine such a project's end. Even today, when politicians revisit the seventy-year-old plan, nothing comes of it. On the shore below we find the adit of a second tunnel, where the train might have emerged from the cliffs; but it stops at the rock face thirty yards inside, as if the tunnellers had lost heart.

Even as I wonder where these hopeless labourers came from, we see, hanging above the sea, the unmistakable wooden ranges that were once gulag barracks. Their walls have been extended with flimsy boards and cracked glass to let in the light, but are splitting into final ruin.

As we stand staring there, thinking the place abandoned, a door cracks open and a tiny man in spectacles and faded battledress eyes us, as if we are guests who have come too early. His shaven head recalls a convict, and his face is clouded by solitude. A wall-eyed dog whines at his feet. Perhaps it is our strangeness – outsiders who know nothing of him – that frees him at last into talking. He is the only inhabitant here, he says. He'd come in 1978, long after the prisoners left, when the place was still heaped with debris and abandoned machinery. So the camp became his inheritance. He liked to study it. As he speaks, I sense a vestige of lost authority. I wonder at his living here. He is perplexed, he says, that the undersea railway was never finished. But perhaps the tunnel started to flood, and was sealed up. He'd hunted for years for the grander railway entrance he imagines exists, but had never found it. He frowns, adjusts his spectacles. It must be closed up and overgrown somewhere. From the camp's refuse he'd recovered an iron roundel of Marx dated 1939, which he'd hung on one blackened wall, and a crimson banner still fringed with gold, which he spreads for us, unsmiling. It unfolds on a double portrait of Lenin and Stalin, enclosed by a Communist star under the slogan 'All Countries Unite'. The other side is inscribed 'Water Transport and Building Management No. 6'. The convicts did everything in those days, the man says – mining, lumber, transport – and they died on the job. Recently soldiers laying a cable here had unearthed two boxes, five skeletons in each. That was how things were in those days, everything secret. The camps that crowded round here – the region was thick with them – did not even know of each other's existence. Not long ago, he says, a camp still lay in the nearby forest, its guards' discarded boots littering the ground; but souvenir hunters had taken everything away now, even the wood.

He offers me some sodden bread and coffee. His china is thick with grime. Peering into his rooms, I am hit by a fetid stench I cannot identify. Even Alexander recoils. The floors are strewn with the rubbish of a lifetime. I glimpse the skull of a whale, and other, unidentifiable bones. He sleeps on a camp-bed, beside the dog. Once he'd been a fishing inspector, he says, and was now a forestry surveyor. But he looks destitute beyond any profession, and I cannot bring myself to ask him why he chose or was consigned here.

Alexander is kicking at the earth outside, wanting to leave. 'The Gulag means nothing to younger people,' he says. 'We just read a couple of paragraphs in history books at school. Or you can look at a documentary, or read Solzhenitsyn. Not many bother.'

But everyone in this decaying place, the man says, longs for the resurrection of Stalin's dream – the completion of a way to Sakhalin – so the community may live again.

10

The Promise

The village is an image of rural peace. On its shores, where the Amur runs silver-grey, a scattering of motorboats is beached above the waterline, and a few trucks stand idle. Even in summer every other cottage lies behind banked tiers of firewood, like a second wall. Russians and native Ulchi, a people close to the Nanai, live side by side. Lagged water pipes worm their aerial way among the dwellings, and arch over muddy alleys. Into the outskirts the forest filters as if waiting to take over. But compared to the desolate Pacific settlements we have left behind to the east, Bogorodskoye gives the illusion of bright sufficiency, and its walls and fences, painted white or turquoise, stand intact among blossoming apple trees. In the central café Ulchi and Russians sup together on bean stews and crab salad, beer and sweet coffee. Our hotel window looks onto leafing ash and maple trees.

I am as elated as Alexander and Igor to have reached here. There are native villages upriver, with abundant fishing, we hear, where the Amur splays into marshy tributaries or mountains plunge to the shoreline.

Alexander phones his wife, who says: 'Don't you want to come home?'

'Of course I do. But here is wonderful.'

She abruptly says goodbye. She does not understand his fishing, he says, but he is unrepentant. He's glad she likes to stay at home, a real mother. He thinks a career demeans a woman. 'I bought her a sewing machine.'

Igor's friend Sergei owns his own boat. Igor has not seen him for several years, and is shocked by his decline. I see a spry, grizzled sea dog, whom I assume is in his fifties. But he is thirty-eight. In his eyes the tiny pupils drown in brilliant blue irises, and he stares at me with the unfocused gaze of the drunk. He works as a truck driver, he says, but this earns him the equivalent of thirty-five dollars a month, so he must go fishing. 'Everyone fishes here. This is not a profession. It's a necessity.' He has two sons he supports at school in Khabarovsk. They'd get jobs there in the end, Igor says, and leave him back here in the village, getting drunker.

That evening, in our small hotel run by two silent Ulchi, Sergei feasts us in celebration of our coming. We delve into a cavernous bowl of red caviar, with a platter of dried carp, and contraband sturgeon. Sergei unleashes the vodka, and toasts tomorrow. He promises us police protection, but from what I do not know.

A storm-filled sky at dawn has dulled the river to lead and turned the air cold. In a tough, 25-foot sloop, whose four wonky seats have been torn from somewhere else, we hunker behind our plastic windscreen, bulked out in anoraks and life-vests, while Sergei steers from a dashboard showing two dials and a medallion of the Holy Mother. Our Yamaha outboard motor can power up to fifty knots, but this morning it purrs us across the river and into a silent tributary. The silhouettes of mountains interweave ahead of us, before folding to the water in ruffles of forest.

We are wending among islands. Some are mattresses of floating grass, brilliant green, others are boned with the straggling roots of purple willow. Soon we are moving becalmed through a grass-island maze, utterly still except for the drift of a fishing eagle, and we stretch our nets in a creek, tying one end to a bank-side willow, and sinking the other from floats in mid-current. Sergei seems to know this place. On a stream nearby a bottle hangs from a shrub, left by poachers, warning of submerged logs. We lay a second net beyond, where he uncorks a vodka bottle – he repeats this wherever we stop – distributing and clashing glasses and tossing a drop into the river 'To Podya!', the local spirit.

Igor mutters: 'Of course we're poaching. It's still no-fishing time.' The off-season weeks, when the salmon fry descend, are almost over, but I hear this with a pang of guilt.

I have no idea what we may find in our nets when we return this evening, because the Amur is host to a unique confluence of fish. Its waters mingle the cold-water breeds of Russia – the lamprey, the Arctic char and the taimen, the largest salmonid in the world – with varieties indigenous to China. The glassy mandarin fish, the yellow-cheek carp and the Mongolian redfish must first have issued from the southern branches of the Ussuri and Songhua, along with the curious snakehead that can live for days in open air. The 130 species that swim the Amur read like a lexicon of invented creatures: the skygazer, the sharpbelly, the chameleon goby, the Amur sleeper, the three-lips, the eight-whiskered stone loach.

But the river belongs above all to the dog salmon. They start life as fertilized caviar in the pebbled beds of obscure tributaries, and when the ice melts the Amur in spring they start to swim. For four years they vanish into the Pacific. Then, one late summer, they return up the river fully grown – the females bulging with roe, the males with angry snouts and teeth – continuing headlong for hundreds of miles, with no dam to obstruct them, until they rediscover, by some mysterious sense of smell, the site where they were born. There each female deposits thousands of eggs, which the male's spray fertilizes before the Amur freezes over them, and the adult fish, fulfilled, float dead to the surface, to the delight of bears.

The Amur fish were once so plentiful, wrote a nineteenth-century traveller, that even the village dogs had learnt to catch them. Now commercial salmon fishing in the river's mouth has ravaged their shoals. As we move through twisting side channels into a larger water, we pass settlements in stark decline. In the village of Solontsy, where the shoreline cottages are rotting away, Sergei has old friends. During the floods six years ago, they say, half the village went underwater. They laugh about this. They are still buoyant and strong in their seventies: he a handsome Ukrainian, she half Nanai, half Chinese, who had come here from Komsomolsk as a teacher, fallen in love and never left. Alone on the ruined shore their home is complete and newly painted.

'After the flood everyone got government money to build a new house,' he says. 'But we took the money and didn't build anything. We spent it on two apartments for our children in Bogorodskoye and Komsomolsk. Then we came back here and built again.'

'So legally', the woman laughs, 'our house doesn't exist.'

I find myself laughing with her, but ask: 'Won't the floods come back?'

'Yes!' Her husband knows the chances are high, even hopeless. 'Then we'll go and live in a tent on the hill, and come down and repair this place again.'

I glance round their house with misgiving, at its carpets and patterned wallpaper; it looks so proudly restored. The Amur's flooding recurs like an old sorrow. In years of heavy monsoon the network of its streams and greater tributaries turn its basin to near-impassable boglands as distant as those

I had met in Mongolia, and the water level in its valley may rise by up to fifty feet.

But our Solontsy hosts have made their decision. He stands foursquare in his stained pullover and battledress, she stout and humorous in her flowery jerkin. Their garden plot is waiting for the growing season, with vegetable seedlings ready to be planted – potatoes, cucumber, tomatoes – and fat chickens laying fat eggs. But the village population has drastically declined, they say. The priest has gone from their church; the old woman who tended it is dead, and the building locked up. There is a shop they call their supermarket, but her husband won't go there, she says. 'He's afraid he'll want to buy everything, and we can't!'

He says: 'We don't need anything.'

They hope to die here. Their relatives live far off, in the way that no longer surprises me in these villages: a nephew in Lithuania, a niece in Scotland. They would not return. But he'd never wanted another life, the man says. In Soviet times the village was too remote to be collectivized, and he still makes a living as a hunter, happy, alone.

Among the so-called 'small people' of Siberia and the Russian Far East, the Ulchi are almost the smallest, numbering scarcely three thousand. Their language is close to that of the Manchu and the ancient Tungusic people of central Siberia, but now it is dwindling to domestic conversation among the old, and barely taught in schools. Their villages along the Amur's quietest tributaries, where we are moving, lie far apart and few: a tracery of weathered homes along black-pebbled shores.

At one of these, too obscure even for my large-scale map, we beach our boat and walk into a scatter of silent cottages, where the trucks are wrecked and feral dogs roam, and the only person we see is the stoic villager who finds us. He wears the standard Russian battledress, with a jaunty baseball cap, but he looks hardy and poor. He has his people's narrow eyes and raw cheeks. He wonders why we are visiting. There are only thirty inhabitants left here now, he says, out of the two hundred when he was a boy. 'Soon this place won't exist.'

Sombrely he accompanies us, although there is nowhere living to go. But beyond the settlement, on a wooded hill above the river, we glimpse the old cemetery. It is lost among silver birch trees. I remember accounts of the Ulchi and Nanai fear of the dead – that graveyards were sited far from villages – but the man guides us there.

We thread through the trees in silence. Only Alexander has joined us. Once we come upon the fresh footprints of a bear. The man says: 'If it comes, just don't run away.' But nothing stirs, not even the wind. The graves are spiked with short pillars, marked by no inscription except a name and date. The railings that enclose them are thinned with rust, and only a few synthetic flowers flare in the undergrowth. Here and there a boat has been upended near a mound, its hull purposely breached, and disintegrating. The possessions of the dead used to be heaped above them, the man says, but always broken, torn or burned. When I ask why, he only says: 'So they won't be stolen.'

But long ago a Siberian native explained to me that in the afterlife the night turned to day, summer changed to winter, things broken became whole. Sometimes among the Ulchi the corpse was laid in a miniature house, its head turned to the river, with the sense, perhaps, that its soul would flow to its own eternity. Yet mourners returning from funerals never looked behind them, for fear that the dead would overtake them and lodge in the village of the living. The souls of the dead, especially those of suicides, could turn vindictive. Sometimes whole villages were transplanted because malignant spirits had infested them. The forest was full of these haunted ruins.

The Ulchi man is silent until I ask him more. I cannot tell what he believes. He says: 'Before the Soviet time, the corpses used to be buried seated, with their belongings, and I remember as a boy that the bodies of babies were hung in birchbark cradles in the trees. Their souls become birds that fly among the branches. And every family had its own tree, like an idol I suppose. Ours was deep in the woods, and my family fed it once a year, and we had another in the house, quite small.'

When I question further, he replies: 'I don't remember everything. The Russians took away our culture. But I remember the last shaman, who carried dead souls to the afterworld. All except the suicides. They were buried far away. And people who were drowned and lost, their valuables were piled up here among the graves, and that was all. I don't know what the shaman did for them . . .' He is barely middle-aged, but he thinks he remembers a golden time of Soviet community. 'In those days the fishing was good and life was happier, more friendly. Everyone left their doors unlocked and children went freely in and out. People forget that.'

The cemetery looks as shrunken as the village now. Most of the graves have sunk away beneath the leaves and fallen branches. We go back Indian-file through the trees, to where Sergei and Igor are waiting on the river. Alexander offers the man a tip for guiding us. But he stands silent, while a sour dignity surfaces. He will not receive charity, especially from a Russian. He says: 'Give it to an orphanage.'

We haul in our nets at evening. The creek around us is smoothed to near-stillness, and the sky dusted with high clouds. As Sergei and Igor drag up our catch, the tangled fish come twitching to their outstretched hands, some inert from struggle, others writing in flashes of silver. We pull up fifteen crucian carp: diamond-scaled creatures whose fins stiffen within minutes, as their eyes turn blue. Theirs is a sweet, delicate meat, Alexander says, which we'd eat this evening, and nobody cares that we've broken the fishing ban. Some bony Amur barbel emerge too, and three catfish whose whiskers twirl and droop as they surface. Sergei returns the younger carp to the water.

Then a sloop arrives suddenly, ghost-like, from farther up the creek. Two rugged men climb aboard. I feel a twinge of alarm, but they want only to share our vodka, joking with Sergei about something, and they recommend a better place for us to fish next day. For a while they help us drag up the nets, then speed away, and Sergei drinks again, tossing a vodka drop into the water for Podya, and turns us homeward.

I ask: 'Who were those fellows?'

He laughs. 'The police.'

How hopeless it is to monitor these waters. The poor communities on their shores are interleaved with the local patrolmen, who turn a blind eye, or elicit a bribe. Sergei knows them all. It is the professional boats downriver, he says, that surpass by many times their legal quotas, and sell the caviar of salmon and kaluga sturgeon – a species threatened with extinction – on a thriving black market.

In the mist of early morning the far shore next day is only a sepia hairline, as though the horizon had rusted away at its edges. The river is formidable now. For over 2,500 miles it has gathered its tributaries from a basin almost the size of Mexico, until its brown flood pours northward through a channel that sometimes reaches three miles across. As our boat shudders upriver in the lightening day, the eastern shore ascends in mountain walls of pine, spruce and birch, where wisps of cloud dangle, as if from steaming jungle. Even as we speed beneath them, Sergei and Alexander go on smoking, cupping the cigarettes in their hands against the headwind, while our beer bottles dwindle alongside a bag of frozen smelts with cartoon faces.

An old Ulchi named Valdui has joined us from Bogorod-skoye, and points to where pioneer camps had stood in Khrushchev's day, now returned to forest. Once or twice a village touches the littoral with a scatter of coloured roofs and mud streets, and cattle graze on the dark-earthed banks. But within a minute we are roaring through wilderness again under the coniferous shadow and the brilliance of summer birch. Sometimes a fish eagle circles the enormous sky. White-bibbed ospreys perch on solitary lookouts, watching the shallows, and once a heron cruises at peril low along the shore. For miles we see no building except the deserted shack of a shaman far inland. There was once a collective farm there, Valdui says, and after it was disbanded the shaman remained and died there in solitude.

A long time later, the Ulchi village of Mongol appears, strung along a headland. A woman living here wants to revive the native ways, Sergei remembers, as he runs our boat ashore. The chained dogs in her compound roar in fury as I enter. Somebody must have told her that a Westerner has come, because she greets me in a resplendent Ulchi gown. Her black hair is flattened over a pale face that flushes with emotion as she speaks. There is something girlish about her, a girl locked in a woman's body, and proud of her party dress. She wears it like a placard for her culture: a sheen of gentian blue, banded in spirals like a broken river, and embroidered with gold dragons that betray Chinese influence long ago.

For a long time, seated on a sofa's edge, she talks about the hardship of the Ulchi, the years of forced collectivization, the dwindling settlements, the intermarriage that threatens to subsume them. Half of Ulchi weddings were now contracted with outsiders, she says. Even her own marriage had been like that. She was born in Kolenikovo, a place I'd never heard of, and became betrothed to a builder, half Ulchi, half Ukrainian. 'You see what a mix we are!' She herself had an Ulchi mother and a Russian father, but I find no Slavic trace in her wide nose and blackcurrant eyes. Her village had largely been indigenous, she says.

'My grandmother was a shamaness, a woman of great power. After I got married, she tried to pull me home. No, I don't know why. But it's our custom that before a wedding the groom's friends abduct the bride by boat. Then the bride's villagers try to haul her back. They don't succeed, of course, and the bonds are cut. But my grandmother's power was strange and long-lasting.' She winces a little even now. 'In my husband's village I slowly became terrified. For months I couldn't leave his home. In the end his friends banded together ritually to cut me free. I don't know what they did. But still I felt my grandmother's curse on me. Whenever I visited my old home, strange things happened. Sometimes terrible storms would stop me going. And if I did, fires broke out there. People grew afraid of my coming. I became like an outcast. Near the village there's a headland shaped like a woman, where wives had been thrown down into the river. Women who had failed their husbands.' She shows me a photograph of this cliff. 'In the end I stopped going home.'

I can barely imagine this now, she seems so articulate, so sure. Her house, by village standards, is spacious and wealthy, with upholstered sofas, thick carpets patterned with water-lilies, and an outsize television. I wonder what her husband does. She says: 'We went to Komsomolsk soon after we married, and I was happy there. I saw opportunities for our children. But my husband yearned to return to his village, to go back to the taiga. He would stand on our balcony in the evenings and when he saw the ducks flying north, I knew that he couldn't stay longer. So we went back, and he took to working for the village. He was remembering his childhood and the old Ulchi ways, and he hoped to restore them. We had money by then. But I was sad. I wanted that other life.' She gives a constrained smile. 'In the end my husband burned himself out, and that is how he died, at fifty.' She lifts a photograph from her table, and I see a man among his family: a slight, melancholy face, already too delicate, and she with rebelliously eruptive hair, shepherding two daughters.

It is easy to view her life through another lens, in which her shamaness grandmother becomes a possessive crone, and she a frightened, homesick girl; and now, as in long mourning, she is following her husband's path in recovering a native childhood, collecting stories, remembering, keeping pure the language.

'That was the trouble in Komsomolsk. We weren't working for our own people. When I go back there now, the air smells horrible, and everyone uncaring.' She wishes that she had listened to her grandmother, the shamaness, and to her grandfather who used to take her to the family tree in the forest, which she was allowed to touch if she were not menstruating. But in those days the village had become a collective farm, and she was busy being a Young Pioneer in what seems another age. Now she wants the shamans back. Not long ago there had been four or five here, but they were all dead. One of them had given her a wooden heart – her heart, she knew, was weak – and after she had suffered three strokes it had changed colour with each attack, from white to brown, as it absorbed the shock into itself.

She is sitting very upright beside me. Beneath her Ulchi gown peep out small feet in plastic slippers shaped like fish. I catch myself imagining these fish swimming along the water-lily carpets under her. In front of us a picture-window enshrines a shining fragment of the Amur. 'The river came close up to our windows in the floods,' she says. 'I believe it was angry. When people overfish the river, it grows angry. You don't have to rob it of everything. One sturgeon will feed the whole community.'

Among her framed photographs I notice, as I leave, an icon of the Holy Mother. But when I ask her about this she waves at it dismissively, as if the Virgin were a tiresome relative. 'I prefer my own gods.' She keeps these deities in another room, and she does not invite me to see them. I can only guess them from museums: wooden statuettes with conical hats and overcast eyes. She says: 'These are what we still have, and the river.'

'Is the river then a spirit?'

She does not precisely answer. 'Sometimes I talk to it. I light a fire on its bank by night, and ask it for help.' She gives her tempered smile. 'The river listens.'

In these northern reaches, the tracks of the tiger peter out and the sovereignty of the forest belongs to the bear. Among all native peoples, the bear was held in reverence, and an intimate affinity connected them. The bear's epithet of 'Old Man' or 'Grandfather' suggested ancient wisdom, and alone among animals he was believed to have a soul. Bears could transform into humans and vice versa; it was said that bears were their ancestors. Sometimes bears made love to women, and sired their children. A man killed by a bear might even become one.

The Ulchi relationship with the bear centred on an arcane ceremony. A cub, or even an adult bear, was captured at great peril – mutilated Ulchi hunters were once a common sight – and for two or three years the bear was kept in a log hut, and fed by women. Then one day it would be escorted through the village in chains, while the women danced for it to the drumming of wooden instruments, until it arrived at the house of the ceremony's host. Only if it crossed his threshold standing upright would his family be forgiven. Then its paws were bound to a scaffold and the strongest man in the community shot it dead with three arrows. So it was returned to the spirit lord of the forest, of whom it was an emanation, and its meat consumed in a gluttonous eucharist by the village hunters, whose courage it would fortify.

Bulava is the Ulchi village closest to the bear. We approach it under a louring sky. For a week we have not seen the sun. Beyond the mud-churned shore and grounded boats, we enter a grassy compound framed by empty longhouses and barns engraved with native carvings. The curator of this ghostly ensemble, an ebullient Ulchi, says that it was created to honour the bear festival. Proudly he shows me the massive log prison where the creature was confined, and the twin poles for its execution. Yet the bear festival no longer exists.

'But we wait for it to come back!' He is bright with hope. 'We revived it in 1992, when I was a boy. It was magnificent. Two weeks of celebration! The bear was pinioned upright, and everyone processed behind it to caress its head. Then it was shot by our best bowman, just as things used to be! If that man had failed, he'd be in eternal disgrace.' He looks momentarily mystified: 'Some people think it's cruel.'

He laments the fading of all his native culture, even here at its heart. 'In fifty years there'll be no one left who knows our language. Even my wife and I speak it only when we don't want our children to understand.' But he shows us his museum of Ulchi artefacts. For the first time I notice tasselled poles that were thrust into the Amur to petition the water spirits, and he talks with optimism of the villagers fishing the river. Their commercial boats stretch 100-metre nets across tributaries 30 miles to the north, while each family enjoys a small quota of its own. So they are surviving. But when the bear festival will return he does not know. During Soviet times the authorities had once appeared and taken away the bear on a steamer.

Alexander and Igor are disgruntled now: nothing to do with bears, but with Ulchi fishing. 'Actually I think these people hate us Russians,' Alexander mutters. 'Because they were here first. But now they get special privileges and throw their nets halfway across the river . . .'

'In my village,' Igor grumbles, 'a law came in that only the Ulchi were allowed to fish at all. Just because some guy had slit eyes he was given permission, while we starved. So there were riots, and the police had to relax the rules just to let us live.'

The old Ulchi Valdui, who had shared our boat to Bulava, reappears and coaxes me away. He has a face of androgynous sweetness, lapped round by greying hair. But he is furious. 'All that bear talk! It's nonsense! They fake the traditions . . .' His father had written folk-tales, he says, and there is a monument to him in the village, but he despises this. He even takes me there to vent his disgust. It is an ugly plinth, where a spindly totem pole sends Valdui into a new paroxysm. 'Look at that thing. It's not traditional! We never had such things. Or if we did, they were pulled down within a year. In the first year after somebody dies, rites are held for them every month. Then you burn all their stuff and forget it. My father hated ceremony. The community is just using him.'

Valdui's girlish delicacy has hardened into petulant bitterness, so that I wonder if I had imagined any benevolence there. The erosion of tradition maddens him. He shows me the yard in the back of his home, whose racks are full of rotting bears' heads. The jaws gape round tremendous teeth. Already someone has told me that he is a superb hunter. A while ago the village had been invaded by a female bear with four cubs, he says, and it was he who was called upon to shoot them. 'If she had killed a child, how would I have faced the parents? Each should keep to his territory. Bears to their forest, we to our villages.'

But you don't, I thought. I was growing fond of bears.

Valdui is full of animistic lore which I cannot follow. Benign and evil spirits abound. A black dog once emerged from the forest and spoke to him in Ulchi. He extracts a giant fang from a putrefying bear's head, and presents it to me. But his anger is spilling over. 'The bear festival they talk about was a scandal. That bear wasn't their own. It was *my* bear. They stole it. And it wasn't shot with a bow and arrow at all, but with an AK-47. That festival should have been for *my* relatives, my clan, everyone with my surname. I would have advertised it everywhere, and they would all have come, from Uzbekistan, even Hanoi.' He is imagining an inrush of people he's never known. 'But I wasn't even invited to the ceremony.'

Then calm comes over him. Some justice had been done, after all. A curse had been laid on those who arranged that bear festival, he says. Soon afterwards, several of them became paralysed, and their leader died in a coma, without speaking. As for the man who'd shot the bear, he was stabbed to death a year later in Novosibirsk.

The river flows in silvered corrugations under the mountains, and we move with it, northward, while Sergei plans where to lay our nets. A few miles downstream from Bogorodskoye a cavernous tent serves as a canteen-cum-dormitory for the police, with their launches beached in front and their Land Cruisers alongside. Sergei makes flagrant landfall here and we enter their canvas quarters as if invited. In the half-light I see they are hosting the wardens of a women's prison from the nearby settlement. I have tried to avoid police for weeks – I may be the only Westerner within hundreds of miles – but I am engulfed in a tide of welcome that consigns all difference to oblivion. A turmoil of carousing and flirting has broken round us. A dark, febrile officer detaches himself from his blonde wardress to embrace me. He is very drunk. In boisterous fellowship our open palms crash together in the air again and again while he shouts 'Crab! Crab!' for no reason I know. The women stare and the men laugh, and we all drink until whatever purpose Sergei had in coming here fulfills itself, and within minutes we are out again on the open water and the parting cry of 'Crab!' fades into the distance and the roar of our motor.

We lower our nets close to shore in the river's full flood. Its surface has woken into steel-grey waves under a hard wind. When we return to pull in the nets we find them snagged on the riverbed far below – on a sunken tree, Sergei guesses – and after half an hour, manoeuvring back and forth, we still cannot raise them. It is a police launch that arrives and hauls them in on one side, while we lift them from another. Then a shudder of excitement goes up. Igor shouts something as the meshes tighten against our prow. There erupts from the water a six-foot torpedo of a fish with a toothed spine and thrashing tail. It is an Amur sturgeon, whose hunting has been banned for over thirty years. But Sergei and the others are jubilant. The police let him take it home ('to feed your family'), then laugh and career away.

Alexander says, with a tinge of consolation: 'I've heard sturgeon are coming back. Everyone eats it round here.'

From the start of summer, when the spawning sturgeon re-enter the Amur, they become ready prey. The males – ours is one – cruise along the riverbed, while the females are lying on their backs near the surface, maturing their eggs in the filtered sun. Then poachers – well-organized professionals or poor villagers – take a drastic toll. The Chinese are farming Amur sturgeon, but in the wild they are endangered, and their caviar, laundered by Russian officials or evading supervision altogether, is dispersed to Moscow or Japan, or passes through China to the United States at inflated prices.

Sergei phones a nephew back in Bogorodskoye, and when we land a mile beyond the police tent this burly youth is waiting in a closed truck and spirits the sturgeon back to town unseen. That evening they cook it in the privacy of our hotel yard. Sergei has already distributed half its meat among relatives and we settle at last, like schoolboys at a midnight feast, but less innocently, to savour the mild-tasting flesh, with contraband caviar and toasts in moonshine vodka. This is how we exist, Sergei says. Who can afford to live legally? And as we clasp one another's shoulders in inebriated friendship, I understand belatedly that I am the excuse and cover for this enterprise: the foreign guest, who confers on his comrades a fleeting immunity.

For its last hundred miles to the ocean, the Amur spreads again into wilderness. We seem no longer to be riding a river but lost on an inland sea. Scarcely a ship crosses it. Only the passage of gulls presages the Pacific. This glittering surface barely conceals a shifting maze of silt and gravel. River captains must set their course by pairs of white-painted triangles erected on shore, aligning one behind the other, and a careless moment, or a harsh crosswind, may grind their prow into the fluctuating riverbed.

Our own draught is scarcely deeper than the propellers of our motor. The last mountain flanks drop behind us, their pinewoods thinned among torrents of shale, and we are tearing across open water at fifty knots in a freezing headwind. Our wake leaves a foam-flecked scar over the surface. Even Alexander's cigarettes are dowsed. Once, when we pause in choppy shallows for a moment's line-fishing, a police sloop swoops alongside, its engines guttering, then careers away again. Sergei only grins. 'They realized you were the Englishman who drank with their buddies yesterday.' They were, he said, 'our' police.

The distant shores look uninhabitable. Igor says that many villages in Khrushchev's time were uprooted and integrated into others far away, and collective farms erased under Gorbachev. One third of Ulchi settlements had disappeared. The shore is full of silent clearings. Sergei remembers one of these, where we land under high, eroded banks. Through tangled shrubs and grasses we climb up the trace of a path, shouting to warn off bears. Where dense woods have returned on the plateau above, the village of Bolshoe Mikhailovskoe has vanished. It was once the Ulchi capital, Sergei says, but was abandoned in 1956 and even its wooden dwellings shipped away to Bogorodskoye. Now stone foundations leave a sunken geometry in the undergrowth, and alder trees have pushed up through the empty rooms. The only structure that survives – a crude tin obelisk – marks the grave of four soldiers killed by Japanese in the Civil War.

We search each other's bodies for the ticks that infest the underbush: tiny, armoured bloodsuckers whose encephalitic virus can permanently injure the brain, or kill. They have congregated around Alexander's waist, clinging to the roughness of his battledress, and two are travelling up my legs. Sergei has another three. They do not care for Igor at all. They have had no time to burrow beneath our skin, and we brush them away.

Downriver, ahead of us, where storm clouds are crowding over the hills, the Amur's last great tributary, the Amgun, pours in from the west. We go fast across a widening sea. Then something white, like a broken birch trunk, is glistening in our wake. It dives and resurfaces with a flash of fins, as if helplessly following us, twisting and floundering in the wash of our foam, and sometimes turns belly up.

When we circle alongside and pull it half out of the water, I see it is a sturgeon: not the common Amur kind, but the giant kaluga, *Huso dauricus*, endangered and fished to a precipitous decline. I stare down at an eight-foot monster, descending from an upturned snout and shovel mouth to the writhing of a magnificently spined body, ribbed laterally by rows of seeming teeth. This ancient species can grow to twenty feet and weigh a ton, and may live fifty years; but it is slow-maturing, spawning every four years, and growing rarer. At this time of year the males are trawling the riverbed hoovering up snails seventy feet down, while the females cruise the surface. This one is a wounded female. Between her pectoral fins, her body has been gouged out by poachers for its caviar, then thrown back. Sergei predicts that she will live, and returns her, disgusted, to the water.

So we move on into the evening. The cold is fiercer now. The spray blows like hail in our faces. The shores are locked in leftover ice, sometimes stacked high up their banks. Their meltwater floats around us in rheumy patches, and the clefts of the hills still shine with snow. As we turn up the Amgun tributary, where Igor has friends, the mud-brown Amur transforms to limpid green. Its turmoil calms between banks whose green reflections shatter in our wake. Igor's own village is far upriver. In Soviet times, he says, when regions like his received subsidies, passenger and cargo boats would be queueing at the village wharves, and plying the Amgun over three hundred miles. But now, nothing.

Igor's friends live on an inlet by a near-vanished settlement. Their ramshackle house, with its chicken coops and rabbit hutches and outlying sauna, overlooks a river now red with sunset under a suddenly opened sky, and their fields flood to the river under a glaze of dandelions. Trofim has lived here for a decade with his third wife. A dreamy optimist at sixty-three, he will be happy here for ever, he declares, as if God may exist. But his wife Galina declares no such thing, and storms away from us.

He takes me round his range of hutches, where white California rabbits gorge on dandelion leaves. The wind has stilled. Below us a line of ducks is swimming across the crimson water. He shows me his beds of strawberries and vegetables, squeezed into the swift growing season after seven months of winter. 'When I get to heaven,' he says, 'I will say I am living in paradise already. Leave me alone.'

We eat in the dark-wooded sauna annexe, by electric light that flickers on and off. A stove sends a scorching chimney into the ceiling. Galina has spread our table with now-familiar contraband: smoked sturgeon and red caviar, banked with potatoes. But she does not join us. We should have eaten in genial intimacy – Sergei and Igor will be parting from us next morning – but we are joined by an electrician from upriver who has intruded his boat alongside ours. He seems to inject a virus into the room. He hates everyone: the local administration, the indigenous people, the police, his wife, the Chinese of course, the Jews, all foreigners for sure. But he loves Stalin. Those were the days, of course: the days when Russia earned respect, and everyone was equal, and anybody better off than him went to the Gulag. His probing nose and narrow forehead, slicked with thinning hair, gives him a look of weasel agitation. The toasts that go round – to our reunion, my return – are subsumed in growing rancour as Sergei and the weasel wrangle about who is most important on the local electricity board (while our two bulbs go on and off). Then, as the subject of Stalin surfaces, the crossfire of partisan convictions mounts into furious discord. Trofim joins the weasel in wanting Stalin back. Sergei and Igor, freebooters both, consign him to the past. The noise swells. Ugly thoughts erupt. Alexander recalls a documentary in which three survivors remember the Gulag. Two of them still loved Stalin; but the third, a Jew, said: 'The word Stalin is forbidden to be uttered in my family.'

This brings a moment's incomprehension. A Westerner's dislike may count in Stalin's favour, I realize, and I only say: 'I hate him for what he did to Russia.'

But no one is listening. In the vodka-fuelled uproar I lose all trace of argument. My Russian gives up. I wonder if I am drunk. The faces of my companions become indecipherable in the ferment. At such heated moments profound cultural differences, concealed in the day-to-day, may emerge with sudden shock. Now I can no longer tell who hates or loves, who idolizes Putin, vindicates Jews or loathes Stalin. Alexander, perhaps sensing my confusion, tries to quell the din of invective with a plea to lighten up, crying 'Anecdote! Anecdote!' But it is too late. The electrician is in furious exchange with Sergei again. Igor, who drinks only wine and never smokes, eyes the weasel and murmurs to me: 'I can recognize a professional poacher when I see one' (and later I understand why).

The acrimony dissipates only in the drowsy swelter of the sauna, where I sit between the bulk of Alexander and the spindly thighs of the electrician. In this steamy détente, I seek to dent the weasel's chauvinism by mentioning the broken Treaty of Nerchinsk; but he only says this was never taught in school, he'd learnt it from a museum somewhere, everybody knew it, and it didn't matter. Soon Sergei and Alexander climb back to the house, to drink into early morning, and only Igor is left thinking on the verandah. For the first time, shorn of his baseball cap, his grizzled hairline makes him look older, and I suddenly regret that this solid, cloudy-eyed man, with his tacit benevolence, will be parting from us tomorrow. As if to excuse the evening's tumult, he says: 'We're simple people, you know. Our lives have never been anything else. We were brought up like this.'

I ask if he will continue up the Amgun to his home. But no, he says, he has business in Khabarovsk. He asks suddenly: 'How much does a gram of caviar cost in England?'

But I have no idea.

Momentarily he wonders whether to believe me. Who could not know such a thing? Then his frustration clears. 'A lot of our caviar goes through China, and they sell it on abroad. But the Chinese are hypocritical. They'll kiss your arse if you've got money. If not, they ignore you.'

'You sell caviar?' This is a dangerous question. The unregistered trade is forbidden.

A wintry smile gutters. 'I do. But this is secret. I take it from my village – five hundred kilos of it. Sometimes I get it out by car, sometimes by boat. I sell it between Khabarovsk and Nikolaevsk. Even people in Kamchatka get it from me. That's where the money is. Not from the fish themselves, or from hunting.' He puts a hand to his lips. 'Don't tell Alexander.'

After he has gone, I wait in the dark above the river. Stilled in its lagoon, and perhaps misted in vodka, it fleetingly resembles the Onon in Mongolia, still green and clear and young. I turn into the sauna anteroom, where blankets and a pillow have been laid on a sofa. The weasel is already asleep on the floor beside me, curled on a bearskin rug.

* * *

In a poignant passage of Andrei Makine's *Once Upon the River Love*, his protagonist speculates that you could spend your life on the remote Amur and never discover whether you were ugly or beautiful, or understand the sensual topography of another human body. 'Love, too, did not easily take root in this austere county . . .'

The sight of Galina next morning, haranguing her chickens, brings this sad notion to mind. She is a dark, feral-looking woman, with a mane of shaggy hair. She says she hates it here. She is younger than her husband. She may once have loved him, but not his rustic Eden. She will go away to Penza soon, she says, back west beyond the Volga, where her people live. When? She doesn't know. She'll go this year, or maybe next. 'I scream every day. I forget human language. We have no television, no telephone, no radio.' She turns her gaze on me with a strange, glaring smile. Her earrings flash like defiance. 'If your wife was out here, she'd be gone in two days. I've been here eleven years.'

When I return to the sauna, Alexander is seated on its steps, clutching his temples. He and Sergei were drinking until three in the morning. The Lousy Alexander is in occupation, and he is not talking. An hour goes by before he finishes breakfast, then he clears his hangover the Russian way, with a shot of vodka, and we wait for Sergei, who is stone sober, to ready the boat.

Slowly the OK Alexander returns. We sit on a bench near the river, where he imagines casting a line. It was his grandfather, he says, who taught him fishing as a boy, travelling together along tributaries he still remembers. His reverence for this figure reminds me of Batmonkh's, in a time that seems long ago. 'He and my grandmother became very close to me. But he died of a heart attack.'

Becalmed in cigarette smoke, Alexander has passed from hangover to reverie. 'My father was working in those days, and I never saw him. In any case he never had much interest in me. He was only twenty when he married, and I guess he was too young. I've never felt close to him. Only when I graduated from high school he said: "Now I feel I have a son."' His voice holds a rough understanding, empty of self-pity. 'My mother in those days turned all her attention on me, so it was partly her fault. She's an alcoholic now. Sometimes my father and I go fishing, but we just talk about fish.'

I glance at him for any changed expression, and find none. But his bullish independence becomes intelligible. His face is burnished after days of wind. He says: 'Now my parents make excuses not to see my wife and me. They pretend they're busy, but they're both out of work. When I contact my mother on the phone she just sends me silly Whatsapp jokes . . . I think she's declining. They never see our children. If I try to break the barrier between us, they just say "Let's not talk about that . . ."' His voice is tinged with surprise. 'I feel I am older than my parents now.'

Close to where the Amgun river flows into the Amur, the shore steepens to a precipitous headland. Almost eight centuries ago a temple was built here under the Chinese Yuan dynasty, at the northern limit of their empire, but vanished when the so-called Wild Jurchen, ancestors perhaps of the natives who live here today, regained their hold. Then in 1411, under the resurgent Ming dynasty, the eunuch admiral Yishiha, with twenty-five ships and a thousand men, sailed down the Songhua and northward along the Amur, bringing the Jurchen into vassalage with gifts and honours, and raised a Temple of Eternal Peace, dedicated to the Goddess of Mercy. A memorial tablet discovered here, inscribed in Chinese, Mongol and Jurchen, praises the beneficent power of the Ming imperium. Along the tablet's edge the engraved Buddhist mantra *Om Mani Padme Hum* breathes its ancient spell in four languages.

The reach of the Ming wavered, and the Wild Jurchen wrecked Yishiha's temple soon afterwards. Yet in 1432 the ageing admiral returned with double his earlier force and with a hostage prince to assume the Jurchen leadership. He rebuilt his temple on the crown of the promontory, inscribed a new memorial stela, and spread again a notional peace. But within three years, as the Ming ambition waned, this shrine too was abandoned, and in time its site became the haunt of other rites, and shamans danced among the uncomprehended stones.

It was not until the 1850s that Russian scholars penetrated here, and found vestiges of the last temple. The ethnic German geographers Richard Maack and Ernst Ravenstein recorded the remains soon afterwards. The two engraved stelas had survived, and were shipped to the Arseniev Museum in Vladivostok. The trace of a ten-foot wall still stood, with the base of a porphyry pillar, and high above, miraculously intact, an octagonal column rose like a lighthouse on the edge of the scarp.

I climb here in apprehension, up from the miniature harbour where we moor our boat, past the village of Tyr scattered along its cliffs. Beside me the headland plunges to the river in serrated claws of rock, where seagulls nest. But I am climbing into emptiness. In the late 1990s archaeologists uncovered on the summit the base of roof-bearing pillars, and bricks decorated with blossoming vines. Among them lay fragments of tiles, a dragon finial and a bronze bell. Then the site was sealed beneath tarmac, and a 150-year-old cannon – a squat bombard with a broken mouth – was installed above. The cliff-top pillar had been destroyed more than a century earlier, long before the Russian–Chinese hostility of the 1960s could turn its presence political; so deep within the Soviet border. As early as 1945 Russian chauvinists were claiming that Tyr was built by their own ancestors. Now I stand on the edge of a precipice swept clean of all ruin. To the west the colossus of the river winds and splits and rejoins under a filmy mass of mountains, while opposite me the Amgun meanders over its emerald waterlands. The only sounds are the distant bark of dogs and the call of wild duck.

In the harbour below, when I return, Sergei is talking to an angry villager. The day before, the police had beaten up two local poachers, and had left them overnight on the deck of their launch. These were not local police, but Putin's men, he reckons. Maybe, I think cruelly, they were the only hope for the river's conservation. Yet I've been travelling, I realize, in my own divided shadowland. As I clasp Igor and Sergei farewell, I wonder at how quickly this loyalty cements. My camera has been filling with it for days. I am hugging fishermen, poachers, Ulchi, policemen, hunters. And now Alexander is snapping Igor, Sergei and me in brotherly embrace, before they point their boat back to Bogorodskoye, and fade beyond its scything wake.

An hour later a broad-beamed hydrofoil, the first of the summer, is carrying Alexander and me along the last, deep bend of the river eastward. As we ease away from the iron jetty under its bedraggled Russian flag, two timber depots heave into sight, stacked with ranks of birch and larch. Then the rustle of the silt-brown river is taking us to Nikolaevsk, the ultimate port of the Amur, where it opens at last into the Pacific. The *Meteor* is swift, clean, almost empty. Ahead of us the last hills rise out of forest into balding valleys. We have less than seventy miles to go. Soon we are criss-crossing between invisible reefs, targeting the coastline triangles, while the sky expands over us, and the horizon stretches an indigo line between retreating shores.

The enormous silence of the river, its shrinking human populace and its virgin forest, give the illusion of return to some primeval Arcadia, of recoil from a stricken present. But to its inhabitants it means desolation. For almost four centuries the Amur has been the stuff of dreams, but also of promise forever delayed. In the mid-nineteenth century, especially, there arose in Russia a grand and delusive exhilaration. Just as in the seventeenth century the Cossacks were lured south by rumours of a Daurian river valley spread with wheat and sable-filled forests, even silver and precious stones, so the accession of the initially liberal Czar Alexander II, in an empire that had been stagnating for thirty years, released a groundswell of intoxicating hope. Momentarily Russia turned her back on Europe, with its old humiliations, and found a visionary future in Siberia's east.

Suddenly the immense but little-known Amur loomed into brilliant focus. Here would be Russia's artery to the Pacific, a titanic waterway flowing, as if by providence, from the belly of Siberia into an ocean of infinite promise. The trading concessions wrenched from China by the British and French, the prising open of Japan, and above all the arrival of a young and vigorous America on the opposite coast, would surely transform the Pacific into an arena of world commerce. Russians had watched the American advance westward with awe. It seemed to mirror their own headlong drive across Siberia to the same ocean, and now the two countries might flourish together in a shared oceanic commonwealth. There was even heady talk, in Siberia, of a political alliance.

With Muraviev-Amursky's seizure of the Amur from a helpless China in 1858, the vision of an eastern destiny became euphoria. The Amur, it was declared, would become Russia's Mississippi, and Muraviev was hailed, without irony, as 'one courageous, enterprising Yankee'. Such dreams climaxed in the energies of the American entrepreneur Perry McDonough Collins, quaintly named his country's 'commercial agent' on the Amur. 'Upon this generous river shall float navies, richer and more powerful than those of Tarshish,' he announced, and at its mouth 'shall rise a vast city, wherein shall congregate the merchant princes of the earth'.

Even before Muraviev's land grab, St Petersburg was rife with reports of foreign merchant ships making for the Amur. Soon a lighthouse at De Castries was raised to guide them. A fleet of steamboats began plying the once-quiet waters. The lower river valley was declared a free trade zone. And the fulcrum of these hopes was the newly founded port of Nikolaevsk at the Amur's mouth, which Alexander and I were approaching on the lonely *Meteor*. For a few years German and American trading firms went up here, housed in stout log cabins with iron and zinc roofs. A library of over four thousand books was assembled, with recent Paris and St Petersburg newspapers, happily uncensored. The officers' club flaunted a dining hall and ballroom. Life was reported delightful. The Nikolaevsk stores were selling Havana cigars, French pâté and cognac, port and fine Japanese and Chinese furniture. Susceptible minds twinned the town with San Francisco. And Perry Collins, of course, went further, looking forward to the day when St Petersburg itself would be replicated on the Amur.

Then, within a decade, harsh realities broke in. Far from being a riverine highway, the Amur was revealed as a labyrinth of shoals, shallows and dead ends, and for seven months of the year was sealed in ice or adrift with dangerous floes. Even cargo boats of low draught might not reach Khabarovsk, let alone Sretensk. And the river mouth offered no simple access. The straits between the mainland and the obstructing island of Sakhalin made for hazardous steering, especially from the tempestuous Okhotsk Sea. Ships sank even in the estuary. As for the Amur shores, for hundreds of miles they were peopled only by a sprinkling of Cossacks, natives and subsistence farmers, many forcibly settled on poor land, and open to the floods that still ravage it. For its inhabitants, this became a cursed river: not the 'Little Father' of

Russia's affection, wrote a dismayed naturalist, but her 'sickly child'. The structures of commerce that worked elsewhere – the trading houses, the shipping agents, the free zones – had been imposed upon an indifferent wilderness. In the simple, brutal realization of those most disillusioned, there was nobody to trade with and nothing to trade. Within a few years the agents and flotillas were gone, transferring first to De Castries and then to the ice-free harbour of Vladivostok.

As for Nikolaevsk, even Collins had expressed misgivings. Its waterside was so shallow that ships had to drop anchor half a mile offshore, and their cargo was transported by lighters to a swampy coast. In winter the town was blasted by Arctic blizzards and lay sometimes six feet deep in snow. Even the reports of foreign commerce were exposed as delusion. The shipping had never been significant. Within a few years Nikolaevsk became a byword for boredom, immorality and petty scandals. In its celebrated officers' club, remarked a worldly sea captain, the newspapers were few and several months old; it compared poorly to a low German beer house. The great explorer Nikolai Przhevalsky equated the whole place with Dante's hell.

The strangest foretelling of the Amur's isolation – and its first known record in English – emerged as early as 1719. This was not the work of an explorer or navigator, but of Daniel Defoe. In *The Farther Adventures of Robinson Crusoe*, and sparked by no certain origin, his fictional hero, returning home overland from Peking, hears of 'the great river Yamour':

> As its navigation is of no use, because there is no trade
> that way, the Tartars to whom it belongs, dealing in
> nothing but cattle; so nobody, that ever I heard of, has
> been curious enough either to go down to the mouth of
> it in boats, or to come up from the mouth of it in ships;
> but this is certain, that this river running due east, in

the latitude of sixty degrees, carries a vast concourse of rivers along with it, and finds an ocean to empty itself in that latitude; so we are sure of sea there.

By the time Chekhov arrived in 1890, Nikolaevsk had sunk into obscurity. Half its houses were ruined and gaping like skulls, he wrote. The inhabitants were surviving in drunken lethargy, semi-starved, by exporting fish to Sakhalin, embezzling gold, preying on the natives and selling stag antlers as a Chinese aphrodisiac. For religion and politics they cared nothing (the most prominent priest was a gold smuggler). Sometimes they shot Chinese in the nearby forests.

Chekhov found no hostel. As evening came on, with his baggage piled on the quay, he started to panic. But at last he persuaded two natives to row him to an offshore steamer, and slept in a passable berth. Alexander and I arrive at the same dismal quayside, but find a Soviet hotel on the stark main square. We might have slipped back half a century. In its gaunt foyer a receptionist assigns us rooms without a word. The only other person in this echoing gloom is a guard watching the empty corridors on a closed-circuit television. I must have been allotted the honeymoon suite; the nylon sheets are printed with red hearts and roses, and two vodka glasses stand by the bed. A fire notice on the door, rendered into quaint English, advises that if you cannot liquidate the burning, do not use the lift for avocation (there is no lift). At evening I look across at buildings where no one comes or goes – a palace of culture, a medical school – and street lamps that are never lit. I imagine I can smell the sea. Perhaps it is the knowledge that this is my journey's end that turns sleep fitful. My face in the bathroom mirror looks harsher than I remember it, as if I were still gazing into the wind.

*

When I wake, a golden light is seeping under the curtains, and I see in the square below that it is Children's Day. A troop of twelve-year-olds has assembled before a makeshift platform, on which a winsome folk singer is trying to entertain them. Meanwhile mothers are shepherding a class of infants to a patch of Astroturf and a bouncy castle made in China, where Lenin's statue raises a silvered arm on a dais of splitting marble. And now the folk singer has hit her stride. For half an hour her voice pours its passion and pathos across the square. The children stand bunched in front of her, staring up, speechless. They never stir. Then they form up behind their teacher, and file away between the park benches and the stagnant pools.

I go downstairs with the sense of being at the world's end. Alexander is smoking on the hotel steps. As we wonder where to go for breakfast, his mobile phone rings. Faintly I hear the rasp of a male voice. Alexander scowls. Now I catch only intermittent sentences, and his curt replies. The voice is demanding answers.

'*What is this man doing?*'

'He just walks about.'

'*But you know we have some issues with the West now . . .*'

'Yes, I know . . . nothing much . . .' Alexander's tone tightens.

'*Who has he been talking to?*'

'He talks to anybody . . .'

'*?*'

'He's not political. He doesn't do that stuff.'

'*So he . . . never . . . ?*'

'No, he goes to museums . . .'

After five minutes the caller rings off. Alexander is standing in his familiar, obstinate way, his legs planted apart, unshaken. He says: 'Yes, that was the FSB. The KGB, to you.' He frowns angrily. 'How the fuck did they get my number?'

'Maybe the hotel receptionist.'

'I told that FSB guy you weren't interested in overturning the state. You are just wandering around and fishing a bit.' He snaps his phone shut. 'I should have told him to fuck off.'

'I'm glad you didn't.'

But I am glad he wanted to. This is what I prize in Alexander: the stubborn self-belief that fuels his rebellious optimism. When the OK Alexander is present, which is almost always, this confidence seems to make anything possible. Yet I fear for him a little, as I had for dissidents in Brezhnev's time, whose integrity was hazardously their own. When Alexander and I come to part, it is this bear-like intransigence that I suddenly miss.

I think: when I despair of Russia, I will remember him.

The spine of Nikolaevsk is the desultory Soviet Street, which the past forty years seem hardly to have touched. Its lamp-brackets are still stamped with the hammer and sickle and Communist star, and here and there a Stalinist edifice – a cinema, perhaps – stands dressed in stucco and stout columns, before the low flat blocks drift into wooden suburbs. Almost no one is to be seen. In half a century the population has halved. But a jazz concert is promised in the cinema, and the Far East Symphony Orchestra will be playing Tchaikovsky and Mahler. I am walking down a street barely woken after winter. It is easy to suppose that the shops are shut or non-existent; but they are entered through padded double doors against the cold, and if you knock at a shuttered kiosk its window is opened by a bored-eyed Lydia or Svetlana selling Russian burgers or cabbage pies, just as fifty years ago. Where the high street dwindles among old mansions, you see the wood panels dropping from inner walls of log, and the delicately framed windows vacant or blocked up.

You imagine a house abandoned, but at dusk you see a glimmer of light behind the misted glass, or glimpse through tattered curtains a samovar or some potted vegetables ripened by the vanished sun.

It is futile to trace where the old port has gone, to hunt for the officers' club or a shipping agent's home. By the time the Civil War broke out, Nikolaevsk was enjoying a modest revival, but photographs taken after 1920 show only a wilderness of charred ruins, spiked with the brick chimneys of wooden dwellings dropped in ashes. As Bolshevik forces advanced through Siberia, Nikolaevsk remained garrisoned by a small, pro-czarist White contingent and 350 Japanese troops from the expeditionary force that had occupied the Far East littoral two years before. Encircled by superior numbers in mid-winter, cut off from all help, the Japanese garrison agreed to let the Reds enter under treaty. But at once, among a trembling populace, the first massacre began. The vicious young partisan commander, Yakov Triapitsyn, ordered the death of anyone prominent. One hundred White officers were arrested and executed. Their commander committed suicide. The Japanese refused to surrender their arms and launched a despairing attack. Most died in battle, the rest surrendered and were slaughtered. Then an orgy of revenge broke out. There were almost four hundred Japanese civilians in the town – many women and children – and these, along with thousands of Russians, were butchered with axes and bayonets, and thrown under the ice of the Amur. In spring, with the threat of Japanese forces moving down the thawing river, Triapitsyn conducted a general massacre of four thousand remaining inhabitants, and the last Japanese women and children. Then Nikolaevsk went up in flames.

Over a month later, when Triapitsyn and his mistress were executed by the Bolsheviks themselves, their trial made no mention of this bloodbath. They were shot for endangering Moscow's relations with Japan, and for killing four Communists.

Perhaps it is the echoing corridors of my Soviet hotel, or the nameless voice on Alexander's phone, or this town's louring past, that remind me of travels forty years ago in the Soviet Union. I find myself thinking that I am being followed. I leave telltale clues among my papers as I used to do, to learn if they've been sifted in my absence. Strolling in the memorial park above the river, I wonder about the man walking alongside me among the trees. And is the policeman in that parked van only pretending to be asleep? And who is the youth who turns away too quickly at my approach? The world has lost its innocence. Perhaps it is only my own memories that have transformed it; but even the strolling couples have subtly changed.

Yet after a while the sun comes out and burns away these notions. The sky is the painted blue of cottages along the river. Only a cat is following me. On a nearby bench a young woman is laughing into her mobile with a smile of light-hearted complicity, and the man among the trees is collecting fag ends. The park is crowded with memorials among a wash of dandelions. It is as if the town were withdrawing around its past. Above the river, where the silver birches are coming into bud, the brick-laid paths are tenderly intact. I pass a Crimean War cannon, then a monument to marines, then another that I cannot decipher. The statue of a mourning mother stands beside a commemorative plaque to partisans who died between 1916 and 1922. They lie in a mass grave somewhere on the riverbank below. But the White Russian thousands murdered here are unrecorded dust, and an early Japanese monument to their own dead was demolished by an outraged Party secretary in 1978.

Nikolaevsk grew piecemeal from the ashes, and lived again on salmon fishing and ship repairs. Even the elderly women who trundle along the waterfront park are the children of milder times. They are savouring the brief summer. The Bolshevik massacre lies now beyond the reach of living memory, and the Great Patriotic War itself has become the faltering tale of the old.

Near the park's end, on a 30-foot granite obelisk, perches the bronze model of a ship. It commemorates the precocious founding of Nikolaevsk in 1850 by the navigator Gennady Nevelskoi. Clutching a scrolled map, his statue towers close by, above a double flight of steps and a huge iron anchor. It was Nevelskoi who opened for Russia the straits between Sakhalin and the mainland, and who reconnoitred for Muraviev-Amursky the mouth of the Amur itself.

But Nevelskoi disowned the town he founded. It was no more than a stepping stone, he declared. The Amur itself, clogged with glaciers and sandbars, could never be Russia's gateway to the Pacific. That must lie on the Sea of Japan, with greater access to the ocean, eight hundred miles to the south.

A sense of thwarted purpose pervades the port where its breakwaters move out ruined into the water. Gas storage tanks rise above the quay across the artificial harbour, where long-disused cranes are dipped into nothing. The tarmac turns to earth underfoot. I pass a lorry signed with Chinese characters, dealing in salmon, and a police car close by on the neck of the mole, watching. Beyond me, in sunlight still, the Amur mouth yawns three miles wide, running at five knots in waves of silvered mud. The solitude of its end reminds me of no river I have seen. On one side the unblemished hills fall in spurs of forest light; on the other I am walking a path along a thin jetty. The carcasses of iron barges lie sunk under its water, and its shingle is heaped with fallen bricks and concrete, tangles of wire and chains. The only person in sight is an old man in waders, angling for pike. No sound but the faint clank of iron shifting in the wind, and the squelch of the current. Beyond the headland's tip a corridor of hills vanishes where the Amur pours out its dark fusion of waters to the ocean.

Acknowledgements

There are those to whom I feel especially indebted.

For generous advice and help: Caroline Humphrey, Jon Halliday, Jeremy Swift, David Lewis and Colin Sheaf. And above all to Gillian Tindall and Charlotte Wallis for their generous reading. A few people's names, sadly, I have altered or withheld for their security.

To my agent Clare Alexander and my publisher Clara Farmer, for unflagging confidence in a book that might not have seen the light of day.

To Goyo Travel and the Russia House for negotiating tortuous permits.

To my Russian tutor Edvard Gurvich, for his patience and friendship.

To Bill Donohoe for his scrupulous cartography.

There are many studies that have been valuable to me, but I am grateful in particular to those of Mark Bassin, Franck Billé, Grégory Delaplace, James Forsyth, Caroline Humphrey, John Man, Mark Mancall, Michael Meyer, John Stephan and Dominic Ziegler.

Finally, and most deeply, I am grateful to my wife Margreta de Grazia, for her loving encouragement of the journey and her sensitive critique of its words.

Index

Page references in *italics* refer to the map.

Afghanistan 190, 219
Aginskoye *viii*, 48, 49, 50, 51–2, 54, 59, 60, 61, 81
Aigun 133, 150, 154–60; Treaty of Aigun (1858) 108, 109, 110, 117, 125, 154, 156–7, 188, 205, 234. *See also* Aihui
Aihui (Aigun) *ix*, 150, 154–60
Akhmatova, Anna 216
Aksha *viii*, 52
Albazin *viii*, 97–8, 99–112, 131, 138
Alena (schoolgirl) 114–15
Alexander (guide) 220–8, 230–2, 235–6, 239, 240–1, 245, 246, 247, 248, 253, 255, 257, 260, 261, 262–3, 265, 267, 269, 270–1, 273
Alexander II, Czar 266
Alexei (Cossack) 105–9, 110–11, 145
Almsgiver's Wall *viii*, 29–30
Altai 34
Amgun (tributary) *ix*, 230, 257, 258, 261, 263, 265
Amur Highway 94–5
Amur leopard 211
Amur river: basin 1, 64, 71, 113, 124, 159, 243–4, 247; bridges 48, 60, 95, 139–40, 152, 181, 217, 218; fish/fishing on 10, 47, 53, 74, 89, 173, 199, 212, 215, 216, 222, 230, 231, 233, 235–6, 240–3, 246–7, 251, 252, 253, 255–6, 257, 258, 262, 263, 269, 274; floods 146, 202, 206–7, 243–4, 267; future of 127, 140, 153, 178–80, 220, 271; isolation of 265–9, 274–5; kaluga sturgeon 199, 247, 255–6, 258; length 1, 2, 47–8; name 1, 7, 117–18, 146, 201; nineteenth-century hopes for commercial future of 265–8; Pacific, flows into 2, 48, 265; pollution 173, 185; source 7, 12, 146; traffic 73, 75–6, 80, 117–19, 256, 265, 267–8; tributaries *see individual tributary name*. *See also* Black Dragon River, Heilongjiang; Onon river; Shilka river
Amur Shipbuilding Plant (Komsomolsk) 229
Amurskaya Gazeta 133
Amur tiger 199, 211–12, 222, 234, 251

animism 39–40, 254
Argun river *viii*, 62, 66, 96
Argun (steamship) 109–10
Arseniev Museum, Vladivostok 264
Arseniev, Vladimir 126, 200, 264
Asralt massif 15

Baekdu mountain *ix*, 198
Baikal-Amur Railway *ix*, 228
Baikal, Lake *viii*, 66, 139
Bakunin, Mikhail 76
Baron Korff (steamship) 75, 118
Batmonkh (guide) 3, 5–6, 8, 9,
    10–11, 12, 14, 15, 16, 17,
    18, 19, 20, 24, 29, 30, 31,
    33, 34, 39, 40, 43–6, 56,
    169, 236, 262
Batshireet *viii*, 23, 28, 29, 37, 44
Bayan-Uul *viii*, 44
bears 3, 6, 9, 17, 95, 151, 202,
    211, 212, 216, 222, 233,
    243, 245, 251–2, 253–4, 257
Beijing 127, 148, 177, 179, 197,
    229
Belgium 75, 176
Binder *viii*, 29, 37, 44
Birobidzhan *ix*, 181
Black Bear Island 205–10. *See
    also* Bolshoi Ussuriisk island
Black Dragon River 117, 146. *See
    also* Heilongjiang
Blagoveshchensk *ix*, 114–45, 147,
    149, 152, 153, 157, 158,
    159, 181, 200; Cathedral
    137–9; esplanade 115, 116;
    market 120–2, 124; mass
    drowning of Chinese
    townspeople in Verkhne-
    Blagoveshchenskoe (1900)
    132–3, 158; museum 131–2,
    158; secondary school

134–7; shuttle trade and
    119–22
Bogorodskoye *ix*, 240–1, 243,
    248, 254, 256, 257, 265
Boli (Khabarovsk) 181
Bolshevik (village) 52
Bolshevik Revolution (1917) 25,
    68, 78, 94, 107, 108, 227
Bolshoe Mikhailovskoe 257
Bolshoi Ussuriisk (Black Bear
    Island) island 205–10
Boxer Rebellion (1899–1901)
    131–3, 157
Braz, Osip 119
Brezhnev, Leonid 135, 271
Bronze Age 34
Buddhism/Buddhists: household
    altars 24; Kangyur scripture
    51; Maitreya (Buddha of the
    Future) 59, 179; mantras
    263; monastery, Aginskoye
    48, 49, 50, 51–2, 81;
    monastery, Batshireet 44;
    monastery, Tongjiang
    178–80; monastery, Tsugol
    53–60, 179; Mongolia,
    repression of within 42, 44,
    54–5; Mongolia, spread of
    Tibetan Buddhism 44;
    monks 44, 48, 49, 50–2, 54,
    56–7, 55, 58, 59, 60, 61, 81,
    179; shamanism and 22;
    Stalin's repression of 42, 44,
    54–5; Tengyur scriptures 51;
    Tibetan Buddhism 24, 44,
    51, 56, 57
Bulava 252, 253
Bureinsky range 172
Burkhan Khaldun mountain
    3, 9, 38. *See also* Khan
    Khenti
Buryatia 25, 94

Buryats 24–5, 26, 36, 39, 40, 42–3, 47, 48, 49, 51, 52, 53, 54, 62, 94
Butin, Mikhail 67–9, 70
Butin, Nikolai 67–9, 70
Butin palace, Nerchinsk 67–70, 71
Butin, Sophia 68
Bystrinsk *ix*, 232–4

Canada 134, 221, 222, 226
'camels' (shuttle traders) 120–2, 152, 153, 184
Caspian Sea 31
cathedrals: Cathedral of the Annunciation, Blagoveshchensk 137–9; Nerchinsk 63; Transfiguration Cathedral, Khabarovsk 190, 205; Uspensky Cathedral, Khabarovsk 187–9
Changbai mountain 198
Changchun *ix*, 173
Chekhov, Anton 63, 69, 76–7, 118, 119, 235, 269
chelnoki (shuttle traders) 120–2, 152, 153, 184
Chengdu 57
Chiment (Buryat) 40–3
China *viii–ix*, 146–85; Amur river course and 2, 12, 47, 62, 73, 74, 96; Amur sturgeon, farming of within 256; author arrested in 174–5; Blagoveshchensk/Verkhne-Blagoveshchenskoe, mass drowning of Chinese townspeople in (1900) 132–3, 158; Bolshoi Ussuriisk, division of and 205–10; Boxer Rebellion

(1899–1901) 131–3, 157; bridges across Amur river between Russia and 48, 139–40, 181; Confucian philosophy within 146, 169; contraband trade across Russian border 95, 201; Cultural Revolution 157, 162, 169, 170, 178, 205; Genghis Khan and 31, 38, 39; 'Golden Week' (commemorating foundation of the Chinese republic in 1949) 147, 148, 150, 155, 159, 166, 167–8; Great Wall of China 35, 160, 171; Heilongjiang, Black Dragon River *see* Heilongjiang, Black Dragon River; Mandarin language 50, 128, 142, 144–5, 149, 154, 160, 164, 165–6, 181, 187; military exercise, Russo-Chinese 57, 60–1, 81, 123, 148, 159; Mongolia and 10, 17, 26, 27–8, 30, 31, 35, 36, 37, 38, 39; Nationalist Chinese 118; pollution of Amur river and 185; raw materials, extraction of Russian 93, 135, 176, 227–8; ruling dynasties *see individual dynasty name*; Russia, Chinese migrants within 62, 107, 119–32, 135, 137–8, 139–43, 152–3, 158, 184–5, 200–1, 206, 210, 227–8, 259, 261; Russian border with, Amur river and 1–2, 37, 48, 62, 77, 96, 97, 99, 103, 117, 139–40, 145, 205; Russian government under

Putin, relations with 122–5; shuttle trade between Russia and 119–22, 152–3, 184, 200–1; source of Amur river and 7; Soviet Union and 177, 200, 205–10, 229, 264–5; Treaty of Aigun (1858) and 108, 109, 110, 117, 125, 154, 156–7, 188, 205, 234; Treaty of Nerchinsk (1689) and 63–7, 71, 97, 100, 102, 109, 110, 131, 156, 157, 159, 206, 260; Treaty of Peking (1860) and 157, 183, 205; Willow Palisade 161, 170; Xiongnu and 35, 36; Zheltuga Republic and 112

China – A Deadly Friend (Russian documentary) 124

Chita *viii*, 82–4, 86, 92, 94, 195, 228

Choibalsan *viii*, 25

Choibalsan, Khorloogiin 24–5, 27, 38, 41, 43

Christianity 178, 192, 193, 197

Christine (Yupik woman) 192–4

Chukotka 221, 226–7

churches. *See individual place name*

Civil War, Russian (1917–22) 24, 40–1, 75, 107, 109, 113, 118, 222–3, 235, 257, 272–3

Clark, Francis 75, 118

collectivization 42, 55, 113, 244, 248–9

Collins, Perry McDonough 266–7, 268

Communism 22, 56, 99, 107, 116, 126, 180, 186, 196, 197, 203, 205, 215, 227, 238

Confucian philosophy 146, 169

control tracking lane 103

Cossacks 53, 64, 74, 75, 78, 97, 99, 100–11, 114, 126, 131, 132–3, 138, 145, 158, 170, 230, 266, 267

cranes 32

Crimea 56

Crimean War (1853–6) 109, 235, 273

Cultural Revolution, China (1966–76) 157, 162, 169, 170, 178, 205

Dadal *viii*, 39–42

Dagestan 121

Da-Heihe, island of 152

Damansky (Zhenbao) island 190, 205

Damascus 209

Danube river 7

Danzan (politician) 42

Daoist philosophy 146

Daochen 57

Dashi Choypelling, monastery of, Tsugol 53–60, 179

Daur people 64

Dauria 48–9, 61, 88, 266

Dawujiazi *ix*, 160–4

De Castries *ix*, 234–6, 267, 268

Decembrist uprising, Russia (1825) 69

deer-stones 33

Defoe, Daniel: *The Farther Adventures of Robinson Crusoe* 268–9

Dersu Uzala 200

Dimitri (monk) 48, 49, 50–2, 54, 56, 59, 60, 61, 81

dog salmon 242–3

Dorje (monk, driver) 49, 52, 56–7, 60

Doroskova, Agrippina 99–100, 102, 103, 105–6
Duurilag Nars *viii*, 34–5
Dzerzhinsky, Felix 191
'Dzhem'. *See* Vasin, Yevgeny

Egiyn (tributary) 23
Engels, Friedrich 157
Ereentsav *viii*, 45–6, 48
Evenk (indigenous people) 192, 193–4

Federal Security Border Guards 92, 98
Federal Security Service (FSB) 97, 190, 224, 229, 270, 271
First World War (1914–18) 78
floods 146, 202, 206–7, 243–4, 267
Forbidden City, Beijing 195
France 109, 112, 157, 235, 266
Fraser, John Foster 75–6
Fuyuan *ix*, 182–4, 210

Gagarin Aviation Plant (Komsomolsk) 228–9
Galina (Trofim's wife) 259, 262
Ganpurev (horseman) 6, 7, 13, 15, 16–17, 19, 23, 233
Gaunt, Mary 118
Genghis Khan 1, 3, 9; birth 9–10, 29, 37, 39; Buddhism and 44, 58; death 31, 32, 37; empire 31; grave 12, 29–31, 37–8; *khural* proclaims supreme leader 28; Onon river and 9, 10, 31, 37; Pax Mongolica and 31; rehabilitation of 38; Russia/ Soviet Union and 32, 44, 52, 54, 55; *The Secret History of the Mongols* and 31; veneration of 28–9, 30, 38, 44, 58
George V, King of Great Britain 223
Georgia 85, 225, 230
gers 23, 24, 28, 39
Gerbillon, Jean-François 66
Germany 26, 75, 78, 112, 134, 157, 190, 226, 264, 267, 268
Glasgow 75
Gleb (businessman) 127–31, 139, 140, 141, 142, 143, 150, 154
Gobi Desert 18
Golden Horde 32
Golden Week (Chinese commemoration) 147, 148, 150, 155, 159, 166, 167–8
gold-mining 37, 62, 76, 90, 91, 93, 94, 112, 115, 123, 125, 131, 135, 161, 173, 177, 221
Golovin, Count Feodor 156
Gorbachev, Mikhail 26–7, 117, 218, 257
Great Britain 17, 157
Greater Khingan mountains *viii*, 112, 171, 172
Great Northern Wasteland 171
Great Patriotic War (1941–45) 26, 78–9, 97, 99, 106, 190, 191, 195, 196–7, 208, 217, 219, 226, 235, 274. *See also* Second World War
Great Wall of China 35, 160, 171
Gulag/prison camps 26, 54, 94–5, 191, 197, 237, 239, 259, 260

Hailanpao (Blagoveshchensk) 181. *See also* Blagoveshchensk
Hainan island 170
Harbin *ix*, 11, 127, 128, 143, 173, 174, 177, 182, 210, 221
Hassan, 'Grandpa' 225
Hebei 170–1
Heihe *ix*, 115–16, 117, 119, 120, 121, 128, 137–8, 142, 144, 145, 147–54, 161, 167, 168, 169, 174, 181; Russia St 153–4; Wenhua St 148. *See also* Da-Heihe
Heilongjiang, Black Dragon River *ix*, 146–85, 186, 187; bridges along 181; Chinese frontier along 170, 186; Chinese migration across 170–1; Manchu and 160–4, 170; name 117, 146; pollution of 173; shuttle trade between Russia and China and 152–3; source 146–7; traffic on 167, 182; tributaries 172, 176–7, 183–4
Heir of Genghis Khan, The (film) 51
Hitler, Adolf 26, 107
Hong Kong 143, 159
Huns 18, 35–6
hunting 16, 31, 53, 215, 231, 244, 253, 255, 261
Hurhin (tributary) *viii*, 37

Ides, Ysbrants 89
Igor (trapper) 221, 228, 230–1, 232, 234, 235–6, 240, 241, 242, 246, 253, 255, 257, 258, 259, 260, 265

India 32, 55, 85, 135, 149, 229
Indus river 7, 185
Ingoda river *viii*, 62, 102
Inner Mongolia 38, 48–9
Innocent, Archbishop 133, 137
Internat schools 192–3
Irina (restaurateur) 91
Irina (schoolteacher) 111
Ivan IV, 'the Terrible', Czar 32
Ivankov, 'Yaponchik' 225

Japan/Japanese 25, 49, 75, 78, 97, 113, 118, 123, 127, 135, 147, 157, 159, 164, 195, 266, 267; Manchurian occupation (1931–45) 162, 195–8; Russian Civil War and 257, 272–3; Second World War and 26, 143, 196–8, 219, 235
Japan, Sea of 212, 237, 274
Jesuits 66–7, 71
Jews 181, 259, 260
Jiamusi *ix*, 173
Jiayin *ix*, 166–7, 170, 171
Jilin *ix*, 150, 151, 173
John Cockerill (steamship) 118
Jong-il, Kim 198–9
Jurchen people 160–1, 198, 199–200, 263–4

Kalinovo 70–1
kaluga sturgeon (*Huso dauricus*) 199, 247, 255–6, 258
Kamchatka 261
Kandinsky, Vasily 67
Kangxi, emperor 65, 102
Kangyur (Buddhist scriptures) 51
Kara goldmines 76
Kara river *viii*, 93, 94
Kennan, George: *Siberia and the Exile System* 69–70, 76

Kennan, George Frost 70
KGB 26, 97, 190, 200, 220, 270
Khabarov, Nikifor 71
Khabarov, Yerofei 64, 70–1, 100, 189
Khabarovsk *ix*, 48, 76, 133, 173, 181, 182, 184, 186–210, 211, 216, 222, 228, 241, 261, 267; Bolshoi Ussuriisk island and 205–10; cemetery 191, 197–8, 203–4; Chinese in 124, 125, 126, 128, 186, 194–8, 199, 200–1, 205–6, 208, 210; Church 201–4; House of Life 191–4; Kim Jong-il and 198–9; Mafia in 224; Pu Yi and 194–7, 198; regional museum 199–200; size of 186; Transfiguration Cathedral 190, 205; Uspensky Cathedral 187–9; war memorial 190
Khalkha (Mongolians) 42
Khan Khenti mountain *viii*, 2, 9, 12, 15, 25, 37, 38, 47. *See also* Burkhan Khaldun
Khan, Kublai 38
Khenti Strictly Protected Area 2, 21
Kherlen river *viii*, 4, 9
Khingan mountains 112, 114, 171, 172. *See also* Greater Khingan Mts; Lesser Khingan Mts
Khitans 30
Khrushchev, Nikita 218, 248, 257
khural (conclave of the Mongol peoples) 28, 29
Kiev 32
Kirghizia/Kirghiz people 121, 122
Knox, Thomas 75

kokoshnik headdress 187
Kolenikovo 249
Kolyma 191
Komsomol (Communist youth organization) 56, 218
Komsomolsk-na-Amure *ix*, 189, 210, 217–30; Amur Shipbuilding Plant 229–30; cemetery 223–6; founding of 218–19; Gagarin Aviation Plant 228–9; war memorial 217, 226; Young Pioneers and 218–19
Korea *ix*, 39, 113, 126, 139, 180, 198, 211, 229. *See also* North Korea; South Korea
Korsackoff (steamship) 75
Kravitz, Maury 29
Kvantrishvili, Otari 225

lamas 27, 44, 51, 54, 55, 58, 59, 104
languages 66, 68, 104, 127, 134; border definitions in Russian and Chinese 127; Manchu 160–4, 244; Mandarin 50, 126, 127, 128, 142, 144–5, 148, 149, 154, 160, 164, 165–6, 181, 187; Nanai 215; Russian 71, 108, 116, 119, 127, 136, 148, 153, 177, 187; Sanskrit 50, 56; Tibetan 50, 51, 56; Ulchi 244, 250, 252
Lazarev *ix*, 233, 236–9
Lena river 66
Lenin, Vladimir 74, 84, 86, 108, 139, 186, 188, 191, 196, 203, 205, 215, 219, 238, 270
Lepeshkin, Sergei 223–4

Lesser Khingan mountains *ix*, 114
Liang (companion) 150, 155, 157, 159–70, 172, 173–81, 221, 236
Liao dynasty 30, 34
Liaoning 151
'Little Father Amur' 12, 62, 146, 201, 267–8
Lukic, Maria 74
Lumumba University, Moscow 11

Maack, Richard 264
Mafia 63, 130, 137, 138, 150, 223–6
Magadan 218
Mahakala, Black (Tibetan deity) 24
Maitreya (Buddha of the Future) 59, 179
Makine, Andrei: *Once Upon the River Love* 261–2
Manchu Chinese 64, 100–4, 109, 112, 149, 156, 160–4, 170, 172, 195–8, 213, 244. *See also* Qing dynasty
Manchukuo 195–6
Manchu language 66, 71, 160–4, 244
Manchuria 74, 133, 157, 161, 171, 208, 211; Japanese occupation of (1931–45) 162, 195–8
Mandarin language 50, 128, 142, 144–5, 149, 154, 160, 164, 165–6, 181, 187
Manoma (tributary) 216–17
Mao Zedong 104, 171, 177, 183, 197, 200, 205
marshrutka (shared taxi) 62
Marx, Karl 52, 76, 126, 157, 238

matrioshka dolls 148, 152, 177
Meakin, Annette 118, 125
'Medusa' (police officer) 81–4, 87, 92, 236
Medvedev, Dimitri 13
Mesolithic Age 33
Meteor (hydrofoil) 265, 267
military exercise, Russo-Chinese 57, 60–1, 81, 123, 148, 159
Ming dynasty 156, 160, 263, 264
Mogoytuy *viii*, 61, 62
monasteries and temples 27, 81, 104, 155–6, 178, 179, 180, 200, 263–4; Aginskoye 48, 49, 50, 51–2, 81; Batshireet 44; Tongjiang 178–80; Tsugol 53–60, 179
Mongo (horseman) 6, 7, 13, 15, 16–18, 19, 22–3, 222, 233
Mongol (village) *ix*, 248–51
Mongolia *viii*, 1–46, 48, 49, 51, 52, 53, 54, 58, 60, 65, 109, 147, 162, 164, 166, 173, 222, 233, 242, 244, 248, 261, 263; Buddhism in 22, 24, 42, 44–5; Buryat Mongols 24–5, 26, 36, 39–43, 47, 48, 49, 51, 52, 53, 54, 62, 94; China and 10, 17, 26, 27–8, 30, 31, 35, 36, 37, 38, 39; collectivization in 42; Genghis Khan and *see* Genghis Khan; Golden Horde 32; grasslands 1, 2, 4, 13, 20, 33, 37, 45; horses/ horsemen in 1–20, 23, 26, 30, 31, 33, 34, 35, 39, 41, 42; independence (1990) 38; Khalkha Mongolians 42; nationalism 27, 28–9; Onon river and *see* Onon river;

Russian Civil War and 40–1;
Russian frontier 1–2, 7, 9,
17, 23, 24, 25, 32, 40–1, 44,
45–6, 47–50, 97; Stalinist
Terror, Choibalsan and
24–7, 40, 38, 41–4, 51, 54–5
Mongols 4, 8, 9, 28, 30, 31, 32,
33, 52, 53
monks, Buddhist 44, 48, 49,
50–2, 54, 56–7, 55, 58, 59,
60, 61, 81, 179; Dimitri 48,
49, 50–2, 54, 56, 59, 60, 61,
81; Dorje 49, 52, 56–7, 60
Moscow 11, 38, 50, 64, 71, 76, 77,
80, 81, 90, 93, 100, 123, 124,
127, 130, 135, 137, 140, 148,
152, 199, 204, 225, 227, 229,
256
Mukden 195
Muraviev-Amursky, Count
Nikolai 99, 100, 109–10,
116, 131, 133, 137, 157,
187, 188–9, 199, 200, 221,
266, 267, 274
musk deer 9, 199

Nanai (indigenous people) 192,
193, 212–16, 221, 230, 231,
240, 244, 245
Narasun *viii*, 49
Nationalist Chinese 118
Neolithic Age 213
Nerchinsk *viii*, 62–70, 72–3;
Butin palace 67–70;
cathedral 63; Kennan and
69–70; Silver-Mining District
69; Treaty of Nerchinsk
(1689) 63–7, 71, 97, 100,
102, 109, 110, 131, 156,
157, 159, 206, 260
Nerva river 63
Nevelskoi. Gennady 274

Nicholas I, Czar 69, 109
Nicholas II, Czar 108, 116, 119,
188, 190, 223, 235
Nikolaevsk-na-Amure *ix*, 189,
193–4, 212, 230, 233, 261,
265, 267, 268–75
Nivkhi (indigenous people) 192,
212
Northern Song dynasty 154
North Korea *ix*, 198–9
Novosibirsk 150, 254

Okhotsk Sea *ix*, 47, 76, 189, 237,
267
Old Believers 75, 136
Onon river *viii*, 3, 7, 9, 10,
12–13, 14, 15, 23, 24, 36–7,
39, 48, 49, 52–4, 60, 61, 62,
173, 261; Genghis Khan and
9, 10, 31, 37; name 22,
36–7, 53; Russian border
with Mongolia and 12, 44–6,
61; source 3, 25, 47;
veneration of 47, 53
Orochen (indigenous people)
112
Orthodox faith 52, 75, 82, 94,
102, 103, 104, 137, 142,
148, 177, 216, 224, 230
Orwell, George 128
ovoos (votive sites) 7, 22, 37, 39,
44

Pacific Ocean 2, 31, 48, 64, 66,
73, 76, 80, 88, 90, 96, 97,
109, 118, 182, 183, 188,
189, 211, 212, 228, 229,
230, 232, 240, 242, 256,
265, 266, 274
Paris 134, 188, 267
Paris Exposition (1878) 69
Pax Mongolica 31

INDEX

Peking 31, 64, 65, 100, 102, 104, 110, 112, 156, 157, 161, 170, 268; Treaty of Peking (1860) 157, 183, 205. *See also* Beijing
'Peking Albazinians' 104
Penza 262
Pereira, Thomas 66
Peter I, 'the Great', Czar of Russia 63, 65, 89, 231
petroglyphs: Mongolia 33, 34; Sikhache-Alin 212–14
Platonov, Matvei 106
poachers 7, 9, 183, 211, 221, 242, 256, 258, 260, 265
Polish insurrection (1863–4) 69
pollution 37, 125, 173, 185
Poppe, Nikolai 51
Poyarkov, Vasily 64
Przhevalsky, Nikolai 268
Pudovkin, Vsevolod 51
Pushkin, Alexander 149
Putin, Vladimir 17, 32, 79, 82, 107, 121, 123, 136, 137, 138, 139, 180, 224, 227, 228, 260, 265
Pu Yi, Aisin-Gioro 194–7, 198

Qingdao 168, 170, 181
Qing dynasty 156, 160–1, 163–4, 181, 195–8, 200. *See also* Manchu dynasty

Ravenstein, Ernst 264
Red Guards 157, 169–70, 205
Russia 47–145, 186–275; author arrested in 79–84, 87; Bolshoi Ussuriisk, division of and 205–10; bridges across Amur river between China and 48, 139–40, 181; Buddhism in 48, 49, 50, 51–2, 53–60, 81; Chinese border with, Amur river and 1–2, 37, 48, 62, 77, 93, 96, 97, 99, 103, 117, 139–40, 145, 205; Chinese government, hostile relations with (1960s) 177, 205–10, 264–5; Chinese government, present-day relations with 122–3; Chinese migrants within 62, 107, 119–32, 135, 137–8, 139–43, 152–3, 158, 184–5, 200–1, 206, 210, 227–8, 259, 261; Civil War 24, 40–1, 75, 107, 109, 113, 118, 222–3, 235, 257, 272–3; Cossacks *see* Cossacks; Czars *see individual* Czar name; Decembrist uprising (1825) 69; 'Little Father Amur' 12, 62, 146, 201, 267–8; Mafia in 130, 137, 138, 150, 223–6; Manchuria and 194–8; military exercise, Russo-Chinese 57, 60–1, 81, 123, 148, 159; Mongolian frontier 1–2, 7, 9, 17, 23, 24, 25, 32, 40–1, 44, 45–6, 47–50, 97; Mongol subjugation of 32; Polish insurrection (1863–4) 69; Putin and *see* Putin, Vladimir; raw materials, Chinese extraction of 76, 93, 123, 135, 176, 181, 205, 227–8, 265; Shilka river in *viii*, 12, 47–8, 61–2, 63, 73, 74, 80, 88, 90, 93, 96, 118, 173; shuttle trade between China and 119–22, 152–3, 184, 200–1; Siberia, conquest of 63–4; 'small peoples' of 215,

288

244; Soviet era *see* Soviet Union; 'Tartar yoke' 32; Treaty of Aigun (1858) and 108, 109, 110, 117, 125, 154, 156–7, 188, 205, 234; Treaty of Nerchinsk (1689) and 63–7, 71, 97, 100, 102, 109, 110, 131, 156, 157, 159, 206, 260; Treaty of Peking (1860) and 157, 183, 205; Yeltsin and *see* Yeltsin, Boris

Russian Far East 96, 108, 124, 127, 135, 136, 197, 215, 223, 224, 244

Russo-Chinese Bank 73

Sakhalin island *ix*, 76, 95, 118, 221, 235, 236–7, 239, 267, 269, 274

salmon 37, 173, 212, 219, 233, 242–3, 247, 274

Sasha (evangelist) 192–4

Second World War (1939–45). *See also* Great Patriotic War

Secret History of the Mongols, The 30–1, 37

Selenga (steamship) 131

Sergei (fisherman) 241, 242, 243, 246–8, 254–6, 257, 258, 259–60, 262, 265

shamanism 22, 27, 38, 42, 44, 45, 131, 162, 193, 194, 215–16, 246, 248, 249, 250, 264

Shandong 151, 170–1

Shanghai 168

Shenzhen 168

Shilka (town) *viii*, 62, 74

Shilka river *viii*, 12, 47–8, 61–2, 63, 73, 74, 80, 88, 90, 93, 96, 118, 173

Shilkinsky massif 94

Shilkinsky Zavod *viii*, 89, 90

shuttle trade (between China and Russia) 119–22, 152–3, 184, 200–1

Siberia *viii*, 1, 2, 4, 12, 19, 25, 35, 36, 47–8, 62, 71, 76, 77, 171, 179, 186, 188, 192, 266, 272; Amur Highway and 94–5; China and 121–4, 135, 161, 176, 200, 227–8; Gulag/prison camps in 26, 94–5, 197, 259, 260; Kennan in 69–70; Onon crosses border into 2, 25, 37, 45; pastoral nomads between Mongolia and 40; population decline in 136; raw materials, extraction of 76, 93, 123, 135, 176, 181, 205, 227–8, 265; red deer 19; 'small peoples' 215, 244; taiga 4, 47–8, 95, 176, 200, 211, 222, 232, 236, 250; Trakt 94–5; Treaty of Nerchinsk and 63–4; Xiongnu and 35. *See also* Trans-Siberian Railway

Sichuan 56–7

Sikhache-Alyan 212–14

Sikhote-Alin mountains *ix*, 211

Skovorodino *viii*, 95–8, 113

Slava (trader) 48, 49, 50, 54, 56, 57–8, 59, 60, 61, 81, 122, 236

'small peoples' 215, 244. *See also individual group name*

Solonik, Alexander 225

Solontsy *ix*, 243–4

Solzhenitsyn, Alexander 93, 239

Songhua river *ix*, 172, 173, 176–7, 242, 263

Sovetskaya Gavan *ix*, 221–2
Soviet Union 11, 18, 93, 96, 104,
    96, 104, 111, 116, 118, 119,
    125, 134, 136, 202, 227,
    253; Buddhism, repression of
    42, 44, 54–5; China and
    177, 200, 205–10, 229,
    264–5; collapse of 9, 55,
    120, 191–2, 225, 228;
    collectivization 42, 55, 113,
    244, 248–9; Great Patriotic
    War and *see* Great Patriotic
    War; Gulag/prison camps 26,
    54, 94–5, 191, 197, 237,
    239, 259, 260; indigenous
    peoples and 192, 215, 216;
    Komsomol (Communist
    youth organization) 56, 218;
    Mongolia and 7, 9, 11, 18,
    24–8, 33, 38, 44, 54;
    nostalgia for 93, 203, 246;
    Pacific Fleet 229; Stalin and
    see Stalin, Joseph; Terror
    (1930s) 24–8, 40, 41, 51,
    54–5, 99, 105, 126, 190–1,
    219, 237
Spain 134
Spleen Hillock 37
Sretensk *viii*, 73–87, 88, 92, 109,
    118, 125, 134, 267; author's
    arrest in 79–84, 87; museum
    78–9; secondary school 84–6
Stalin, Joseph 61, 78, 97, 238,
    239, 259–60, 271; Chinese
    population on Amur river,
    persecution of 126–7;
    Choibalsan and 24, 27, 43;
    Cossacks and 105, 107;
    death 26, 42; Evenk and
    193; Genghis Khan and 32;
    Gulag and 94, 191, 219,
    260; Jews and 181, 260; Pu

Yi and 196, 197; Terror
    (1930s) 24–8, 40, 41, 51,
    54–5, 99, 105, 126, 190–1,
    219, 237
Stanovoy mountains *ix*, 66, 114
St Petersburg 51, 135, 188, 231,
    267
sturgeon 118, 199, 212, 233, 241,
    247, 251, 255–6, 258, 259
Suibin *ix*, 171–5; author's arrest
    in 174–5
Sükhbaatar, Dadin 38
Sukhoi aircraft 228–9
Suvorin, Alexei 119
Svetlana (schoolteacher) 134–7
Syria 190, 209

Taiwan 159
Tajikistan, Tajiks 190, 227
Tamara (in Khabarovsk) 201–4,
    206
Tashkent 121
'Tartar yoke' 32
Tengyur (Buddhist scriptures) 51
Terror, Stalinist (1930s) 24–8,
    40, 41–4, 51, 54–5, 99, 105,
    126, 190, 191, 237
Tianjin 195
Tibet 24, 34, 39, 44, 50, 51, 56–7
timber 76, 123, 176, 181, 205,
    228, 265
Tochtor (driver) 23, 24, 33, 34,
    45–6
Tokyo War Crimes Tribunal
    196–7
Tolbuzin, Alexis 101
Tongjiang *ix*, 155, 176–81;
    church 178–9; Culture Park
    177–8
Toppin, John (author's
    schoolteacher) 129, 131, 139
Trakt 94–5

Trans-Manchurian Railway *ix*, 61
Trans-Siberian Railway *ix*, 47, 61, 63, 68, 73, 75, 93, 95, 113, 125, 228
Triapitsyn, Yakov 272–3
Trofim (garden farmer) 259–60
Trofimov, 'Sylvester' 225
Troitskoye *ix*, 214–16
Trump, Donald 17
Tsongkhapa (Buddhist teacher) 58
Tsugol *viii*, 53–60, 179
Turkey 31
Tyr *ix*, 264–5

Ukraine 74, 190
Ulaanbaatar *viii*, 10, 11, 25, 29, 42, 44
Ulchi (indigenous people) 192, 212, 230, 231, 240, 241, 244–54, 257, 265
United States 51, 62, 68, 69, 70, 75, 76, 86, 109, 118, 137, 157, 208, 256, 266, 267
Ural mountains 63–4, 124, 230
Uryum (tributary) *viii*, 95
Ussuri river *ix*, 157, 183, 189, 194, 200, 211, 242; Sino-Russian conflict along 190, 205–10
Ust-Karsk *viii*, 85, 90–3
Uzala, Dersu 200
Uzbekistan/Uzbeks 50, 56, 62, 121, 227, 254

Valdui (Ulchi) 248, 253–4
Vasin, Yevgeny ('Dzhem') 224–5
Vereshchagin, Colonel Alexander 133
Verkhne-Blagoveshchenskoe 132–3
Vienna 31

Vladik (driver) 61–2
Vladimir (on Bolshoi Ussurisk island) 208–10
Vladivostok *ix*, 61, 94, 117, 188, 199, 210, 229, 264, 268
Volkov, Alexander 223
Vyatskoye *ix*, 198, 199

Wang family 159–60, 166
White Russians 40, 273
White Tara (Tibetan deity) 24
Wild Jurchens 160–1, 263
Willow Palisade 161, 170
wolves 6, 17–18, 211, 222

Xi Jinping 123, 167
Xiongnu 35–6
Xunke *ix*, 166, 170

Yablonovy massif *viii*, 49, 88
Yading mountain 57
Yakutsk 64
Yangtze river 146–7
Yellow river 146–7, 151
Yeltsin, Boris 97, 99, 223
Yishan, Prince 157
Yishiha, Admiral 263–4
Young Pioneers 169, 218–19
Yuan dynasty 38, 263
Yun (Manchu speaker) 162–4
Yupik people 192–3

Zeya river *ix*, 114, 115, 116, 125, 131, 155
Zhalinda *viii*, 99
Zheltuga Republic 112
Zhenbao (Damansky) island *ix*, 205
Zhengzhou 151
Zhuajishan massif 184

READ MORE BY
COLIN THUBRON

TO A MOUNTAIN IN TIBET

"A superb account of a pilgrimage. . . . Characteristically beautiful, though uncharacteristically haunted."

—PICO IYER, *New York Review of Books*

SHADOW OF THE SILK ROAD

"Thubron has done it all, with sparkling grace. . . . His is an experience of transformation, fittingly for if the Silk Road was anything, it was an agent of kaleidoscopic transformation."

—*San Francisco Chronicle*

AMONG THE RUSSIANS

"Superb. . . . One of the best books on Russia to appear in years."

—*New York Times*

THE LOST HEART OF ASIA

"Thubron has a novelist's sensitivity and an historian's perception. One could not ask for a more rewarding travel companion through a little-known land."

—*Washington Post Book World*

IN SIBERIA

"A cinematically evocative, often heartbreaking account of one of the world's wildest, loveliest places."

—*Newsweek*